CHILDREN, CHILDHOODS, AND GLOBAL POLITICS

Edited by
J. Marshall Beier and Helen Berents

First published in Great Britain in 2025 by

Bristol University Press
University of Bristol
1-9 Old Park Hill
Bristol
BS2 8BB
UK
t: +44 (0)117 374 6645
e: bup-info@bristol.ac.uk

Details of international sales and distribution partners are available at bristoluniversitypress.co.uk

© Bristol University Press 2025

British Library Cataloguing in Publication Data
A catalogue record for this book is available from the British Library

ISBN 978-1-5292-3230-1 hardcover
ISBN 978-1-5292-3231-8 paperback
ISBN 978-1-5292-3232-5 ePub
ISBN 978-1-5292-3233-2 ePdf

The right of J. Marshall Beier and Helen Berents to be identified as editors of this work has been asserted by them in accordance with the Copyright, Designs and Patents Act 1988.

All rights reserved: no part of this publication may be reproduced, stored in a retrieval system, or transmitted in any form or by any means, electronic, mechanical, photocopying, recording, or otherwise without the prior permission of Bristol University Press.

Every reasonable effort has been made to obtain permission to reproduce copyrighted material. If, however, anyone knows of an oversight, please contact the publisher.

The statements and opinions contained within this publication are solely those of the editors and contributors and not of the University of Bristol or Bristol University Press. The University of Bristol and Bristol University Press disclaim responsibility for any injury to persons or property resulting from any material published in this publication.

Bristol University Press works to counter discrimination on grounds of gender, race, disability, age and sexuality.

Cover design: Hayes Design and Advertising
Front cover image: Getty/Gizet Gonzalez

For the children known to us personally and the millions of others like them in all parts of our world whose contributions create and sustain families, communities, and societies every day. Let us not lose sight of their work which, though perhaps more visible through a pandemic, is always indispensable.

Contents

Notes on Contributors — vii
Acknowledgements — xiv

Introduction: Children and Childhoods in Global Political Perspective — 1
J. Marshall Beier and Helen Berents

PART I Imagined Childhoods

1   'Anchor Babies' and 'Imposter Children': Childhoods' Representations in Global Migration Politics — 17
    Patrícia Nabuco Martuscelli

2   Creating Inclusive Reconciliation and Reporting Spaces with Children: Valuing Their Stories — 31
    Caitlin Mollica

3   Stories about Children Born of Violence: Counter-narratives in the Peruvian Truth Commission's Archive and Popular Culture — 45
    Ana Lucia Alonso Soriano

4   (Un)Recognition of Child Soldiers' Agency in UN Peacekeeping Practice — 58
    Dustin Johnson

PART II Governed Childhoods

5   Contested Children's and Young People's Political Representation in Global Health — 73
    Anna Holzscheiter and Laura Pantzerhielm

6   The Representative Breakthrough? Children and Youth Representation in the Global Governance of Migration — 87
    Jonathan Josefsson

7   The Office of the Special Representative of the Secretary-General for Children and Armed Conflict: A Normative Agenda and Children's Agency in Armed Conflict — 101
    Vanessa Bramwell

8	In/visible Subjects: Global Migration Management and the Integration of Refugee Children into Schools in Addis Ababa, Ethiopia *Alebachew K. Haybano and Jennifer Riggan*	114
9	Alone and on the Move: Unaccompanied Children in UK Parliamentary Debates 2015–2016 *Lesley Pruitt and Antje Missbach*	127
10	Pathologies of Child Governance: Safe Harbor Laws and Children Involved in the Sex Trade in the United States *Robyn Linde*	140

PART III Lived Childhoods

11	Childhood, Playing War, and Militarism: Beyond Discourses of Domination/Resistance and Towards an Ethics of Encounter *Sean Carter and Tara Woodyer*	155
12	Troubling Girl Power Environmentalism: Indigenous Girls, Climate Change Activism, and a Relational Ethic of Responsibility *Lindsay Robinson*	167
13	Children's Intifada: Children as Participants in a Violent Conflict *Timea Spitka*	180
14	Children's Agency and Co-construction of Everyday Militarism(s): Representations and Realities of War in Ukrainian Children's Art, 2014–2022 *Kristina Hook and Iuliia Hoban*	193
15	Centring the Demand for Critical Climate Justice Education *Bennett Collins and Ali Watson*	210

Index 225

Notes on Contributors

Ana Lucia Alonso Soriano is Programme Director of International Relations at Tecnologico de Monterrey, Queretaro, Mexico. Ana has a PhD (International Relations) from The Australian National University in Australia, a Master's degree (Peace, Conflict, and Development Studies) from Universitat Jaume I in Spain, and a BA (International Relations) from El Colegio de San Luis in Mexico. Prior to pursuing her PhD, she worked for REDIM, a Mexican NGO focused on children's rights, and at the Comisión Estatal de los Derechos Humanos (Local Ombudsman Office) of San Luis Potosí. Ana's research looks at representations of children and women in transitional justice processes, narratives and counter-narratives about children and violence, and children in peace and security. Her work draws on critical human rights, feminist, and gender International Relations.

J. Marshall Beier is Professor of Political Science at McMaster University, Canada. His research considers issues of children's rights and political subjecthood, visual and affective economies of children in abject circumstances, and imagined childhood as a technology of global governance. His publications include *Discovering Childhood in International Relations* (editor) (Palgrave Macmillan, 2020). He is Editor-in-Chief of the journal *Critical Studies on Security*, and his work has appeared in journals including *Childhood, Children's Geographies, Contemporary Security Policy, Cooperation and Conflict, Critical Military Studies, Global Governance, Global Responsibility to Protect, International Political Sociology, International Politics, International Studies Review, Journal of Human Rights, Security Dialogue*, and *Third World Quarterly*.

Helen Berents holds a PhD in International Relations from the University of Queensland, Australia. She is an Australian Research Council Discovery Early Career Research Award (DECRA) Fellow and Senior Lecturer in International Relations at Griffith University (Brisbane, Australia). Her research draws on peace studies, feminist International Relations, and critical security studies to consider representations of children and youth in crises and conflicts, and engagements with lived experiences of violence-affected young people. Her current Australian Research Council

DECRA Fellowship (DE200100937) examines youth peace advocacy and leadership in the context of the emergent global 'Youth, Peace and Security Agenda'. Her book *Young People and Everyday Peace: Exclusion, Insecurity and Peacebuilding in Colombia* was published by Routledge in 2018. She is the author of numerous book chapters and research reports, and her articles have been published in journals including *the Australian Journal of Political Science, Cooperation and Conflict, Critical Studies on Security, International Affairs, International Feminist Journal of Politics, International Journal of Children's Rights, International Political Sociology,* and *Signs: Journal of Women in Culture and Society*. She was the 2015 recipient of the Enloe Award from the *International Feminist Journal of Politics,* and she is editor of the journal *Critical Studies on Security*.

Vanessa Bramwell is a PhD candidate at Massey University, New Zealand, situated across the fields of politics and security studies. Her current research focuses on normative characterizations of children in various United Nations work programmes relating to conflict intervention. Her other research interests include humanitarian protections in conflict, policing, terrorism and insurgency, and contemporary political theory. Vanessa is currently working on several publications relating to her thesis topic, as well as teaching in politics. She lives in the Manawatū region of Aotearoa New Zealand with her husband and children.

Sean Carter is Associate Professor in Political Geography at the University of Exeter, UK. He is interested in the ways that cultural and geopolitical practices are mutually constitutive, particularly the interrelationship between geopolitics and various forms of popular culture. This has been pursued through various projects that examine how the geopolitical world is framed, visualized, and performed. These have included studies of the geopolitics of diaspora communities, film and cinema, photojournalism, and most recently, play. Sean's research on ludic geopolitics, funded by the Economic and Social Research Council, seeks to more fully understand the ways in which play and geopolitics are intertwined, especially in the everyday lives of children, and the ways in which an attentiveness to 'play' can reframe cultural and political geographies more generally.

Bennett Collins holds a PhD from the University of St Andrews, Scotland, and is the Curriculum and Training Coordinator and co-founder of the Third Generation Project, a think tank at the University of St Andrews dedicated to educational research and programming on the social causes and effects of the climate crisis. His research and activist interests centre around land and belonging, critical and decolonial research methodologies, and global environmental and climate politics.

Alebachew Kemisso Haybano is Assistant Professor and faculty in the Center for Comparative Education and Policy Studies at Addis Ababa University, Ethiopia. He holds a PhD in International and Comparative Education from Addis Ababa University. Currently, he is a post-doctoral fellow at the Harvard University Center for African Studies. He is also an inaugural fellow in the Open Society University Network East African Hub. His research focuses on how national education systems deal with issues of identity development and the integration/inclusion of refugees. Alebachew has extensive experience working with refugees in the camps and urban areas of Ethiopia, and excellent insider knowledge of the refugee operation and refugee management systems in Ethiopia.

Iuliia Hoban is Assistant Professor of Human Security and Resilience (HSR) and Graduate Programme Chair for HSR programme, Department of Security and Emergency Services, Embry-Riddle Aeronautical University Worldwide Campus, US. Iuliia's research interests are with issues of childhood and youth across various settings, conflict studies, and the dynamic interrelationship between law and war. Her current research explores how the strategic use of childhood in political persuasion shapes security discourse and how the militarization of childhood precedes and sustains many forms of security. Iuliia has also applied her research skills in NGOs and think tanks such as Watchlist for Children and Armed Conflict (New York, US) and the Institute of World Policy (Kyiv, Ukraine), where her major responsibilities focused on analysis and research of multi-dimensional factors and aspects of human rights violations.

Anna Holzscheiter is Chair of International Politics at Technische Universität Dresden and Research Fellow at the WZB Berlin Social Science Center, Germany. She has published widely on non-state actors in international politics, global health governance, children's rights, and the politics of age. She obtained her PhD from Freie Universität Berlin and has held fellowship positions at the London School of Hygiene & Tropical Medicine and the Center for European Studies at Harvard University.

Kristina Hook is Assistant Professor of Conflict Management at Kennesaw State University's School of Conflict Management, Peacebuilding, and Development, US. A specialist in Ukraine and Ukrainian–Russian relations, she has research, policy, and practitioner experience in 25 countries. Kristina has expertise on topics including genocide and mass atrocities, civilian protection, post-conflict reconstruction, and security challenges such as hybrid warfare and environmental degradation. For her current book project, she has conducted multi-year ethnographic fieldwork in Ukraine since 2015 through Fulbright, National Science Foundation, and USAID research fellowships. Prior to her time in academia, Kristina served as a US Department of State policy advisor for conflict stabilization.

Dustin Johnson is a doctoral student in Peace and Development Research at the School of Global Studies at the University of Gothenburg, Sweden, and a Research Advisor at the Dallaire Institute for Children, Peace and Security at Dalhousie University, Canada, where he has worked since March 2016. His doctoral research is part of a research project on gender and child protection in UN peacekeeping missions. He has also worked on various projects related to the recruitment and use of child soldiers, such as early warning and prevention. He is originally from Los Alamos, New Mexico.

Jonathan Josefsson is Associate Professor in the Department of Thematic Studies – Child Studies, at Linköping University, Sweden. His research focuses on young migrants' political activism, voting rights, age and democratization, and the political representation of children and youth in global politics. He is co-editor of *The Politics of Children's Rights and Representation* (Palgrave, 2023) and author of numerous articles including 'Age as yardstick for political citizenship: Voting age and eligibility age in Sweden during the twentieth century' (2022, with B. Sandin), 'Empowered inclusion: Theorizing global justice for children and youth' (2020, with J. Wall), 'Child rights governance: An introduction' (2019, with A. Holzscheiter and B. Sandin) and '"We beg you, let them stay": Rights claims of asylum-seeking children as a socio-political practice' (2017). Jonathan is the Principal Investigator for the research projects, 'Youth Representation in Global Politics: Climate, Migration and Health Governance Compared' (2020–2023) and 'Pathways to Global Politics: Children Youth and the Making of Global Civil Society 1920–1992' (2023–2025).

Robyn Linde is Professor of Political Science and the director of the International Nongovernmental Organizations Studies programme at Rhode Island College in Providence, Rhode Island, US. Her book, *The Globalization of Childhood: The International Diffusion of Norms and Law against the Child Death Penalty*, was published by Oxford University Press in 2016. She has also been published in the *Journal of Human Rights*, the *European Journal of International Relations*, *Case Research Journal*, *Radical Teacher*, the *International Journal of Minority and Group Rights*, and the *International Journal of Children's Rights*. She currently serves on the board of directors of Amnesty International USA.

Patrícia Nabuco Martuscelli is Lecturer in International Relations at the University of Sheffield, UK. She has a PhD in Political Science from the Universidade de São Paulo (Brazil) and an MA in International Relations from the Universidade de Brasília (Brazil). Her research interests are children in International Relations, child and family migration, and asylum politics in Latin America. She has published in different International Relations and Migration journals, including *Critical Studies on Security*, *Journal of Refugee Studies and Conflict*, and *Security and Development*. Further information is available at: https://sites.google.com/view/patricia-martuscelli

Antje Missbach is Professor of Sociology at Bielefeld University, Germany. Her research interests include Refugee and Migration Studies, particularly migratory decision-making, irregular(ized) border transgressions, and shifting migration and asylum policies in transit and host countries. Her geographic area of interest is the Asia-Pacific region, first and foremost Indonesia, Malaysia, and Australia. She is the author of *Troubled Transit: Asylum Seekers Stuck in Indonesia* (ISEAS, 2015) and *Separatist Conflict in Indonesia: The Long-distance Politics of the Acehnese Diaspora* (Routledge, 2012) and also the co-author of *Indonesia: State and Society in Transition* (Lynne Rienner Press, 2019) together with Jemma Purdey and Dave McRae. In 2022, her latest book *The Criminalisation of People Smuggling in Indonesia and Australia: Asylum out of Reach* was published by Routledge.

Caitlin Mollica is Lecturer in the Business School at the University of Newcastle, Australia. Her research interests include youth's political participation, gender-inclusive justice practices, transitional justice, and human rights. She has published in well-regarded journals, including *Cooperation and Conflict*, *Human Rights Quarterly*, and *Pacific Review*. Caitlin's primary research considers the substantive participation of young people in transitional justice, peacebuilding, and human rights practices. Her sole authored book: *Agency and Ownership in Reconciliation: Youth and the Practice of Transitional Justice* will be published in 2023 by SUNY Press. Caitlin's current work examines the relationship between donors and youth in the broader context of the new international mandate on youth-inclusive peacebuilding. She is working with international NGO Dag Hammarskjöld Foundation to develop a publicly available database that charts available funding programmes for youth-led peace work.

Laura Pantzerhielm is Research Fellow and Lecturer at Technische Universität Dresden and Visiting Fellow at the London School of Economics and Political Science. Her research focuses on human rights, health, and critical approaches to the study of global politics. She obtained her doctorate from Freie Universität Berlin and has previously been a visiting researcher with the Graduate Institute of International and Development Studies in Geneva and the University of Sydney.

Lesley Pruitt is Senior Lecturer in the School of Social and Political Sciences at the University of Melbourne, Australia. Lesley's research focuses on recognizing and supporting young people's participation in politics and peacebuilding and advancing gender equity in efforts aimed at pursuing peace and security. Lesley's books include *Youth Peacebuilding: Music, Gender, and Change* (State University of New York Press, 2013); *The Women in Blue Helmets: Gender, Policing, and the UN's First All-female Peacekeeping Unit* (University of California Press, 2016); *Young People, Citizenship and Political Participation: Combatting Civic Deficit?* (Rowman & Littlefield, 2017), with Mark Chou, Jean Paul Gagnon, and Catherine Hartung; and *Dancing through the Dissonance: Creative Movement and Peacebuilding* (Manchester University Press, 2020), with Erica Rose Jeffrey.

Jennifer Riggan is Professor of International Studies at Arcadia University, US. She studies nationalism, the state, militarism, and education and is the author of *The Struggling State: Nationalism, Mass Militarization, and the Education of Eritrea* (Temple University Press, 2016). She has held fellowships from the Wolf Humanities Center (2020–2021), The Georg Arnhold Program (2019), Fulbright (Addis Ababa University 2016–2017 and Asmara University 2004–2005), The Spencer Foundation/National Academy of Education (2012–2014), and the Social Science Research Council (2004–2005). Along with Amanda Poole she is the author of *Hosting States and Unsettled Guests: Eritrean Refugees in a Time of Migration Deterrence* (Indiana University Press, 2024).

Lindsay Robinson is a PhD candidate in the Department of Political Science at Carleton University, Canada, which resides on the traditional and unceded territory of the Anishinaabe Algonquin nation. Her research interests include theorizing decolonial and Indigenous feminisms, destabilizing colonial and capitalist notions of girlhood, and critically engaging with girl-led social movement activities and protests. She is currently completing her Social Sciences and Humanities Research Council-funded thesis: 'Girls Cannot Save the World Alone: The Climate Crisis, Intergenerational Action, and Relational Responsibilities'.

Timea Spitka is Fellow at the Norman Patterson School of International Affairs, at Carleton University, Canada. She was previously a post-doctoral researcher at Hebrew University (Israel) and, in Security Studies, at Masaryk University, in the Czech Republic. Her main areas of expertise are on human security, global responsibility to protect, gender, and children's rights. Timea has worked for international organizations including the UN and Oxfam in Bosnia and Herzegovina and Israel/Palestine. She is the author of the book *International Intervention, Identity and Conflict Transformation: Bridges and Walls*

Between Groups (Routledge, 2016) and several articles, including 'Children on the front lines: Responsibility to protect in the Israeli–Palestinian conflict'. Her new book, *National and International Civilian Protection Strategies in the Israeli–Palestinian Conflict,* will be published in 2023 by Palgrave Macmillan.

Ali Watson is Professor of International Relations at the University of St Andrews and co-founder and Managing Director of the Third Generation Project, an international think tank focusing on climate justice education that is based at St Andrews. Previous work has been within the realm of Childhood Studies, peace studies, and action research. The Third Generation Project's aim is to educate diverse audiences – including Western policy makers, academics, and students – using practices and advocacy tools that prioritize marginalized frontline communities, and to follow a research approach that is both critical and collaborative. The chapter in this volume is written in the spirit of that work.

Tara Woodyer is Senior Lecturer in the School of the Environment, Geography and Geosciences at the University of Portsmouth, UK. Her research examines how childhood is entangled in the (re)production of wider socio-cultural processes. She has a particular interest in ludic – or playful – geographies, advancing theorizations of play and childhood agency through attention to embodiment and affect. Tara's recent research on ludic geopolitics, funded by the Economic and Social Research Council, has explored play as a critical lens for addressing conflict and militarization. This has focused on using ethnographic, child-centred techniques to examine how children express and enact contemporary geopolitics through everyday domestic practices of play. This work interrogates militarization beyond areas of actual armed conflict and highlights childhood political subjectivity through consideration of embodiment.

Acknowledgements

This book project started, as many good academic projects do, over a lunch and a conversation where Marshall and Helen imagined and schemed about what might 'come next' for critical conversations on children's constitutive role in global politics. We were able to make these plans thanks to the thoughtful work of many scholars – some within this volume and many more beyond it – who have been carefully paving the way for taking children and childhoods seriously in our home discipline of International Relations and beyond it. This project is indebted to, and builds from, their intellectual contributions.

Plans for an in-person contributors' workshop in 2020 were halted by the onset of a global pandemic. Yet, we are incredibly grateful to all our authors for their commitment and enthusiasm for this project, and their shared work to sustain it through the pandemic and all the associated disruptions and challenges it brought for everyone. We thank our contributors for their willingness to navigate time zones and technology to come together for two virtual contributors' workshops where chapters were read and discussed by each other as well as the editors. In the enforced distance of a global pandemic, our authors have repeatedly made the world feel smaller and the community feel close and supportive, which has been an unexpected gift.

Many thanks to Stephen Wenham and Zoe Forbes at Bristol University Press, who shepherded the project from the proposal stage through to production. We are also thankful to our reviewers, who recognized and validated the political project of this book and provided helpful feedback for framing the volume.

Marshall would like to thank the Social Sciences and Humanities Research Council of Canada for the support of an Insight Grant (435-2019-0009) over the span of work on this project. Colleagues at McMaster University and, especially, the many excellent undergraduate and graduate students with whom I am privileged to work are constant sources of inspiration from which I always benefit immeasurably. My family and their usual mix of patience, interest, and support continue to buoy me in this and all else I do; thank you, Carole Beier, Myra Hurst, and Kaelyn Beier. Across a dozen time zones, working with Helen has been a true joy, undiminished even by the dislocations of a pandemic and the many challenges we have all found in its wake. The ease of conversation and spirit of true collaboration you have brought to this project, Helen, leave me at once grateful and eager to get to work on what will follow.

Helen's work on this project was enabled by a DECRA Fellowship from the Australian Research Council (DE200100937). I would like to thank Siobhan McEvoy-Levy, Ingrid Valladares, and Nyasha Mutongwizo for conversations along the way that made their way into the fabric of this book. Brendan Keogh and Harry have always been there for me with love, patience, and endless quiet support. Finally, this project has been a bright spot in the past few years. One joy of working across time zones was waking up to find a book-related email in my inbox from Marshall ready for me to pick it up, and I am incredibly grateful to Marshall for embracing this project with me and keeping it moving. Thanks for sharing this journey, Marshall; now, what's next?

J. Marshall Beier, Hamilton, Canada
Helen Berents, Brisbane, Australia
April 2023

Introduction: Children and Childhoods in Global Political Perspective

J. Marshall Beier and Helen Berents

What would global political life look like without children and childhoods? If the question seems an odd one, it is perhaps because it presumes something quite outside the ambit of what global politics is usually understood to enclose, and well beyond the realm of possibilities normally imagined about childhood. Certainly, for students and scholars of disciplinary International Relations (IR), the association is not an intuitive one, but neither has it figured significantly in the wider interdisciplinary spaces concerned with critically interrogating the politics of the global. And yet, the provocation is important because, despite a dearth of attention to children and childhoods, they are indivisible from and indispensable to discourses and practices of global politics. Though the dominant understanding of childhood is premised on developmentalist-inspired assumptions of children's incapacity and the consequent deferment of their meaningful participation in the social worlds we share, this belies not only their competence as everyday social actors but also the ways in which they are relied upon as such. And while imagined childhood is sentimentalized as a time of innocence, understood to demand a unique claim on protection from the harsh realities of the world, the fact is that children the world over contend daily with 'adult' life through, among other things, participation in labour markets, shouldering domestic responsibilities on which households and communities depend, enduring structural deprivations, navigating complex emergencies, and experiencing armed conflict. What is more, the everyday functioning of global systems of material production and the maintenance of status quo power relations *depends* on millions of children performing essential functions and fulfilling important roles across these and other contexts.

While recognizing and taking seriously this indispensability of children to socio-political life is a critical first move towards finding them in global politics, coming to a sophisticated and nuanced understanding of childhood(s) themselves is no less crucial. On first gloss, the meaning of childhood may seem self-evident as a temporally delineated formative stage of the human life course. This aligns well not only with vernacular usage and but also with culturally and historically specific common senses that hold childhood – and, by extension, children – sequestered behind some nominally fixed age threshold. For juridical purposes, this lends straightforward criteria for the governance of children through age-contingent deferment of rights, participation, bodily autonomy, and more. In practice, however, definitions of children and childhood are much less clear cut, varying in application not only across spatial and temporal registers but also as befits particular political purposes. Children may be deemed too young to vote but old enough for military service; they might reach the age of criminal culpability before being permitted to serve on juries. More broadly, childhood entails duties of care and protection from adults that extend to some children but which, mediated by intersecting social categories of identity and difference like race or gender, are less accessible or even explicitly denied to others. At the same time, imputed 'childishness' is a stock rhetorical feint by dint of which the competence of adult subjects is routinely placed under challenge, even at the level of interstate diplomacy. This malleability of childhood in practice – variously claimed, withheld, and ascribed separate from age – reveals it as an intersubjectively held idea residing more in social imaginaries than in meaningfully objective characteristics. It begins to lay bare, too, how childhood is an ideational keystone to the working of wider imaginaries and, as such, is not only affected by politics but is itself always political.

Returning to our opening question then, there is a dual sense in which it is literally impossible to imagine global political life without children and childhoods. First, because children have always been important and effectual social agents (see, inter alia, Wells, 2015; Chou et al, 2017; Bessant, 2020), the world we know and seek to apprehend more fully would undoubtedly appear very different were their multifarious contributions suddenly to be somehow withdrawn. Second, imagined childhood itself is integral to the (re)production of the social worlds we inhabit locally and globally. Like race or gender, ideas about childhood are vital to the constitution of acting subjects and acted-upon objects, not only in the relatively mundane encounters between adult and child in everyday life but in global political life also. Summoned rhetorically, the figure of the child is an important political meaning-making device in whose name desired futures are claimed, for whose sake security is demanded and insecurity decried, and over whose suffering retributive violence is sanctified. Imagined childhood – marked by innocence, incapacity, dependence, and vulnerability – thus operates as a social technology of governance both in regulating the lives of children and in the possibilities it can open or foreclose along lines of global political practices, performatives, and processes.

Just as they are and have always been essential to global political life, children and childhood have likewise always been important – though, paradoxically, largely unnoticed – in global political studies, including the more narrow and often parochial field of IR. As the field has seen new critical challenges broaden its remit in recent decades to move beyond old referents towards more inclusive and more nuanced approaches to the study of global politics, ever more students and scholars of IR have come to recognize how race, gender, and indigeneity have never been absent from its articulations of apposite subject matters, research programmes, and conceptual traditions. Rather, these and other neglected arbiters of the kinds of worlds we imagine have always been inseparable from colonial and patriarchal framings of global politics and, consequently, from the contours of disciplinary IR as it was traditionally tooled to narrate those worlds. Though we remain at the early stages of its recognition as an equally important social category of identity and difference, childhood similarly has always been present and important not only in the study of global politics but also to IR, where it likewise is not new but merely newly noticed.

Like earlier interventions on gender, race, indigeneity, and more, a new literature broaching childhood has emerged in IR – notably in the adjacent and overlapping critical security studies specialty – as well as in some areas of scholarship engaging global politics across other disciplinary contexts. Doing the necessary ground-clearing that all such new currents must undertake, a number of these contributions have addressed themselves directly to IR, making out the case that subsumed commitments about children and childhood have always been congenitally bound up in the worlds the discipline sketches and revealing something of the kinds of insights we miss where we fail to take this seriously. Disciplinary inclinations do not bend quickly or easily, of course, and we remain a long way from wide acceptance of the importance of finding children and theorizing childhood as always relevant to understandings of global politics in the same way as gender, race, and indigeneity (in respect of each of which, it is important to acknowledge, much work also remains to be done). While it might be tempting to opt to leave IR to its devices and carve out a new space in spite of it, this would be to forfeit what remains an important and authoritative discursive space in the production of knowledge about global politics, which therefore needs to be called to take notice of and take seriously childhood, as it has been called to do around gender, race, and indigeneity. As with each of these, the call is not for childhood to be 'brought in' to disciplinary conversations but, rather, to be acknowledged and thoughtfully engaged for the implications of its already being a subsumed part of their very intelligibility. It is from this standpoint that *Children, Childhoods, and Global Politics* can be understood both as a continuation of this call on disciplinary IR and a collection of original contributions to the study of global politics from other disciplinary perspectives that *build from* rather than retreading the ground opened by the important work done to date. With this is in mind, a brief sketch of the openings from which we proceed is in order.

Breaking through: finding children and childhoods in global politics

Though they endure hegemonically in dominant social structures and operant common senses, developmentalist-inspired ideas that frame children as less human 'beings' than human 'becomings' (Qvortrup, 1994; Uprichard, 2008) have been widely repudiated in debates animating the 'new sociology of childhood' that emerged in earnest in the 1980s and which have since given rise to a flourishing interdisciplinary Critical Childhood Studies specialty (foundationally see, inter alia, James and Prout, 1990; Burman, 1994; Qvortrup, 1994; Jenks, 1996; Aitken, 2001; see also Canosa and Graham, 2020). Recognition of children's innate assets and abilities as bona fide social actors and the reality that we are all, child and adult alike, simultaneously 'beings' and 'becomings' has motivated a wide range of conceptually sophisticated and empirically rich research programmes approaching questions of children's rights, social participation, perspectives, competencies, and contributions. These, in various ways, have exposed the indeterminacies of imagined childhood as well as its imbrication with patterns of unequal social power relations whose analogues include the particular ways power is bound up in and circulates through gender, race, indigeneity, and other categories of identity and difference. Among other things, these contributions have revealed the cultural and historical specificity of dominant ideas about childhood (see Rabello de Castro, 2021; Tisdall, 2022) and challenged the idealized political innocence (Jenkins, 1998) central to them, showing how it comes to operate as an exclusionary social practice sustaining unequal relations of power (Garlen, 2019). A certain ambivalence around imagined childhood is exposed by contributions that show how children's everyday participation in social life is both meaningful, not least for children themselves (Horgan et al, 2017), and relied upon across myriad social contexts in ways that may not be reducible to mere exploitation (Lund, 2007; Holzscheiter, 2018; Jijon, 2020). This points to the importance of recovering children's agency and understanding them as complex political subjects engaged in and with our shared social worlds, from the local to the global (Barly, 2018; Wall, 2019). At the same time, however, the imperative of holding children's unique social disempowerment conspicuously visible has been emphasized, lest we err too far in responsibilizing them while deactivating the responsibility of more powerful subjects of the adult world (Jacob, 2014; Holloway et al, 2019).

These and other insights from Critical Childhood Studies have been taken up in other disciplinary contexts, though IR and (global) political studies in general have been conspicuously slow to take notice. While children have never been absent from international studies discourse, they are all too often reduced to a few simplistic and unidimensional framings. They have appeared principally as child soldiers, rhetorical devices, or, even less visibly, conflated with women as 'womenandchildren' (Enloe, 1993). They are invoked visually and rhetorically to influence policy and to reinforce or question global order and power, yet they are rarely considered meaningful social actors in their own right or made central objects of inquiry, and childhood remains under-theorized. This critical lapse invites new interventions, urging attentiveness to children's agency and emphasizing the complex heterogeneity of lived childhoods, promising fresh insights around issues of insecurity, rights, and exploitation affecting children in contexts of conflict, migration, labour, climate change, and more. Disciplinary IR, however, is not well equipped to engage these developments in ways that resist children's objectification. This puzzle of children's co-constitution within and of international politics, yet their absence as meaningful subjects of IR, has been an important animating focus of work to date at the emergent IR/Critical Childhood Studies nexus.

Out of this same sense of a puzzle to be answered, recent years have seen the emergence of an engaged and growing community of scholarship inquiring into issues of children and childhoods in IR, with wider relevance for the ways global political studies are approached beyond the discipline as well. Much of this has worked to advance the case for IR's attention, not only where children might seem more palpably at issue – as in the case of child soldiers, for example – but for what a nuanced understanding of imagined childhood can tell us about core disciplinary concepts and concerns like security, norms, political economy, and more (Watson, 2004, 2006, 2009; Brocklehurst, 2006; Wagnsson et al, 2010; Beier, 2020). At the same time, contributions explicitly addressing themselves to IR speak also to projects investigating and theorizing childhood and global politics in Critical Childhood Studies as well as fields like political geography and the burgeoning area of children's geographies (Skelton, 2013; Benwell and Hopkins, 2016; Woodyer and Carter, 2020; Seemann, 2022). They are thus conversant with, enriching, and enriched by a much larger community of scholarship.

Among the broad issue areas over which this work ranges are settings of conflict and emergency (Bennett, 2014; Jacob, 2014, 2015; Berents, 2015; Brocklehurst, 2015; Huynh et al, 2015; D'Costa, 2016; Denov and Akesson, 2017; Mort et al, 2018; Beier and Tabak, 2021). This includes but is not limited to nuanced reflections about child soldiers (Tabak,

2020), on which vast established literatures have not always heeded the lessons of post-developmentalist Childhood Studies. Resisting simplistic renderings of victimhood, important contributions explore children's roles in peacebuilding (McEvoy-Levy, 2006; Berents and McEvoy-Levy, 2015; Pruitt, 2015; Berents, 2018; Martuscelli and Villa, 2018), including as expressed in youth cultures (Pruitt, 2013; McEvoy-Levy, 2018) and as both subjects and objects of international rights regimes (Holzscheiter, 2010, 2018; Linde, 2016). Particular attention has been drawn to children's activism, resistance, and unique diplomacies in pressing action on climate change (Collins, 2020; Trott, 2021; Skovdal and Benwell, 2021). Girlhood has been theorized for its unique positionalities and the political work it (is made to) do as well as for how it both intersects and is at times in tension with feminisms (Jacob, 2015; Berents, 2016; Martuscelli and Bandarra, 2020; Pruitt, 2020). Crossing a wide range of social, geographical, and historical contexts, a number of studies have been carried out on intersections of childhoods and militarisms (Beier, 2011; Collins, 2011; Hörschelmann, 2016; Frühstück, 2017; Grieve, 2018; Harding and Kershner, 2018; Beier and Tabak, 2020; Danilova and Dolan, 2020). Others show how childhood as an idea is ascribed by subjects in global politics against other subjects – including but not limited to sovereign power – as a rhetorical means by which to delegitimize them as competent or legitimate actors (Basham, 2015; Mills and Lefrançois, 2018). Thinking intersectionally (Crenshaw, 1989) about how imagined childhood manifests as a social technology in the governance of conflict, civil emergencies, and even recourse to political violence reveals more about its discursive sway in scholarship as much as in everyday political practice (Macmillan 2009; Lee-Koo, 2011, 2013, 2018; Berents, 2016, 2019, 2020; Beier, 2018, 2022; Pruitt et al, 2018; Shalhoub-Kevorkian, 2019; Tabak, 2020; Shoker, 2021).

What this brief survey outlines is a vibrant body of critical scholarship on children and childhoods that informs and enables new thinking in and about global politics. And though IR remains somewhat late to the party, there too a significant new literature has already done the work of making the sorts of openings normally requisite to claiming space for new areas not traditionally thought apposite to established disciplines. In so doing, the case has been made both for what considering children and childhoods brings to IR and, no less important, the implications of not interrogating the ways in which they not only always have been present but also have been and remain indispensable. IR scholars working in this space, together with colleagues from other disciplines, fields, and specialties, have begun to come together in different fora, including organizing conference panels, journal special issues, and edited book projects, as well as pursuing individual research projects. At the same time, there is a recognized need for a more focused collection of contributions that acknowledge the importance of this topic to an IR readership but which move beyond the introductory and prefatory work that has already been done to open this new area in – but not confined by – the disciplinary space of IR. *Children, Childhoods, and Global Politics* answers this need by bringing together and putting in conversation emergent and more established contributors to this growing area. The volume thus proceeds from initial openings to build in new ways on the possibilities they present.

Acknowledging the important openings already made points to the importance of getting on with the business of doing the work that new disciplinary spaces were intended to enable. Childhood is already a constituent part of our subject matters and present in the ways we theorize them. Again, children and childhoods are not new but, rather, newly noticed in international studies. We take this to have been well established in the sum of contributions to date and, therefore, a point of departure for new reflections on this developing area of scholarship. In formulating their individual contributions, each of the chapters herein draws on and reflects upon the authors' own work in this space, in terms of how they theorize and what methods or empirical contexts they use to do their work. Among the questions from which they proceed are:

- What does venturing to theorize children and childhoods contribute to the study of global politics and the ways we approach it?
- What are the commonalities/differences in the intellectual debts of those who have been working in this area (given the extradisciplinary origins of these currents in Childhood Studies and elsewhere)?
- Are there particular things, unique to its own disciplinary context and character, that IR might usefully bring to thinking about children and childhoods?
- How do childhoods manifest, contest, and disrupt our present rendition?
- Finally, what might our studies of global politics have to offer the children of the world, and what would possibilities along these lines entail for us and for the work we do?

In varied and complementary contexts, the contributors haven taken up these and associated questions both directly and indirectly. We would also offer these questions as starting points for readers coming to thinking about children, childhoods, and global politics from the perspective of their own work and contributions to date. Together, the chapters in this volume present us with a collection of highly nuanced accounts of children and childhoods across global political time and space. These are the critical 'next steps' in an emerging area.

Structure of the volume

An important motivation from the earliest stages of work on *Children, Childhoods, and Global Politics* has been to bring together a range of unique contributions in a single collection so as to capture the diversity and complexity both of childhoods' ideational circulations and of children's lived experiences from an equally diverse range of analytical standpoints. The volume's 15 chapters are the work of more than 20 contributors from a dozen different countries, and their original research projects are similarly diverse in the issues they ply and the empirical contexts in which they are located. Also important in light of their collective contribution to an emerging area of scholarship, they span the full range of career stages, from early career researchers to more established scholars. To facilitate this inclusivity and with a view to sharpening focus on the unique contribution each brings, chapters are purposefully shorter than they might otherwise have been. To build and hone coherence across them, authors participated in two international virtual workshops organized by the editors. All were also involved in a reciprocal peer-review process as well as receiving feedback from the two editors. The outcome is a collective work more collaborative than piecemeal, in which common issues, ideas, and insights cross more seamlessly from one contribution to the others.

The chapters are organized into three broad sections, each turning on a theme around which individual contributions intersect in different ways. Each of these themes is, at the same time, resonant through the whole of the volume. Chapters in Part I, 'Imagined Childhoods', challenge us to think critically about who counts as a child and what this means where claims to protection, voice, and participation reveal childhood to be a contested social terrain through which consequential political struggles are waged. Part II, 'Governed Childhoods', brings together contributions that are revealing of the significant global political work that goes into the regulation of childhood as a critical arbiter of competing claims to rights, security, and more. The final section, Part III, 'Lived Childhoods', includes investigations that foreground children's agential remit while urging us to think more critically about how and where we find it expressed through and between the local and the global.

Though there is a logic to this structure, a caveat is in order as regards both the sections and the ordering of the chapters. Like hyperlink matrices, key concepts, ideas, issues, and insights arise and speak across sections and individual chapters. The themed sections highlight some of these connections but, ultimately, form just one suggested reading we think will be helpful to those broaching this area for the first time. They and others will benefit too from reading across and even against these sections also, drawing different readings from new combinations.

Working from original research across a range of unique contexts, the contributors to *Children, Childhoods, and Global Politics* advance new insights not only about children and childhoods in global political contexts but also about the communities of practice and of scholarship that have neglected their indispensability to the maintenance and reproduction of the global political worlds we share. They speak to an emerging area of scholarship both within and beyond the disciplinary boundaries of IR. They also contribute to currents in the interdisciplinary Critical Childhood Studies specialty and associated fields and disciplines in which scholarship moves from this area of expertise towards global political contexts rather than the other way around. Together, they also give us a range of critical glimpses into just how much of what we presume to know about global politics is contingent on children and what we think we know about them. In the end, they make clear that, though children and childhood have been neglected in the study of global politics, we have never really been able to imagine it without them.

References

Aitken, S.C. (2001) *Geographies of Young People: The Morally Contested Spaces of Identity*, London: Routledge.

Barly, R. (2018) '"He wasn't nice to our country": Children's discourses about the "glocalized" nature of political events in the Global North', *Global Studies, of Childhood* 12(2): 147–158.

Basham, V.M. (2015) 'Telling geopolitical tales: Temporality, rationality, and the "childish" in the ongoing war for the Falklands-Malvinas Islands', *Critical Studies on Security* 3(1): 77–89.

Beier, J.M. (ed) (2011) *The Militarization of Childhood: Thinking Beyond the Global South*, New York: Palgrave Macmillan.

Beier, J.M. (2018) 'Ultimate tests: Children, rights, and the politics of protection', *Global Responsibility to Protect* 10(1–2): 164–187.

Beier, J.M. (ed) (2020) *Discovering Childhood in International Relations*, New York: Palgrave Macmillan.

Beier, J.M. (2022) '"This changes things": Children, targeting, and the making of precision', *Cooperation and Conflict* 57(2): 210–225.

Beier, J.M., and Tabak, J. (2020) 'Children, childhoods, and everyday militarisms', *Childhood* 27(3): 281–293.

Beier, J.M. and Tabak, J. (eds) (2021) *Childhoods in Peace and Conflict*, New York: Palgrave Macmillan.

Bennett, C. (2014) '"Now the war is over, we have something else to worry us": New Zealand children's responses to crises, 1914–1918', *Journal of the History of Childhood and Youth* 7(1): 19–41.

Benwell, M.C. and Hopkins, P. (eds) (2016) *Children, Young People and Critical Geopolitics*, Abingdon: Routledge.

Berents, H. (2015) 'Children, violence, and social exclusion: Negotiation of everyday insecurity in a Colombian barrio', *Critical Studies on Security* 3(1): 90–104.

Berents, H. (2016) 'Hashtagging girlhood: #IAmMalala, #BringBackOurGirls and gendering representations of global politics', *International Feminist Journal of Politics* 18(4): 513–527.

Berents, H. (2018) *Young People and Everyday Peace: Exclusion, Insecurity and Peacebuilding in Colombia*, New York: Routledge.

Berents, H. (2019) 'Apprehending the "telegenic dead": Considering images of dead children in global politics', *International Political Sociology* 13(2): 145–160.

Berents, H. (2020) 'Politics, policy-making and the presence of images of suffering children', *International Affairs* 96(3): 593–608.

Berents, H. and McEvoy-Levy, S. (2015) 'Theorising youth and everyday peace(building)', *Peacebuilding* 3(2): 115–125.

Bessant, J. (2020) *Making-up People: Youth, Truth and Politics*, Abingdon: Routledge.

Brocklehurst, H. (2006) *Who's Afraid of Children? Children, Conflict and International Relations*, Aldershot: Ashgate.

Brocklehurst, H. (2015) 'The state of play: Securities of childhood–insecurities of children', *Critical Studies on Security* 3(1): 29–46.

Burman, E. (1994) *Deconstructing Developmental Psychology*, London: Routledge.

Canosa, A. and Graham, A. (2020) 'Tracing the contribution of childhood studies: Maintaining momentum while navigating tensions', *Childhood* 27(1): 25–47.

Chou, M., Gagnon, J-P., Hartung, C., and Pruitt, L. (2017) *Young People, Citizenship and Political Participation*, London: Rowman & Littlefield.

Collins, R. (2020) 'Great games and keeping it cool: New political, social and cultural geographies of young people's environmental activism', *Children's Geographies* 19(3): 332–338.

Collins, R.F. (2011) *Children, War and Propaganda*, New York: Peter Lang.

Crenshaw, K. (1989) 'Demarginalizing the intersection of race and sex: A Black feminist critique of antidiscrimination doctrine, feminist theory and antiracist politics', *University of Chicago Legal Forum* 1989(1–8): 138–167.

D'Costa, B. (ed) (2016) *Children and Violence: Politics of Conflict in South Asia*, New Delhi: Cambridge University Press.

Danilova, N. and Dolan, E. (2020) 'The politics and pedagogy of war remembrance', *Childhood* 27(4): 498–513.

Denov, M. and Akesson, B. (2017) *Children Affected by Armed Conflict: Theory, Method, and Practice*, New York: Columbia University Press.

Enloe, C. (1993) *The Morning After: Sexual Politics at the End of the Cold War*, Berkeley: University of California Press.

Frühstück, S. (2017) *Playing War: Children and the Paradoxes of Modern Militarism in Japan*, Oakland: University of California Press.

Garlen, J.C. (2019) 'Interrogating innocence: "Childhood" as exclusionary social practice', *Childhood* 26(1): 54–67.

Grieve, V.M. (2018) *Little Cold Warriors: American Childhood in the 1950s*, New York: Oxford University Press.

Harding S. and Kershner, S. (2018) '"A borderline issue": Are there child soldiers in the United States?', *Journal of Human Rights* 17(3): 322–339.

Holloway, S.L., Holt, L., and Mills, S. (2019) 'Questions of agency: Capacity, subjectivity, spatiality and temporality', *Progress in Human Geography* 43(3): 458–477.

Holzscheiter, A. (2010) *Children's Rights in International Politics: The Transformative Power of Discourse*, New York: Palgrave Macmillan.

Holzscheiter, A. (2018) 'Affectedness, empowerment and norm contestation – children and young people as social agents in international politics', *Third World Thematics: A TWQ Journal* 3(5–6): 645–663.

Horgan, D., Forde, C., Martin, S., and Parkes, A. (2017) 'Children's participation: Moving from the performative to the social', *Children's Geographies* 15(3): 274–288.

Hörschelmann, K. (2016) 'Crossing points: Contesting militarism in the spaces of children's everyday lives in Britain and Germany', in M.C. Benwell and P. Hopkins (eds) *Children, Young People and Critical Geopolitics*, Abingdon: Routledge, pp 29–44.

Huynh, K., D'Costa, B., and Lee-Koo, K. (2015) *Children and Global Conflict*, Cambridge: Cambridge University Press.

Jacob, C. (2014) *Child Security in Asia: The Impact of Armed Conflict in Cambodia and Myanmar*, London: Routledge.

Jacob, C. (2015) '"Children and Armed Conflict" and the field of security studies', *Critical Studies on Security* 3(1): 14–28.

James, A. and Prout, A. (1990) *Constructing and Reconstructing Childhood: Contemporary Issues in the Sociological Study of Childhood*, London: Falmer Press.

Jenkins, H. (1998) 'Childhood innocence and other modern myths', in H. Jenkins (ed) *The Children's Culture Reader*, New York: New York University Press, pp 1–37.

Jenks, C. (1996) *Childhood*, New York: Routledge.

Jijon, I. (2020) 'The priceless child talks back: How working children respond to global norms against child labor', *Childhood* 27(1): 63–77.

Lee-Koo, K. (2011) 'Horror and hope: (Re)presenting militarised children in Global North–South relations', *Third World Quarterly* 32(4): 725–742.

Lee-Koo, K. (2013) 'Not suitable for children: The politicisation of conflict-affected children in post-2001 Afghanistan', *Australian Journal of International Affairs* 67(4): 475–490.

Lee-Koo, K. (2018) 'Children', in R. Bleiker (ed) *Visual Global Politics*, Abingdon: Routledge, pp 48–54.

Linde, R. (2016) *The Globalization of Childhood: The International Diffusion of Norms and Law Against the Child Death Penalty*, New York: Oxford University Press.

Lund, R. (2007) 'At the interface of development studies and child research: Rethinking the participating child', *Children's Geographies* 5(1–2): 131–148.

Macmillan, L. (2009) 'The child soldier in North–South relations', *International Political Sociology* 3(1): 36–52.

Martuscelli, P.N. and Bandarra, L. (2020) 'Triply silenced agents: Cognitive structures and girl soldiers in Colombia', *Critical Studies on Security* 8(3): 223–239.

Martuscelli, P.N. and Villa, R.D. (2018) 'Child soldiers as peace-builders in Colombian peace talks between the government and the FARC–EP', *Conflict, Security & Development* 18(5): 387–408.

McEvoy-Levy, S. (ed) (2006) *Troublemakers or Peacemakers? Youth and Post-Accord Peace Building*, Notre Dame: University of Notre Dame Press.

McEvoy-Levy, S. (2018) *Peace and Resistance in Youth Cultures: Reading the Politics of Peacebuilding from Harry Potter to the Hunger Games*, London: Palgrave Macmillan.

Mills, C. and Lefrançois, B.A. (2018) 'Child as metaphor: Colonialism, psy-governance, and epistemicide', *World Futures* 74(7–8): 503–524.

Mort, M., Walker, M., Williams, A.L., and Bingley, A. (2018) 'From victims to actors: The role of children and young people in flood recovery and resilience', *Environment and Planning C: Politics and Space* 36(3): 423–442.

Pruitt, L.J. (2013) *Youth Peacebuilding: Music, Gender, and Change*, Albany: State University of New York Press.

Pruitt, L.J. (2015) 'Gendering the study of children and youth in peacebuilding', *Peacebuilding* 3(2): 157–170.

Pruitt, L.J. (2020) 'Revisiting 'womenandchildren' in peace and security: What about the girls caught in between?' in J.M. Beier (ed) *Discovering Childhood in International Relations*, New York: Palgrave Macmillan, pp 199–218.

Pruitt, L., Berents, H., and Munro, G. (2018) 'Gender and age in the construction of male youth in the European migration "crisis"', *Signs: Journal of Women in Culture and Society* 43(3): 687–709.

Qvortrup, J. (1994) 'Childhood matters: An introduction', in J. Qvortrup, M. Bardy, G. Sgritta, and H. Wintersberger (eds) *Childhood Matters: Social Theory, Practice and Policy*, Aldershot: Avebury, pp 1–24.

Rabello de Castro, L. (2021) 'Decolonising child studies: Development and globalism as orientalist perspectives', *Third World Quarterly* 42(11): 2487–2504.

Seemann, J. (2022) 'Children's cartographies of the world: Mapping Brazilian modes, methods and moments', *Children's Geographies* (online in advance of print): 1–16.

Shalhoub-Kevorkian, N. (2019) *Incarcerated Childhood and the Politics of Unchilding*, Cambridge: Cambridge University Press.

Shoker, S. (2021) *Military-Age Males in U.S Counterinsurgency and Drone Warfare*, New York: Palgrave Macmillan.

Skelton, T. (2013) 'Young people, children, politics and space: A decade of youthful political geography scholarship 2003–13', *Space and Polity* 17(1): 123–136.

Skovdal, M. and Benwell, M.C. (2021) 'Young people's everyday climate crisis activism: new terrains for research, analysis and action', *Children's Geographies* 19(3): 259–266.

Tabak, J. (2020) *The Child and the World: Child-Soldiers and the Claim for Progress*, Athens: University of Georgia Press.

Tisdall, L. (2022) 'State of the field: The modern history of childhood', *History* (online in advance of print): 1–16.

Trott, C.D. (2021) 'What difference does it make? Exploring the transformative potential of everyday climate crisis activism by children and youth', *Children's Geographies* 19(3): 300–308.

Uprichard, E. (2008) 'Children as "being and becomings": Children, Childhood and temporality', *Children & Society* 22(4): 303–313.

Wagnsson, C., Hellman, M., and Holmberg, A. (2010) 'The centrality of non-traditional groups for security in the globalized era: The case of children', *International Political Sociology* 4(1): 1–14.

Wall, J. (2019) 'Theorizing children's global citizenship: Reconstructionism and the politics of deep interdependence', *Global Studies of Childhood* 9(1): 5–17.

Watson, A.M.S. (2004) 'Seen but not heard: The role of the child in international political economy', *New Political Economy* 9(1): 3–21.

Watson, A.M.S. (2006) 'Children and International Relations: a new site of knowledge?', *Review of International Studies* 32(2): 237–250.

Watson, A.M.S. (2009) *The Child in International Political Economy: A Place at the Table*, London: Routledge.

Wells, K. (2015) *Childhood in a Global Perspective*, 2nd edn, Cambridge: Polity.

Woodyer, T. and Carter, S. (2020) 'Domesticating the geopolitical: Rethinking popular geopolitics through play', *Geopolitics* 25(5): 1050–1074.

PART I

Imagined Childhoods

1

'Anchor Babies' and 'Imposter Children': Childhoods' Representations in Global Migration Politics

Patrícia Nabuco Martuscelli

Introduction

'Children shape global politics', reflected Lee-Koo (2020: 22). This chapter explains how different representations of migrant children shape global migration politics. In the last decade, children became more visible in migration/refugee studies. Different categories of migrant children, including unaccompanied children (those that cross an international border alone), separated children (those that cross an international border accompanied by an adult that is not their legal guardian), and children left behind (those that remain in their origin countries when their caretakers migrate), were employed to study the movement of children across borders.

Children, generally defined as people under 18 years old in the United Nations Convention on the Rights of the Child (UNCRC), have rights independently of their migration status (right to non-discrimination – Article 2). The Convention also guarantees children's specific rights connected to migration, such as the right not to be separated from their family (Article 9), the right to have their best interests as a primary consideration[1] (Article 3), the right to family reunification ('family reunification shall be dealt with by States Parties in a positive, humane and expeditious manner' – Article 10), and the right to asylum (Article 22[2]). Besides that, human rights courts, including the European Court of Human Rights and the Inter-American Court of Human Rights, have employed the UNCRC in cases involving children to recognize and guarantee their rights.

In a nutshell, international law obliges states to guarantee child migrants' rights which could mean that the general concept of children (as rights holders) could restrain conservative migration politics. Since children are an internationally protected group and children traditionally perceived as innocent victims that deserve protection (Josefsson, 2017b), states willing to stop the entrance and permanence of child migrants in their territories have to adopt discursive strategies to justify the denial of child migrants' rights. Lind (2019: 337) explains that 'children's rights are increasingly mobilised for governing and controlling, rather than enabling, vulnerabilised migrant children's territorial presence and mobility'.

In recent years, with the increasing number of children migrating alone, politicians and researchers have started to understand that children are decision-makers in their migration processes and have agency in migration (Bhabha, 2014), which has motivated discourses focusing on child migration. Specific representations of migrant children that do not necessary correspond to the reality of child migration, like 'anchor babies', 'anchor children', 'imposter children', and 'innocent children', have been employed by decision-makers and the media to justify and consolidate restrictive migration politics around the world, especially in Global North countries that tend to receive larger migration movements.

'Anchor babies' are perceived as a family migration strategy where families have their babies in countries that grant citizenship by birth; therefore, the baby's status would allow the migrant family to stay in the country. 'Anchor children' are children that are sent alone to migrate as a strategy to bring their families through family reunification policies. 'Imposter children' are young adults that would explore child protection migration mechanisms designed for child migrants. 'Innocent children' is the language used to justify migration policies and rights for children. This chapter analyses how each of these categories of child migration is constructed and employed to justify restrictive migration policies that restrain children's rights. It also briefly discusses how these categories do not reflect the reality of child migration.

As Bhabha (2014) explained, this happens because politicians tend to adopt an ambivalent discourse to deal with migrant children. Western conceptions of children in need of protection and care, together with international obligations to guarantee children's rights according to the UNCRC (1989), would force states to protect migrant children considering their best interests. At the same time, States have adopted restrictive migration politics to avoid the entrance and permanence of foreigners in their territories. Bhabha (2014) perceives this tension when states adopt discourses to protect migrant children and actions that treat them first as migrants (adults) that should be controlled and secondly as children. The ultimate logic of these discourses would be to protect national children ('our' children) from the migrant children ('other' children). This is done by portraying them as adults and/or employing a child protection discourse to deny child migrants' rights.

This chapter briefly discusses two strategies adopted by states to control child migration: first, using different representations of children like 'anchor children and babies' to restrict children's rights to family and nationality; second, employing the category of 'imposter children' to recognize agency as an adulthood characteristic. In both cases, states adopt a discourse of child protection from harm and children's rights to deny children's rights to apply for asylum, family reunification, recognition as a child, and their best interests (Anderson, 2012; Holzscheiter et al, 2019; Lind, 2019). Therefore, 'Children are invoked as rationale or justification for political action' (Berents, 2020: 595) in the migration arena. When politicians employ 'child politics' – that is, the use of specific images of children – to justify restrictive migration actions, they adopt the same logic described by Berents (2020: 595): 'a personal emotional appeal [protection/care]; invocation of protectionist responses [children's rights]; and a condemnation of others [parents]'. This chapter dialogues with other interesting discussions on children's representation in different parts of this book, like Holzscheiter and Pantzerhielm on global health (Chapter 5), Josefsson on the participation of children in global migration governance (Chapter 6), and Pruitt and Missbach on representations of unaccompanied children in UK Parliamentary discourses (Chapter 9).

After this brief introduction, the following section explains how states employ two representations of 'anchor children' and 'anchor babies' to restrain migrant children's rights to family reunification and nationality. The subsequent section discusses strategies to delegitimize child migrants' rights based on the idea that migrants are not children with the 'imposter children' representation. It highlights recent movements where images of suffering migrant children ('innocent children') motivated actions and protests to challenge restrictive migration politics against children and how these logics connect with the other representations. The conclusion argues that these state strategies to control child migration objectify migrant children and ignore their possibilities of agency. However, recognizing their possibilities of agency constructs children as adults since it creates a tension between an imagined childhood (that does not migrate) and adulthood (decision-makers in migration), which excludes migrant children from a child rights perspective. Overall, movements defending migrant children against restrictive migration politics tend to focus on their representations as 'innocent children', which also does not recognize their agency. Therefore, while important literature has advocated the recognition of children's agency in the migration process, states representations of child migration do not recognize their agency.

'Anchor children' and 'anchor babies': children as a family migration strategy

This section unpacks how the representations of 'anchor children' and 'anchor babies' play in global migration politics. While most examples come from Global North countries, this does not mean that Global South countries do not use these representations to justify restrictive measures considering child migration. The first subsection analyses the representation of 'anchor children', understood as children born in other countries ('other' children that are not 'our' children) that are sent by the parents as a migration strategy to allow the migration movement of the family. This representation is particularly useful to deny the right of family reunification to migrant children. The second representation is 'anchor baby'. This refers to national children born from undocumented parents, therefore, 'other' children that would also not be considered 'our' children. In this logic, these babies would be employed as a migration strategy allowing the family to stay in the country where they already live without documents. This discourse is used by politicians contesting the right of the nationality/citizenship of babies from migrant families.

When a child becomes a migration strategy: the 'anchor children' representation

The first discursive strategy involves the concept of 'anchor child'. In the 1980s, this concept was initially used by the US media and decision-makers to refer to Vietnamese children migrating alone to the United States (Ormonde, 2012). The main idea is that families send their children alone as a migration strategy because these children could bring/invite their family members to the destination country through family reunification procedures once they have status in the destination country. Stretmo (2014: 102–103) explains that '"anchor children" are not perceived as "orphans" nor as "refugees", but rather as "economic migrants" shipped away by their calculating parents hoping for a better life in the West on the grounds of family unification with the unaccompanied child'. The concept of 'anchor child' involves a specific representation of migrant children: they are foreign children, that is they are the 'other'; they lack agency because they are sent by their parents as a family migration strategy; and the way states decide to respond to that involves a discourse of states protecting children from harm (in that case, parents that do not consider their children's best interests).

In Finland, the concept of 'anchor child' was employed to make family reunification procedures harder for children who arrive alone (unaccompanied children); (Horsti and Pellander, 2015; Tapaninen et al, 2019). Politicians justify that denying children the right to family reunification is a manner to protect them because their parents will not send them on dangerous journeys to arrive in the destination countries alone. In the case of Finland, Tapaninen et al (2019: 829) explain that politicians argued that 'a child should not be used as "an instrument of immigration"'. It was believed that preventing this would be in the best interest of the child. In this logic, denying the family reunification right to unaccompanied children is in their best interest to avoid their families sending them away. It would be a mechanism for states to protect these children from harm (Anderson, 2012). That is, restrictive migration politics are framed by politicians and the media as a form of protection for children from their parents. In the summer of 2015, Barak Obama also employed the discursive strategy to say that parents were sending their children on perilous journeys to arrive at the southern US border (Ataiants et al, 2018). According to Tapaninen et al (2019: 829), 'The question of anchor children has been framed via the rhetoric of the war on the trafficking of vulnerable children', where parents are perceived as traffickers and states as the ultimate protectors for these children.

In this same logic, states – as responsible for guaranteeing these children's protection – are using the best interests of the child as a justification to reject residence permits based on family reunification cases (Smyth, 2015; Josefsson, 2017a) and 'humanitarian' child deportations that were not really based on humanitarian principles (Lemberg-Pedersen, 2021). States justify that returning children to their origin country to reunite with their families there would be in their best interests and would prevent the phenomenon of 'anchor children' (Smyth, 2015; Josefsson, 2017a). Lemberg-Pedersen (2021: 40) explained that European Union politicians framed children as being at risk to justify their deportation to Afghanistan through the European Return Platform for Unaccompanied Minors. They employed 'humanitarian discourses depicting deportation procedures as "family tracing," "family reunification," "humane and safe return," "reintegration," and "care and education facilities."' Politicians framed this project as the child's best interests to be reunited with their families in the origin countries. They were 'framing deportation as empowering child displacees and their families' (Lemberg-Pedersen, 2021: 254). According to Lemberg-Pedersen (2021: 243),

> States' emotive and rights-based appeals to responsibility, guilt and innocence means that the normative grammars of rights to asylum or of child-specific rights can in fact be marshaled for the purpose of exclusion. They can serve as control devices separating the innocent from those rendered suspicious, allowing states to ascribe the role of savior to themselves, using appeals to rescue, care and universal rights to launder their restrictive policies into rescue efforts.

These two examples show how politicians use children's rights discourses to justify restrictive migration politics that harm migrant children's rights (Holzscheiter et al, 2019; Lind, 2019). In both cases, migrant children are not considered agents of their migration process; that is, they need the states of destination to make decisions to 'protect' their rights and best interests.

Lalander and Herz's (2018) work demystifies the concept of 'anchor children'. Their research with unaccompanied children in Sweden showed that, in general, children themselves decided to travel to Europe in search of safety and better living conditions. Tapaninen et al (2019) also argue that most unaccompanied children in Finland did not apply for family reunification when the process was more straightforward for them. However, we see the use of the 'anchor children' strategy as the main reason to justify harder family reunification procedures when children are the main applicants or the complete denial of the right to family reunification for children.

When a child harms our child: the 'anchor baby' representation

Another representation of migrant children to justify restrictive migration/citizenship politics is 'anchor babies'. 'Anchor babies' are perceived as children that are born in countries that grant citizenship based in the territory (*jus solis*) (like the US and most Latin American countries) from undocumented parents as a strategy for these parents to stay in the country where they already live and access welfare benefits. Most of the literature on this topic focuses on gender and racialized conceptions of undocumented migrant mothers, especially Latin women (Lugo-Lugo and Bloodsworth-Lugo, 2014; Foster, 2017). 'Anchor babies' was a term created in anti-immigrant web pages during the 2000s[3] that was adopted in discourses of anti-immigrant politicians in the United States (Lederer, 2013). This discourse also motivated projects to change the constitutional right to citizenship in the US (Ormonde, 2012).

Donald Trump mentioned different times the need to protect 'American' children from 'anchor babies' (Kim et al, 2018). 'Anchor babies' are portrayed as economic, cultural and national security threats (Kendall, 2012) because they are constructed as potential breaches to restrictive migration and family reunification policies. However, this assumption does not resonate with the reality when we understand the family reunification rules considering children sponsoring their parents in the US. First, children can only sponsor their parents when they turn 21 years old and under specific conditions. Second, most undocumented parents were already living in the US for many years when they had children (Ormonde, 2012). That is, they did not come to the US just for their children to have American citizenship. Schmidt's

(2018) study with women who migrated pregnant from Central America to the US did not show birth citizenship rights as the motivator for their migration. On the contrary, they suffered gender-based violence (with many pregnancies as the result of rapes). They were looking for safety in the US.

This concept of 'anchor baby' was further securitized by US media and politicians as 'terror babies'. Conspiracy theories say that terrorist groups were sending pregnant women to give birth to 'terrorist' babies in the US to have American citizenship (Lugo-Lugo and Bloodsworth-Lugo, 2014). That is, not only would these babies be employed as a migration strategy of their parents but their parents would be terrorists. In that case, these babies were a double threat to US security as both 'anchor' and 'terror' babies. Both types of babies represent a direct and indirect security threat to the country (Lugo-Lugo and Bloodsworth-Lugo, 2014) because they are the entry ticket for potential threats to US economic security (people that would 'steal' American jobs), physical security ('terrorist parents' that can commit terrorist attacks in the country), and cultural security (people coming from different cultural backgrounds that will harm US values).

The idea to change the citizenship law to solve the 'anchor babies' problem (by making US citizenship connected with blood relations and not the place of birth) connects with Bhabha's (2014) conception of ambivalence. It would be a manner to protect American and documented residents first and punish undocumented residents' babies even if they would have no nationality (become stateless) if the country changed its citizenship law. This concept of 'anchor baby' has the same problem of objectifying children. There are never any considerations of these children's best interests, rights, or potential agency. They are only perceived and employed in political discourses as 'entry tickets' for other adult migrants (usually their parents).

In the same way as 'anchor children', the representation of 'anchor babies' involves children that are perceived as 'other' (children of undocumented parents), children who lack agency (the parents are the migration decision-makers), and children who need the state to protect them from being used as a migration strategy. The difference would be the solutions adopted by states to protect these children. While the 'anchor children' representation is more used to justify denials of the right to family reunification and potential deportations, the 'anchor baby' representation is more connected to denial of the right to citizenship. Both representations objectify children and deny the possibilities of their agency. A holistic approach considering migrant children's agency clashes with political discourses that instrumentalize the children's rights lexicon to justify restrictive migration politics and the need to protect children from their parents or families. However, acknowledging or recognizing children's agency can involve another strategy to deny migrant children's rights, which is discussed in the next section.

When a child is not a child: 'imposter children', 'innocent children', and child agency

The West tends to define children as innocent, passive, and with no agency. Although this conception has been highly criticized in the Childhood Studies literature and the IR literature on children (see, among others, the chapters in Beier, 2020), the idea that children are innocent contributes to highlighting the role of adults as the only migration decision-makers (even when we talk about child migration). As Bhabha (2014) discussed, the overall perception is that migrants are adults because children 'cannot' decide to migrate. In that case, children that decide to migrate alone as agents are delegitimized as 'imposter children' because they do not follow the imagined idea of childhood that will not cross an international border. Hence, states adopt the discursive strategy to recognize children's agency to justify their classification as adults.

States adopt the representation of 'imposter children' in that case. 'Imposter children' would be adults that pretend to be children to have better protections and services in migration procedures, especially preferential treatment in the refugee status determination (RSD) process. Silverman (2016) explained that asylum systems, especially in Canada, adopt age-determination procedures that are highly controversial, involving measuring bone sizes and teeth (Mishori, 2019). In those procedures, adolescents who should be considered children may be classified as adults in their RSD procedures, which could also justify summary deportations. The discussion on age determination in asylum procedures has been growing in the last years with political discourses to fight abuses in the asylum systems. In fact, the European Court of Human Rights has received cases of children being treated as adults and detained in adult facilities, which violates their rights. Restrictive migration politics justify rigid age-determination procedures to protect 'real' children from adults that pretend to be children (Silverman, 2016). That is, in order to protect 'real' children, states have to avoid that adults disguised as 'fake' children use services, structures, and procedures that are designed for children. However, this age-determination procedure violates children's rights and excludes children from mechanisms designed to protect them and assess their best interests. These policies are more concerned with protecting migration systems at the cost of harming child migrants' rights. The representation of 'imposter children' also involves this logic of the state as the protector of 'real' children from harm against 'fake' children. In that case, 'imposter' children are not children because they have agency; therefore, they are adults.

On the other hand, we can also understand that images of children – the representation of 'innocent children' – have been used to challenge restrictive migration politics. For example, Josefsson (2017b) showed how the media challenged migration and asylum decisions by Swedish courts to deport children using a child rights' lens. This section presents two recent examples in Global North countries to illustrate cases where the discursive strategies previously explained in this chapter (justifying that children are adults or that children are a threat because they are anchors for adult migrants) did not pay off.

Denmark has adopted restrictive migration politics that make integration and naturalization harder for migrants and refugees (Vitus and Jarlby, 2021). While many of these politics were contested by activists and civil society organizations, the illegal separation of asylum-seeker couples (married or in a civil partnership) in Danish asylum centres when one was a minor (under 18 years old) motivated the decision to impeach the former Minister of Immigration Inger Stojberg (Wallis, 2021).

On June 30, 2018, thousands of Americans in more than 700 protests in all 50 states marched against the 'zero-tolerance' policy of then-President Donald Trump that separated children from their families arriving at the US–Mexico Border (Yoon-Hendricks and Greenberg, 2018). Videos and audios of babies crying and images of children in cages appeared on social media and traditional media worldwide. The protesters had signs saying: 'Families belong together', 'Childhood is not a crime', 'Separating families is a crime against humanity', 'What kind of monsters put kids in cages?', 'Children are not animals',[4] and others. These two situations have in common that policies separating children from their families went beyond the threshold acceptable to the public concerning 'innocent children'. While both countries had previously adopted many restrictive migration politics that harmed children's rights, these two policies received media attention. In these media representations, the general public understood that administrations were harming innocent children. In the Danish case, we could argue that married couples could be perceived as adults (because marriage is an adult activity). However, they were portrayed as children that were forcibly separated from their families.

Both Stojberg and Trump attempted to justify their restrictive migration politics by employing child protection measures. Stojberg aimed to avoid child/forced marriage and people 'abusing' the Danish asylum system. She was 'protecting' children, especially girls that could be forcibly married by their families to migrate to Denmark. It assumes that young people have no agency to decide about their marriages. However, in that case, these couples were applying for asylum together as a family. The Trump administration framed children's parents as child traffickers harming these children by starting dangerous journeys. Just like Obama had before, the Trump administration framed this family separation as a deterrence strategy. The logic is also based in the representation of 'innocent' children and involves the message that families should not migrate to avoid being separated from their innocent cherished children.

These justifications were not compelling because the media showed how innocent children suffered due to these migration politics. Images of suffering children are politically useful (Berents, 2019, 2020). The pictures and videos of separated children suffering in cages and children crying appeared on social media and news for days. International organizations employ pictures of innocent children and babies to justify their projects and ask for support (Dubinsky, 2012). Specific images of innocent babies and children as victims of restrictive politics were useful to mobilize the public against these policies harming children. These also happened in the case of the boy Alan Kurdi, who became the symbol of the so-called 'refugee crisis' in Europe (see Sohlberg et al, 2019; Adler-Nissen et al, 2020). Berents (2020: 594) recalls 'that for some states, his death instead prompted a hardening of borders and of foreign policy rhetoric that centred on the irresponsibility of his father'. Like the discussions of 'anchor children' and 'anchor babies', parents are blamed for the migration – and in this case – the death of 'innocent' children, reinforcing the idea that children are not agents in migration. In these two cases, there was no recognition of children's agency in the migration process. They were represented as 'innocent children' harmed by state migration policies, which reinforces the idea that recognizing migrant children as agents could characterize them as adults.

States, decision-makers, and the media employ different strategies to control child migration and deny child migrants' rights. They use specific representations of children: 'anchor children', 'anchor babies', 'imposter children', and 'innocent children'. In each of these representations, states adopt a protective discourse for protecting both national ('our' children) and migration children ('other' children) from harm (Anderson, 2012). Finally, in all these representations, there is a lack of recognition of children's agency since recognizing children's agency would imply their classification as adults (Josefsson, 2017b).

Conclusion

Berents (2020: 608) explains that '[c]hildren – and, more specifically, particular notions of childhood – are a powerful moral force, and their affective power can mobilise strong political responses'. This chapter has shown that states employ particular discursive strategies and childhood representations to justify restrictive migration politics. First, politicians employ the child rights lexicon and the child's best interests to justify policies that are against children's rights, like deportations and restrictions on family reunification procedures. Second, politicians adopt objectifying representations and images of children, including 'anchor child', 'anchor baby', and 'imposter children', to motivate restrictive migration politics. Finally, when migrant children's agency is recognized in migration procedures, they tend to be perceived as adults and 'imposter children'. Procedures that harm migrant children are also employed to protect national children ('our' children) from migrant children ('other' children) in the case of citizenship politics and 'real' children from 'fake' children that want to abuse migration systems. Specific representations of children are helpful to control child migration, which is harder to justify due to international law (and moral) obligations to protect children.

While politics separating children from their families caused a commotion in the US and an impeachment in Denmark, these were affective reactions to particular images of children that reinforce a Western vision of passive and innocent children. Approaches that recognize children as agents of their migration processes are not helpful to restrain restrictive migration politics. Age-determination politics that harm children's right to asylum and restrictions to family reunification rights of unaccompanied children are not illustrated with images of suffering children. They are not politically visible. Simultaneously, children portrayed as agents of their migration do not fit the social construction of children as innocent and victims. They are 'migrants' (adults) and not children. Representations of migrant children employed by states do not empower children; they show them as suffering beings. In that sense, specific images of suffering children ('innocent children') can mobilize public opinion to challenge restrictive migration politics. Nevertheless, restrictive measures involved in a discourse of protection of children in their best interests are not problematized as harming child migrants' rights. Overall discursive strategies and representations of childhoods employed to control child migration objectify children and do not recognize their agency.

Notes

[1] General comment 14 (2013) explains that the best interests of the child is a right, a principle, and a rule of procedure that should be considered in all processes involving children, including migration procedures. See United Nations, Committee on the Rights of the Child (CRC), *General comment No. 14 (2013) on the right of the child to have his or her best interests taken as a primary consideration (art. 3, para. 1)*, CRC / C/GC/14 (29 May 2013). Available from https://www.refworld.org/docid/51a84b5e4.html.

[2] The article says, 'States Parties shall take appropriate measures to ensure that a child who is seeking refugee status or who is considered a refugee in accordance with applicable international or domestic law and procedures shall, whether unaccompanied or accompanied by his or her parents or by any other person, receive appropriate protection and humanitarian assistance in the enjoyment of applicable rights set forth in the present Convention and in other international human rights or humanitarian instruments to which the said States are Parties.'

[3] Ignatow and Williams (2011: 60) explain that 'An unconsolidated Google search of "anchor babies" yields only 10 results for the year 2000, about 30,000 for 2005, and about 436,000 for 2010.'

[4] I participated in one of the protests in Raleigh, North Carolina. Some reflections about this moment are published at Martuscelli (2018).

References

Adler-Nissen, R., Andersen, K.E., and Hansen, L. (2020) 'Images, emotions, and international politics: The death of Alan Kurdi', *Review of International Studies*, 46(1): 75–95.

Anderson, B. (2012) 'Where's the harm in that? Immigration enforcement, trafficking, and the protection of migrants' rights', *American Behavioral Scientist*, 56(9): 1241–1257.

Ataiants, J., Cohen, C., Riley, A.H., Lieberman, J.T., Reidy, M.C., and Chilton, M. (2018) 'Unaccompanied children at the United States border, a human rights crisis that can be addressed with policy change', *Journal of immigrant and minority health*, 20(4): 1000–1010.

BBC News (2018) 'US attorney general quotes Bible to defend separating families', BBC News, 15 June. Available from: https://www.bbc.co.uk/news/world-us-canada-44499048 [Accessed 3 April 2023].

Beier, J.M. (ed) (2020) *Discovering Childhood in International Relations*. Cham: Palgrave Macmillan.

Berents, H. (2019) 'Apprehending the "telegenic dead": Considering images of dead children in global politics', *International Political Sociology*, 13(2): 145–160.

Berents, H. (2020) 'Politics, policy-making and the presence of images of suffering children', *International Affairs*, 96(3): 593–608.

Bhabha, J. (2014) *Child Migration and Human Rights in a Global Age* (vol 22). Princeton: Princeton University Press.

Dubinsky, K. (2012) 'Children, ideology, and iconography: How babies rule the world', *The Journal of the History of Childhood and Youth*, 5(1): 5–13.

Foster, C.H. (2017) 'Anchor babies and welfare queens: An essay on political rhetoric, gendered racism, and marginalization', *Women, Gender, and Families of Color*, 5(1): 50–72.

Holzscheiter, A., Josefsson, J., and Sandin, B. (2019) 'Child rights governance: An introduction', *Childhood*, 26(3): 271–288.

Horsti, K. and Pellander, S. (2015) 'Conditions of cultural citizenship: Intersections of gender, race and age in public debates on family migration', *Citizenship Studies*, 19(6–7): 751–767.

Ignatow, G. and Williams, A.T. (2011) 'New media and the 'anchor baby' boom', *Journal of Computer-mediated Communication*, 17(1): 60–76.

Josefsson, J. (2017a) 'Children's rights to asylum in the Swedish Migration Court of Appeal', *The International Journal of Children's Rights*, 25(1): 85–113.

Josefsson, J. (2017b) '"We beg you, let them stay!": Right claims of asylum-seeking children as a socio-political practice', *Childhood*, 24(3): 316–332.

Kendall, E. (2012) 'Amending the constitution to save a sinking ship? The issues surrounding the proposed amendment of the citizenship clause and anchor babies', *Berkeley La Raza Law Journal*, 22(2): 349–382.

Kim, J.K., Sagás, E., and Cespedes, K. (2018) 'Genderacing immigrant subjects: "Anchor babies" and the politics of birthright citizenship', *Social Identities*, 24(3): 312–326.

Lalander, P. and Herz, M. (2018) '"I am going to Europe tomorrow": The myth of the anchor child and the decision to flee in the narratives of unaccompanied children', *Nordic Journal of Migration Research*, 8(2): 91–98.

Lederer, J. (2013) '"Anchor baby": A conceptual explanation for pejoration', *Journal of Pragmatics*, 57: 248–266.

Lee-Koo, K. (2020) 'Decolonizing childhood in international relations', in M. Beier (ed) *Discovering Childhood in International Relations*, Cham: Palgrave Macmillan, pp 21–40.

Lemberg-Pedersen, M. (2021) 'The humanitarianization of child deportation politics', *Journal of Borderlands Studies*, 36(2): 239–258.

Lind, J. (2019) 'Governing vulnerabilised migrant childhoods through children's rights', *Childhood*, 26(3): 337–351.

Lugo-Lugo, C.R. and Bloodsworth-Lugo, M.K. (2014) '"Anchor/terror babies" and Latina bodies: Immigration rhetoric in the 21st century and the feminization of terrorism', *Journal of Interdisciplinary Feminist Thought*, 8(1): 1–14.

Martuscelli, P. (2018) 'Milhares vão às ruas em 700 cidades nos EUA contra a política migratória de Trump', MigraMundo, 2 July. Available from: https://migramundo.com/milhares-vao-as-ruas-em-700-cidades-nos-eua-contra-a-politica-migratoria-de-trump/ [Accessed 26 May 2023].

Mishori, R. (2019) 'The use of age assessment in the context of child migration: Imprecise, inaccurate, inconclusive and endangers children's rights', *Children*, 6(7): 85.

Ormonde, M.E. (2012) 'Debunking the myth of the anchor baby: Why proposed legislation limiting birthright citizenship is not a means of controlling unauthorized immigration', *Roger Williams University Law Review*, 17, 861–886.

Schmidt, S. (2018) 'Endangered mothers or "anchor babies"? Migration motivators for pregnant unaccompanied Central American teens', *Vulnerable Children and Youth Studies*, 13(4): 374–384.

Silverman, S.J. (2016) '"Imposter-children" in the UK refugee status determination process', *Refuge: Canada's Journal on Refugees*, 32(3): 30–39.

Smyth, C. (2015) 'The best interests of the child in the expulsion and first-entry jurisprudence of the European Court of Human Rights: How principled is the Court's use of the principle?', *European Journal of Migration and Law*, 17(1): 70–103.

Sohlberg, J., Esaiasson, P., and Martinsson, J. (2019) 'The changing political impact of compassion-evoking pictures: The case of the drowned toddler Alan Kurdi', *Journal of Ethnic and Migration Studies*, 45(13): 2275–2288.

Stretmo, L. (2014) *Governing the Unaccompanied Child: Media, Policy and Practice*, Göteborg: Göteborgs Universitet.

Tapaninen, A.M., Halme-Tuomisaari, M., and Kankaanpää, V. (2019) 'Mobile lives, immutable facts: Family reunification of children in Finland', *Journal of Ethnic and Migration Studies*, 45(5): 825–841.

United Nations Convention on the Rights of the Child (UNCRC) (1989) New York, November 20, *United Nations Treaty Series*, vol 1577, p 3. Available from: https://treaties.un.org/Pages/ViewDetails.aspx?src=TREATY&mtdsg_no=IV-11&chapter=4&clang=_en [Accessed 3 April 2023].

Vitus, K. and Jarlby, F. (2021) 'Between integration and repatriation–frontline experiences of how conflicting immigrant integration policies hamper the integration of young refugees in Denmark', *Journal of Ethnic and Migration Studies*, 48(7): 1496–1514.

Wallis, E. (2021) 'Impeachment trial for former Danish migration minister', *Infomigrants*, [online], 3 February. Available from: https://www.infomigrants.net/en/post/30041/impeachment-trial-for-former-danish-migration-minister [Accessed 3 April 2023].

Yoon-Hendricks, A. and Greenberg, Z. (2018) 'Protests across US call for end to migrant family separations', *The New York Times*, [online] 30 June. Available from: https://www.nytimes.com/2018/06/30/us/politics/trump-protests-family-separation.html [Accessed 3 April 2023].

2

Creating Inclusive Reconciliation and Reporting Spaces with Children: Valuing Their Stories

Caitlin Mollica

Introduction

Truth and Reconciliation Commissions (TRCs) are a widely used mechanism in the transitional justice toolkit today. The purpose and success of TRCs is widely debated within transitional justice scholarship (see Jeffery and Mollica, 2017: 531). Yet there is broad agreement among practitioners and scholars that their emphasis on storytelling provides important opportunities for dialogue within transitional communities, which enables these societies to confront past human rights violations (Quinn, 2010; Philpott, 2015). Participation of children in this dialogue is often ambiguous, inconsistent, highly mediated, and driven by political agendas. As demonstrated throughout this chapter, this ambiguity is evident in how TRCs manage their relationships with children, specifically their obligation to inform on the outcomes of their political participation. Of the 52 TRCs that have occurred since the 1970s, only the reports from Sierra Leone, Timor-Leste, and Canada have been reproduced in forms that children can access and engage with substantively. As such, many TRCs perpetuate marginalizing, apolitical discourses of childhood by excluding children from the political outcomes of reconciliation that their knowledge contributed to through storytelling.

Where children are concerned, the value assigned to their stories by transitional justice mechanisms often denotes a politicized agenda, overlooking the empowerment potential for the individual. Through the act of public sharing, storytelling can 'reconstitute families, communities and relations' while allowing individuals to 'find one's voice in the making of … history' (Baines and Stewart, 2011: 258). Yet children's stories have become inextricably tied to broader peace narratives, thus producing a tension between the collective and the individual. This is compounded by the nature of their participation, which requires that their stories are retold and shared through mechanisms that are often inaccessible and disconnected from their reconciliation experiences, particularly during the dissemination phase. Children's interactions with institutionalized reconciliation practices such as TRCs, therefore, are often static and unresponsive, as the use of their stories as symbols for external political pursuits or the international peace agenda has become normalized. To that end, within the international peace architecture, Children and their lived experiences are often reduced to political resources despite widespread performative political engagement through testimony at TRC hearings and other consultative forums.

Creating equitable and inclusive reconciliation spaces *with* children that look beyond these external agendas requires greater consideration of how these institutions fulfil their obligations *to* children as political actors. Substantive participation should facilitate reciprocity between the architects of the reconciliation mechanisms and contributors. Historically, children have performed their obligations as citizens, and their participation during TRCs has become expected practice (Mollica, 2017; Alonso, Chapter 3, this volume). What continues to be overlooked, however, is the obligation to report the commission's findings to children.

The implementation of more inclusive and responsive processes remains a challenge for TRC architects and the successful realization of reconciliations mandates. Central to this are continued concerns regarding how best to fulfil reciprocal communication responsibilities to *all* stakeholders who participate. For children in particular, a failure to close the *feedback loop* by providing access to the findings of the TRCs persists, due in part to the value we as adults assign to their contributions. Within the international architecture, a disconnect persists, which perpetuates the social exclusion of children by failing to recognize displays of citizenship through mutual obligations and reciprocity. In addition, the failure to acknowledge the character of their participation, where children are valued as children rather than political objects, has broader implications for the capacity of international actors to substantively engage *with* children and their contributions as political actors.

This chapter considers the role of accessible reporting in the realization of inclusive reconciliation processes that value children as political agents rather than as embodiments of peace. Drawing on examples from the reporting processes in Sierra Leone and Timor-Leste, it argues that TRCs have an obligation to produce accessible reports that inform children *as* citizens about the contributions of their participation. Normalizing accessible reporting for TRCs offers opportunities for more inclusive processes beyond the reconciliation landscape. By creating models for the institutionalization of reciprocal practices, accessible reporting by TRCs provides benchmarks for the development of international processes that are developed *with* not *for* children.

Reproducing stories of conflict through Truth and Reconciliation Commissions

By making visible the conflict stories of citizens, TRC reports establish the engagement parameters between transitional governments and the community. While not a consistently mandated outcome of reconciliation processes, reports are a valuable tool for the fulfilment of a transitional government's obligation to provide a public and transparent record of human rights violations (Jeffery and Mollica, 2017). This record is produced following a comprehensive investigative process that collects conflict narratives through public and private hearings, written statements, and focus groups. Since the South African TRC, children have participated in these storytelling processes; however, apart from a few exceptions the character of their participation and contribution has been mediated by adults (Mollica, 2017). The introduction of accessible reporting in Sierra Leone, Timor-Leste, and more recently Canada reflects attempts by transitional justice architects to move away from externally facilitated and exclusionary forms of participation and to recognize children as citizens with political agency.

Mechanisms that facilitate inclusive and substantive dialogue about previous human rights violations are integral to the legitimacy of reconciliation outcomes. Institutionalizing reconciliation narratives through multiple and diverse platforms limits the potential for 'states, societies and perpetrators to deny uncomfortable truths about their pasts' and 'the range of permissible lies' told by stakeholders 'whose interests are not ... served by the truth' (Brahm, 2007). Accessible reporting also provides opportunities for children to feel connected to their country's violent history and attempts to overcome it. This connectedness is integral to empowering leadership and political buy-in among children through a process of sense-making, which ensures they are invested in successful reconciliation and transitional justice outcomes. Despite this, architects of TRCs have largely overlooked the importance of providing forums for children to receive information about past conflicts.

Without these dissemination mechanisms, the conflict narratives that TRCs produce are rendered invisible to children, thus leaving reconciliation mandates unfulfilled. As Karen Brounéus observes, successful 'reconciliation is a societal process' that not only 'involves mutual acknowledgement of past suffering' but also 'the changing of destructive attitudes and behaviours into constructive relationships towards sustainable peace' (Brounéus, 2008). Fulfilment of a state's reconciliation aims, therefore, requires widespread and meaningful engagement with formal conflict narratives to restore authentic relationships between all citizens, including children. Yet the normalization of accessible reporting processes remains an afterthought, due in part to the persistence of normative discourses that prioritize a protectionist mandate when constructing institutional interactions with children.

Establishing normative guidelines for children's engagement

The normative principles which established the parameters for the interaction of children with transitional justice institutions are underpinned by the obligations outlined in the 1989 United Nations Convention on the Rights of the Child (UNCRC). In particular, the UNCRC codified for the first time a child's right to participation and to express their own views as a political actor (Holzscheiter, 2010). Despite structural hierarchies that prevent the realization of this commitment to children's participation and expression (Kwon, 2019); the UNCRC's principles continue to offer a useful entry point for discourses on their institutional engagement. Furthermore, it provides an initial scaffold for understanding the obligations of institutions to children as rights holders.

Children's engagement, however, should not be conceived solely through the lens of the UNCRC as the framework perpetuates a siloed approach to participation. Participation understood through a protectionist framework, as in the UNCRC, allows adults to determine the participatory parameters *for* children (Arce, 2015: 291). They are, as such, rights holders without possessing the agency and voice afforded other rights-bearing citizens. An overreliance on normative guidelines that deny children status as full citizens has implications in reconciliation contexts as it determines how their stories are employed and by whom.

When children's participation is mediated by adults, their voices are employed as embodiments for peace and institutionalized in formats inaccessible to children themselves. The detachment of children from their stories and the negative implications of this siloing reflect broader claims within global politics concerning the need for institutional structures that overcome objectification (see Johnson, Chapter 4, this volume; Beier, 2020). While institutions continue to utilize children as political resources rather than autonomous political agents, substantive engagement will be unattainable. The Sierra Leone and Timor-Leste cases offer important policy lessons for architects of TRC reporting regarding the production of inclusive mechanisms for the dissemination of children's stories in ways that respect their political agency.

Childhoods as integral to future-making? Advocacy for a child-friendly report in Sierra Leone

When children's experiences are institutionalized through a singular protectionist framework, their stories become frozen. These modalities, which envisage childhoods 'out of sequence', remaining untouched by violence, create unresponsive and apolitical spaces for children's public interactions (Shaw, 2014). Nevertheless, these images persist as they are central to the politicized agenda of transitional states, which pursues the resumption of societal innocence through the child. Following conflict, the politics of future-making is underpinned by discourses where 'lost childhoods' are conceptualized as a lasting threat to sustainable peace, and thus reconciliation practices, such as TRCs, seek to reproduce conditions where children are protected to act as children.

At the centre of this discourse is the persistent belief that childhood is a period marked by innocence and development where all behaviours are apolitical (Shepler, 2014). Yet as the interactions between children and the Sierra Leonean TRC process outlined below reveal, an important distinction exists between the apolitical child and the politically excluded child. Public and institutionalized interactions between children and the state are inherently and often subconsciously informed by politics, which challenges the persistent echoes of imagined childhoods within global politics. The myth of the apolitical child is further revealed by Sean Carter and Tara Woodyer (Chapter 11, this volume), who conclude that regardless of motivation, children's capacity to remake and reimagine the social world through play is always political. As such, it is impossible to separate public interactions with children from their political agency.

Children's embodiment as the future heightens the critical imperative of the protection mandate within transitional justice processes. At the same time, it diminishes their political agency, making them objects for the legitimacy of the protective practices implemented by 'real' political subjects rather than leaders of change. When children's stories are employed to represent a collective peaceful future, they occupy political spaces that reflect the broader responsibility of the state for national development and historical change. Assigning external meanings to children's experiences of conflict, particularly those that are static, creates unresponsive reconciliation practices. While children institutionally occupy a dual positioning as apolitical and embodiments of hope, for children themselves TRCs have the capacity to be empowering, particularly when their contributions are made visible through accessible reporting. During the Sierra Leone TRC, for example, children expressed a desire to 'work ... to repair the wrongs and to build a just and fair future', 'to forgive', and to 'uphold peace' (Commission for the Sierra Leone TRC, 2004: 2). These motivations, which are illustrative of children's political agency, highlight the importance of their advocacy around the production of an accessible and inclusive report.

The Sierra Leone TRC is widely considered a model for the direct engagement of children as it was the first to create a child-friendly report (Cook and Heykoop, 2010). A commitment to inclusive engagement in

Sierra Leone is also evident in the simultaneous production of a video report and a secondary school version of the report to accompany the original report and the child-friendly version. Providing multiple platforms for citizens to engage with the narratives of the conflict ensured that the accountability component of the Commission's mandate was realized, and it reveals the value of equity, accessibility, and transparency to the realization of sustainable peace through reconciliation. Furthermore, the multiple engagement mechanisms provided by the Sierra Leonean TRC process empowered citizens by creating a reporting framework where individuals could choose how they exercise their right to information. Where children are concerned, their advocacy on the production of the report has helped give shape to more holistic reconciliation narratives that not only reflect their conflict experiences, but also subtle, although inconsistent, shifts in the nature of childhood within international politics. The children of Sierra Leone lobbied the Commission for a child-friendly report so that their experiences would be accessible not only for other children within Sierra Leone, but to children outside Sierra Leone. In doing so, they sought to create an inclusive and transparent forum for their stories.

Importantly, the child-friendly report is an official account of the Commission's findings that was prepared jointly by the Commission, UNICEF, and children throughout Sierra Leone. The assigning of official status to this version of the Commission's findings lends legitimacy to the voices of children in the process. Further, it reflected the growing national and international sentiment at the time, which acknowledged the role of children as political stakeholders within the post-conflict communities (Fisher, 2013).

The voices of children were central to the development of this accessible version as their ideas helped give shape to its format. Children's participation in the process was facilitated through three networks: the Children's Forum Network, Voice of Children Radio, and the Children's National Assembly. The Children's National Assembly held in December 2003 brought children together from all districts for the drafting of the report, and parts of this assembly were broadcast on national television and radio (TRC and UNICEF, 2004). Underpinning these elements of the drafting process are the principles of partnership, relationship building, and inclusivity.

The creation of a child-friendly report in Sierra Leone reflects one of the earliest uses of the partnership discourse to frame the relationship between children and the political community. A shift towards partnerships represents a significant departure from the dominant discourse established and institutionalized through the international Children and Armed Conflict (CaAC) agenda, which is underpinned by a single pillar: 'the protection of children in conflict' (Lee-Koo, 2019). While organizations in Sierra Leone were empowering children to co-develop an accessible reporting approach in response to the conflict, a more narrowly defined discourse on children was solidifying internationally through the adoption of UN Security Council Resolution 1460 (2003).

Resolution 1460 and subsequent resolutions institutionalized an approach to children's conflict experiences that situates their citizenship on the margins, where participation is heavily mediated and the recognition owed to children and their political agency minimalized. By normalizing protectionism as the standard for Member States' interactions with children (UN Security Council, 2003), the international CaAC agenda fails to create spaces for the impact of children's political agency and voice on citizenship discourses and their associated obligations (Tabak, 2020: 129).

These parallel yet competing discourses, which are employed to inform how formal peace and conflict institutions interact with children, demonstrate a tension concerning beliefs about children's capacity as citizens. The Sierra Leone TRC's reporting process provides an exemplar for recognizing the responsibilities *to* children. This inclusive process is, as such, unique in its acknowledgement of how children's contribution to knowledge reflects citizenship. Children are highly visible within today's international peace architecture. However, diverse understandings of the reciprocal, duty-laden nature of their relationship with these institutions remain fragmented and peripheral (Beier, 2020). Broadly, the CaAC agenda through its prioritizing of a protectionist framework continues to normalize a limited understanding of the duties owed by institutions to children. Yet models for accessible reporting in Sierra Leone and Timor-Leste (discussed below) demonstrate that when reconciliation institutions engage with children as citizens, they provide forums for more responsive and inclusive peace.

Receiving knowledge for empowerment: accessible reporting in Timor-Leste

Meaningful reconciliation with children requires accessible storytelling and reporting. Dissemination mechanisms which consider how stories are received offer greater opportunities for children to connect with the significance of narratives from the past for their future. Accessible reporting also provides a platform for individuals traditionally excluded from meaningful engagement with reconciliation practices to connect with and build trust in the institutions responsible for their implementation. Socialization and trust in institutional processes by young people are necessary conditions for ensuring inclusive reconciliation. Without these, institutional processes often lack the widespread political buy-in necessary to produce sustainable and meaningful justice (Quinn, 2010).

Where children are concerned, knowledge of institutional processes, such as TRCs, and trust in their capacity to pursue responsive justice often determine the degree of legitimacy ascribed to these mechanisms (Schwartz, 2010: 18). Belief in the promised outcomes of these institutions (namely reconciliation and justice) by children who participated in their processes also informs their willingness to advocate for the broader human rights values they promote. Participation for inclusion in TRC processes reflects an important first step for creating reconciliation practices that are responsive to children's voices (Lee-Koo, 2015: 203). Socialization and trust, however, necessitate a more active process of engagement that respects children's political agency. Historical examples of TRCs often heralded as landmarks with respect to the inclusiveness of children, including those in South Africa and the Solomon Islands, reflect an incomplete process due to the nature of the participation. These TRCs demonstrate a broader trend within the transitional justice field towards capturing children's voices and ensuring their visibility through hearings and testimonial processes (Rana and Zvobgo, 2021).

However, they also reveal a continued overreliance on passive and hierarchical forms of participation, where the outcomes of children's engagement remain inaccessible. As such, these mechanisms often fail to reflect children's capacity to be 'politically transformative' and to 'see their ideas take shape' and 'influence their communities' (Lee-Koo, 2015: 203). Since the South African TRC, children are increasingly heard by TRCs. However, these institutions have largely failed to consider how the information gathered at hearings and compiled in formal state-sanctioned reports is disseminated and received by children.

The accessible reconciliation reporting in Timor-Leste provided important opportunities for children to engage and take ownership of the lessons of the TRC. After the Commission launched its official report, a group of educators and human rights activists from Timor-Leste and Indonesia worked to produce a version in comic form that would be accessible for 'schools and young people around the world' (Commission for Reception, Truth and Reconciliation 2015: vi). The editor's note, addressed to teachers, promotes its educative value, suggesting that 'the Timor story ... is informative in terms of events and players but more deeply, in terms of the values taught' (Commission for Reception, Truth and Reconciliation, 2015: vi). Accessible reporting of the Timor-Leste TRC findings through comics, therefore, provides important insights into developing spaces for children's agency at all stages of institutional reconciliation.

The CHEGA! comics are a five-book series which tell the story of the human rights violations committed during the civil conflict in Timor-Leste (1974–1999). Dissemination of a 'popular' version of the final report of the *Timor-Leste Commission for Reception, Truth, and Reconciliation* (CAVR) reflected shifting discourses surrounding the need for reconciliation mechanisms that facilitate an inclusive, educative dialogue across generations.

These discourses acknowledge and seek to respect children as capable political actors and human rights bearers. The focus on accessible reporting for children aligned with expanding international legal norms associated with Article 12 of the UNCRC regarding the value of participatory interactions with children for peace and justice. Participatory approaches that empower and take seriously children's contributions in the political environment are, therefore, recognized for their intrinsic, substantive value rather than an obligation or a 'means to an end' (Holzscheiter, 2010: 74–75). This is evident throughout the comics as there is an emphasis on informative knowledge exchange, led importantly by the child characters and represented through images where the children are located at the centre of the dialogue.

Receiving knowledge about conflict and justice events through fictionalized stories with identifiable characters demystifies the process for children and socializes the norms that underpin these institutions, creating trust in their outcomes and recommendations. The emphasis on sense-making through association throughout the CHEGA! comics is illustrated by the dialogue between the two children when discussing the harms experienced during the conflict. When the young girl expresses disbelief that 'terrible things happened in [the] country', the young boy responds, 'when you think about it, kids like us must have gone through these ordeals too' (CHEGA!, vol 4, 2015: 72). Through the fictionalized children, audiences to the report are given an opportunity to reflect on the universal challenges of human rights violations during war and to 'see themselves' in the experiences.

In addition, each of the comic volumes tells the story of the conflict and the TRC and is accompanied by a 'notice board' where the fictional children engage in a discussion that connects the local Timor context with global human rights discourse. In the chapter on children's experiences, for example, the fictional young girl explains, 'my teacher at school said that all children have the same rights as adults, like the right to life, the right to freedom from torture, and other rights' (CHEGA!, vol 5, 2015: 40). In response, the young boy notes, 'Yes, I heard that too. ... She also said that under the Geneva Conventions Indonesia has duties towards children like evacuating them from the field of conflict and that by signing the Convention on the Rights of the Child in 1990 Indonesia accepted further obligations to children' (CHEGA!, vol 5 2015: 41). In conversation with each other, the two children provide an entry point for audiences to connect the relevance of Timor's conflict story to their own experiences. By situating the conflict experiences of Timorese children within a broader global dialogue on human rights and state obligations, these comics disseminate the stories of Timor in ways that resonate across generations.

Creating fictionalized characters and 'stories' to inform children about real events and values is becoming an increasingly common practice in peacebuilding. Stories and 'make believe' offer children a forum to exercise political agency over processes which require them to 'make-sense' of and 'interpret' their experiences (Cairns, 1996: 83–85). This approach, however, has yet to become normalized within transitional justice practices. Despite this, the CHEGA! comics demonstrate that TRCs, which are based in storytelling, offer a logical platform for the development of more responsive reconciliation practices for children that emphasize the socialization of localized and global knowledge.

Prioritizing storytelling that centres Timor-Leste children as the leading voices in the dialogue also fulfils an often-overlooked reporting obligation (Jeffery and Mollica, 2017). Traditional reporting of TRC findings is often highly politicized and dense, prioritizing legal jargon to convey the stories of conflict and recommendations for reconciliation. The final report of CAVR, for example, is 3,216 pages long. TRC reports when released only in this form are inaccessible to large portions of the populations, particularly those excluded from formal institutions, without access to the internet, or lacking the knowledge to absorb legal texts. As such, TRCs that distribute their findings only through governments and online do not achieve their reconciliation mandate as this complex reporting format lacks transparency and visibility among marginalized communities, in particular children. In contrast, the format of the CHEGA! comics offers an alternative format for fulfilling this reporting obligation and creating transparency for children about the process. The comics acknowledge the significance of this accessibility as audiences are told that the children are visiting the offices of the Truth Commission to 'see for [themselves]' how the process of institutional reconciliation occurred in Timor-Leste, and 'to know about the suffering that occurred' during the conflict (CHEGA!, vol 1 2015: 6).

By empowering the fictional children to lead a discussion on rights, the comics act as a symbol for children's capacity to lead and engage politically with complex conflict narratives and their global significance (see also Alonso, Chapter 3, this volume). Accessible reconciliation reporting such as these comics provides valuable insights into the process of truth-telling, demystifying it and creating buy-in among individuals often excluded from these institutional practices. As Priscilla Hayner explains in her foreword, the comics 'provide a useful glimpse into how "truth commissions" undertake their work' (CHEGA!, 2015: 5). Thus, not only do they socialize the story of Timor's conflict for children; they also act as an accessible manual on the institutional process for a wide range of actors, particularly those often left out of the development process for these institutional mechanisms.

Where children are concerned, accessible reporting allows for greater agency over their interactions with truth-telling institutions and the stories they tell. This is evident in the CHEGA! comics, which follow a family of four as the two adults (both teachers and victims of the conflict) guide their children through the CAVR office and memorial centre, 'so [the children] can see for [themselves]' what happened during the conflict, and the process of reporting (CHEGA!, 2015: 7). One of the most prominent narrative tools used by the CHEGA! comics is the inquisitive child, where the fictional children control the narrative as information is only provided in response to their questions. In the context of broader global debates regarding the role of children in politics, appeals to the inquisitive child within reconciliation practices challenge the status quo of institutions, which remain reliant on passive characterizations to inform their interactions with children. Throughout the five volumes, the fictionalized children have ownership over the storytelling process, asking wide-ranging questions about the process, the types of human rights abuses, and victims' experiences. In doing so, these fictionalized images create a safe space for young people to engage with complex questions about reconciliation processes through the production of a symbolic peer-to-peer dialogue between the children in the story and students engaging with the report. When institutions acknowledge the political curiosities of children, they also encounter engaged and competent children who perform knowledge practices.

The relationship between universal applicability and accessibility is echoed by Priscilla Hayner in her introduction to the *CHEGA!* comics. She notes that this 'popular' version of the report provides opportunities for the conflict story of Timor-Leste to 'reach the broader readership' (*CHEGA!*, 2015: 5). As such, the comic version pursues practical and normative accessibility by highlighting the relevance of a distant past to current and future claims for peace and human rights accountability. As the editors note, 'no-one could study *CHEGA!* without swearing off bullying, thinking twice about war and peace, and gaining a deeper insight into human rights and [its] global importance in today's fractured, violent world' (*CHEGA!*, 2015: 5). The *CHEGA!* comics thus provide a space for children to connect more meaningfully with the stories of the past.

Relevance and relatability are important yet often overlooked concerns for transitional justice mechanisms aiming to establish acknowledgement as a justice approach (Quinn, 2010). Where children are concerned, the potential for reconciliation to create and restore bonds of social capital and trust through acknowledgement will be determined by their capacity to connect to the stories and processes. Central to this is the restoration of interpersonal connections through learning, which produces empathy (Philpott, 2015: 129). Children's substantive participation in reconciliation practices as such requires that TRC architects consider not only strategies for inclusion in hearings but also the development of practices which ensure information is meaningfully received by the children who participated and future generations.

Conclusion

Children's status as engaged political actors is evidenced by the evolving expectation within the transitional justice field that they participate in TRCs as knowledge producers. However, while children are enthusiastically performing their participatory duty, thus fulfilling their obligation as citizens, this often remains unacknowledged. TRCs, which are sanctioned by transitional governments, have largely failed in their reciprocal responsibility to these citizens by not reporting their findings using mechanisms which are accessible to children. Yet, as the cases of Sierra Leone and Timor-Leste demonstrate, accessible reporting that values children's voices is critical as it provides broader lessons for global political institutions regarding the importance of building trust through community engagement.

Reconciliation processes have evolved considerably to create enabling environments where children are seen *and* heard. What continues to be overlooked, however, is how reconciliation processes close the feedback loop between participants and the institutions and thus fulfil their obligations to citizens for transparency and accountability. Capturing young people's voices in TRCs comes with obligations for dissemination. As such, greater consideration is needed with respect to how institutions share with children the contributions of their stories to the reconciliation agenda.

References

Arce, M.C. (2015) 'Maturing children's rights theory: From children, with children, of children', *The International Journal of Children's Rights* 23(2): 283–331.

Baines, E. and Stewart, B. (2011) '"I cannot accept what I have not done": Storytelling, gender and transitional justice', *Journal of Human Rights Practice* 3(3):245–263.

Beier, J.M. (ed) (2020) *Discovering Childhood in International Relations*, Switzerland: Palgrave.

Brahm, E. (2007) 'Uncovering the truth: Examining truth commission success and impact', *International Studies* 8(1): 16–35.

Brounéus, K. (2008) 'Truth-telling as talking cure? Insecurity and retraumatization in the Rwandan Gacaca courts', *Security Dialogue* 39(1), 55–76.

Cairns, E. (1996) *Children and Political Violence*, Oxford: Blackwell Publishing.

CHEGA! (Books 1–5) (2015) Asia Justice and Rights, Secretariado Tecnico Pos-CAVR, and Dili, Timor-Leste: INSIST Press.

Commission for Reception, Truth and Reconciliation (2015) *CHEGA! The final report of the Timor Leste Commission for Reception Truth and Reconciliation,* Dili, Timor-Lest: INSIST Press.

Commission for the Sierra Leone TRC (2004) *Witness to Truth: Report of the Sierra Leone Truth and Reconciliation Commission,* Ghana: GPL Press.

Cook, P. and Heykoop, C. (2010) 'Child participation in the Sierra Leonean Truth and Reconciliation Commission', in S. Parmar, J. Roseman, S. Siegrist, and T. Sowa (eds) *Children and Transitional Justice,* Cambridge, MA: Harvard University Press, pp 159–192.

Fisher, K. (2013) *Transitional Justice for Child Soldiers: Accountability and Social Reconstruction in Post-conflict Contexts,* New York: Palgrave Macmillan.

Holzscheiter, A. (2010) *Children's Rights in International Politics: The Transformative Power of Discourse,* New York: Springer.

Jeffery, R. and Mollica, C. (2017) 'The unfinished business of the Solomon Islands TRC: closing the implementation gap', *The Pacific Review* 30(4): 531–548.

Kwon, S.A. (2019) 'The politics of global youth participation', *Journal of Youth Studies,* 22(7): 926–940.

Lee-Koo, K. (2015) 'Children and peace building: Propagating Peace', in K. Huynh, B. D'Costa, and K. Lee-Koo (eds) *Children and Global Conflict,* Cambridge: Cambridge University Press, pp 185–211.

Lee-Koo, K. (2019) 'WPS, children, and armed conflict', in S. Davies and J. True (eds) *The Oxford Handbook of Women, Peace and Security,* Oxford: Oxford University Press, pp 608–617.

Mollica, C. (2017) 'The diversity of identity: Youth participation at the Solomon Islands Truth and Reconciliation Commission', *Australian Journal of International Affairs* 71(4): 371–388.

Philpott, D. (2015) *Just and Unjust Peace: An Ethic of Political Reconciliation,* Oxford: Oxford University Press.

Quinn, J.R. (2010) *Reconciliation(s): Transitional Justice in Post-Conflict Societies,* Toronto: McGill-Queens Press.

Rana, S.S. and Zvobgo, K. (2021) 'Safeguarding truth: Supporting children's participation at truth commissions', *Journal of Human Rights* 20(3): 1–22.

Schwartz, S. (2010) *Youth and Post-conflict Reconstruction: Agents of Change,* Washington, DC: US Institute of Peace Press.

Shaw, R. (2014) 'The TRC, the NGO and the child: Young people and post-conflict futures in Sierra Leone', *Social Anthropology* 22(3): 306–325.

Shepler, S. (2014) *Childhood Deployed: Remaking Child Soldiers in Sierra Leone,* New York: NYU Press.

Tabak, J. (2020) 'A tale of a (dis)orderly international society: Protecting Child Soldiers, Saving The Child, Governing The Future', in J.M. Beier (ed) *Discovering Childhood in International Relations*, Cham: Palgrave, pp 115–134.

TRC and UNICEF (2004) 'Truth and Reconciliation Report for the Children of Sierra Leone', FreeTown: UNICEF & UNAMSIL.

UN Security Council (2003) *Security Council resolution 1460 (2003) [on children in armed conflict]*, 30 January, S/RES/1460 (2003).

3

Stories about Children Born of Violence: Counter-narratives in the Peruvian Truth Commission's Archive and Popular Culture

Ana Lucia Alonso Soriano

Introduction

From 1980 to 2000, Peru experienced an internal armed conflict between the Peruvian state, the Communist Party of Peru–Shining Path (PCP-SL), the Tupac Amaru Revolutionary Movement (MRTA), and others. After the resignation of Alberto Fujimori in 2000 as president of Peru due to corruption charges, the Peruvian Truth and Reconciliation Commission (PTRC) was created by the transitional government of interim President Valentin Paniagua in 2001, with the mandate to research the causes of the conflict and the human rights violations. The PTRC was seen as part of an exemplary transitional justice case to reach a successful transition to democracy (Boesten, 2014). From 2001 to 2003, the PTRC gathered 16,986 testimonies to produce the *Final Report*.[1] The PTRC relied heavily on the testimonies gathered as the emphasis was placed on victims' narrated experiences about the conflict, and the work done for the chapter on sexual violence against women was no exception. The PTRC *Final Report* acknowledged that the state forces were the foremost perpetrators of sexual violence, and in doing so, it recognized that several children born of violence were born after assaults. These children were mentioned in the *Final Report*, public hearings, and the data gathered and produced by the PTRC as 'abandoned children', 'children without a father', 'soldiers' children', or the 'product of rape'.[2]

Stories about children born of violence have emerged in post-conflict Peru. These stories provide alternative accounts of children born of violence that counter the promoted version of the PTRC conflict memory. The counter-narratives can be found within the realm of the PTRC in interviews, testimonies, birth certificates, and all the material gathered and produced by the PTRC that is kept in the archive and the realm of popular culture. The counter-narratives about children born of violence challenge the promoted narratives on sexual violence against women by the PTRC, in which children born of violence were portrayed as evidence to demonstrate their mother's rape. The counter-narratives situate several narratives, but in general terms, they display that children's identities are continuously constructed and contested in Peru nowadays.

In this chapter, the analysis of the stories about children born of violence as counter-narratives reminds us of the existence of children born of violence as more than just channels to reflect on the trauma of war, as has been suggested in the literature on children born of war (Carpenter, 2007, 2010; Seto, 2013). Instead, I argue that stories of children born of violence perform a significant political function according to their unique political status. The children of the state expose responsibility and impunity at the state level for crimes committed against women and children at the individual level. The relevance of this chapter is clear: we must find a space where the stories about children born of violence can be told and contest any attempt to objectify and homogenize these stories and injustices by truth commissions and several other mechanisms of transitional justice. The stories of children born of violence have an important role in the construction and contestation of the memory of conflict and any efforts towards peacebuilding.[3] Counter-narratives can be found within the realm of the PTRC archive and in popular culture. The stories of children born of violence as counter-narratives can illustrate how complex their stories are by representing children as subjects (instead of objects understood as evidence of rape), with a different temporality than the narrative established by the PTRC (there are no clear beginnings or ends), and challenging the binary and fixed identities constructed, used, and promoted by the PTRC.

All the data used in this chapter, including the PTRC data, was collected during fieldwork in Peru in 2015.[4] I had access to the gathered and produced information from the PTRC that was in the PTRC archive located in the Peruvian Ombudsman Office in Lima, Peru.[5] Regarding fictionalized data, there are several novels regarding the conflict violence and its consequences, as well as focusing on sexual violence and, to a lesser extent, on children born of wartime rape.[6] The selected novel was *Finding Cholita* (2009) by anthropologist Billie Jean Isbell, for the following reasons. Firstly, the author explains that as an anthropologist for many years she focused on researching violence in the Andean region of Peru, and she absorbed the horror from the stories about the violence. She drew on fiction to tell the stories expressed by her interviewees and protect them from any possible harm, and because fiction allowed her to have 'the freedom to create a conclusion that ethnography could not sustain' (Isbell, 2009: x). Secondly, the novel focuses on tracing the life of the child born of violence before, during, and after the conflict violence and the PTRC. This setting of the time before, during, and after opens possibilities to explore the temporalities of children born of violence .

This research undertakes a narrative analysis of the data. The focus is on the content and how the stories are told, who is telling the story, and how children born of violence are depicted. It is essential to highlight that the voices of children born of violence are still absent in many of these accounts in popular culture, but some of these stories explore the unstable identities, stories, and temporality of these children.[7]

Dominant narratives and counter-narratives in memorialization processes

'New approaches define narrative and narrativity as concepts of social epistemology and social ontology. These concepts posit that it is through narrativity that we come to know, understand, and make sense of the social world, and it is through narratives and narrativity that we constitute our social identities.' (Somers, 1994: 606). An analysis of discourses and narratives as dichotomic will not be fruitful, as the way discourses and narratives function is more complex and malleable (Foucault, 1978).[8] However, an analysis of those narratives that are 'dominant or hegemonic' in specific times shows that they are naturalized and normalized knowledge or expressions in a society, even totalizing truths. The power of narratives is that their 'multiplicity of discursive elements can come into play in various strategies' and moments (Foucault, 1978: 100).[9] The dominant narratives 'offer people a way of identifying what is assumed to be a normative experience' that is naturalized, internalized, and reproduced (Andrews, 2004: 1), and they are strong cultural forms; for example, a popular narrative of motherhood refers to women's desired and unescapable natural role as mothers (Andrews, 2004). In contrast, the counter-narratives in this chapter are different stories or interpretations from excluded minority groups that position themselves in the margins and challenge, resist, and disrupt the dominant narratives at certain times. However, it is important to acknowledge that counter-narratives can make sense of what they are countering, but both master and counter-narratives are fluid and relational categories (Bamberg and Andrews, 2004).

As a transitional justice mechanism, truth commissions can contribute to prosecutions and reparations through their research of past human rights violations. Truth commissions are legal spaces in which law and legal instruments play a role in constructing and framing narratives and temporalities to construct the memory of the conflict. The transitional justice discourses are discursive narrative technologies with a narrative scheme through which the memory of the conflict is constructed (Moon, 2006). Claire Moon (2006: 268) argues that 'narrative, typically, imposes form upon its subjects – "victims" and "perpetrators" – and objects – "gross violations of human rights" – because it arranges actions and events in a sequential and connected relationship and embeds them with a tri-partite temporal structure which consists of a well-marked beginning, middle and end'. The narrative is organized in a story form that starts with the conflict violence from the past, a present marked by the confessions and testimonies from victims, survivors, and perpetrators, and a future focus on reconciliation (Moon, 2006).

In Peru, a process took place by which societies construct hierarchies of victimhood that are reflected in justice systems but also in memorialization practices. Jennie Burnet (2009) highlights the politicization of memory and victimhood in the state practices of memory in Rwanda after the 1994 genocide, as it had sustained the ethnic difference (Hutu and Tutsi) through a dominant and hegemonic conception between victims and perpetrators. Some of the effects of these state practices to define victimhood were the erasure of some stories that did not fit in the dichotomic and hegemonic public discourse about the memory of the genocide.[10] In the case of Peru, the PTRC produced a particular narrative about sexual violence against women that objectified children born of violence (as evidence of rape) to construct women's victimhood and a particular set of linear temporalities in which children born of violence and their stories are disruptive.

Narratives about sexual violence that objectified children born of violence in the PTRC

The promoted narratives about sexual violence that objectified children born of violence in the PTRC consisted of a dominant and prevalent narrative on motherhood through which victimhood was constructed. The dominant narrative referred to women's natural role as mothers (and carers), in which women, commonly, have been considered passive, apolitical, and relegated to the domestic and private life.[11] Also, it was expected that women who were raped during the conflict carried and raised the child, as it was a symbolic redemption for a woman who had been used and rejected as being a possible terrorist based on assumptions of class, gender, and race (Silva Santisteban, 2008; Boesten, 2014; Bueno-Hansen, 2015). Thus, the children born of violence and their stories became political objects that were useful for defining the boundaries of belonging in the process of transitional justice in the post-conflict society. The stories and legal documents that attested the existence of children born of violence were used in the transitional justice discourses with a narrative scheme, in which the victims and perpetrators were defined and the stories of children born of violence were arranged within the violations of human rights arranged in sequential actions and events in a tri-partite temporal structure.[12] An example is the set of stories about the children born of violence from the Manta and Vilca Case in the *Final Report* of the PTRC.

Manta and Vilca: children born of violence in the PTRC archive

The case of Manta and Vilca in Peru is often cited as an example of sexual violence against women during the Peruvian conflict and the remaining legacies of the violence. Manta and Vilca are two districts in Huancavelica, in which two military bases were constructed as part of the counterinsurgent strategy to fight Shining Path and the MRTA during the conflict. In these two places, the PTRC team conducted in-depth research to gather records about the several cases of sexual violence against women by members of the state forces. The PTRC *Final Report* identified that impunity enabled sexual violence to be naturalized and allowed the armed forces stationed in these areas to exercise it under the counterinsurgency strategy. In this context, the report also determined that several children born of violence were born in these two places. The PTRC collected evidence to reinforce the judicial cases of the 24 women who experienced sexual violence from the soldiers stationed at the military bases in Manta and Vilca. The document named 'Sexual Violence in Huancavelica: The military bases of Manta and Vilca' was produced by the PTRC specialized unit for research.[13] The document mentioned above included 34 testimonies, 15 testimonial statements, 9 birth certificates from children born of violence, and other legal documents that provide evidence of the rape of 24 women. This section will analyse only one birth certificate of a child born of violence, as they are rare documents to find, deepening the discussion of the content and the critical engagement to it as means of knowledge production.[14]

Testimony 314025 was provided by a man named Nicanor Mejía, who had been in charge of Manta's civil registry since 1985. This testimony was used in the PTRC *Final Report* as evidence of the children born of violence born in Manta and Vilca due to their mothers' rape by soldiers. This testimony is accompanied by Nicanor's testimonial statement and his grandchild's birth certificate.[15] The birth certificate is for a girl named Lalita Margot Andrés Mejía, who was born in Manta in 1986; her mother is Dora Mejía Poma.[16] The birth certificate states that the father's name is Wilfredo Andrés Soto. The declarant or witness that registered the child was Tarcila Poma Espinoza, Dora's mother, as Dora was 15 years old at the time. This certificate tells us that Dora was able to have children for the Peruvian state, but she was still not old enough to register her child. Another vital element to highlight from the birth certificate is that Dora knew who the father was, as Nicanor spoke with a general who released the soldier's name.[17] The soldier, named Wilfredo, promised to talk and mend things with Nicanor and Dora once he finished his service in the army, but he disappeared.[18] In the last part of Testimony 314025, Nicanor elucidates that some of the consequences for Lalita of the sexual violence that Dora endured are that Nicanor and Tarcila had to raise their grandchild as her parents to avoid problems in Dora's new relationships. This shows that some of the legacies of the violence were the restructuring of the traditional conception of the family.

The birth certificate is more than an official state document, transparently demonstrating power relations between the parents. In this case, the birth certificate attests to the power relations between the parents in a militarized scenario where Dora was used and disposed of. Naming the father of the child born of rape became an act of making the rapist accountable through the state institutions. However, this same act of naming conferred stigma on the child, as they became labelled as 'abandoned children' or 'children without a father'. Also, reading between the lines in the birth certificate shows a very different interpretation of the same information, in which the child represents the circumstances in which it was born and named. The analysis of only one of those testimonies and birth certificates shows that excluding the stories about children born of violence – as subjects – created them as political objects that were useful to define the boundaries of belonging in the transitional justice process of post-conflict society while defining victimhood.

Children born of violence as disruptive of the PTRC temporalities

Other stories about children born of violence have emerged in post-conflict Peru in the realm of popular culture.[19] These stories about children born of violence provide alternative accounts of children born of violence and a different version of the memory of the conflict promoted by the PTRC. An example is the fictionalized ethnography *Finding Cholita* (2009), written by the anthropologist Billie Jean Isbell. *Finding Cholita* is set over 30 years in the southern region of the department of Ayacucho, Peru,[20] where an anthropologist,[21] Alice Woodsley,[22] is doing her field research. In *Finding Cholita*, Cholita becomes the centre of Alice's search after she joins Shining Path and murders her biological father because he had raped her mother. In the book, the story of Cholita and the relationship between her parents is located before the conflict, and it attests to this rooted construction of Quechua women as a body that can be possessed, owned, used, and disposed of by men.[23] Thus, children born of violence existed before, during, and after the PTRC, as cycles of discrimination and violence against women, and more specifically Indigenous women. The stories about children born of violence attested to these never-ending cycles of violence, discrimination, and lack of access to justice.

I argue in this section that Cholita's life story exemplifies three central ideas that contest the narratives on sexual violence promoted by the PTRC. These ideas can be seen through Cholita's name changes throughout the book, as part of her life course and the decisions she makes and as a signal of her life before, during, and after the conflict. First, the story about the child born of violence elucidates a judicial system in which women and girls are excluded from justice. Second, the story about the children born of violence shows that these children already existed before the conflict, as did their mothers' experiences of sexual violence. Thus, the limits of the conflict (from 1980–2000) established by the truth commission did not capture the long-term violence, marginalization, and discrimination experienced by Indigenous, poor, peasant women and the children born after rape. Finally, the discussion points regarding children born of violence as disruptive of the neat, linear temporality set by the PTRC demonstrate that children do not exist only in a past moment of the conflict violence. Instead, they exist before that, in the present, and have futures.

Finding Cholita: counter-narratives in popular culture

> 'Do you see Cholita, comadre Alicia?[24] She is the real revolutionary of Peru. Someday she will grow up and want to kill me!'
>
> Isbell, 2009: 2

This is the self-fulfilling prophecy that Romulo Rosetti Martinez expresses to Alice Woodsley while having a roast chicken for dinner at Rosetti's house, where a girl, Cholita, is eating the chicken bones that Romulo throws to her under the banquet table. Alice had questioned Romulo regarding the poor nutrition and maltreatment that Cholita was experiencing in his house. This prophecy that Romulo spoke about his illegitimate daughter (born after rape) will become true as part of the cycles of violence in which justice and accountability are non-existent for Indigenous, peasant, and poor girls and women – like Cholita and her mother – as violence against them was normalized by society in their everyday life.

Cholita before the conflict

Cholita was one of the many illegitimate children of Romulo Rosetti that he had while being the director of schools at *Pumapunku*.[25] Romulo raped Cholita's mother, Juana, and bribed her by promising to educate his illegitimate daughter – something he never did – and took Juana as the family's cook at Romulo's mother's house. Alice recounts a conversation with Juana, stating,

> She told me that the worst of it was not when he loaned her to his friends for their drunken pleasure, but rather when she was used to initiate their sons into the mysteries of sex. Such initiations generally occurred on Sunday mornings while the 'decent' women of the family attended Mass. (Isbell, 2009: 12)

Sexual violence and rape towards the 'non-decent women' were entrenched into everyday practices of masculinity. The only justice and accountability that Cholita had was through exercising violence herself, specifically in Romulo's execution.

The violence of Cholita against Romulo is significant analytically, as it shows the problems for these women and girls to access the justice system.[26] In post-conflict Peru, at least until mid-2020, there have not been any convictions of the perpetrators of sexual violence during the conflict. Even though women spoke about sexual violence in the PTRC setting and some of the testimonies[27] were judicialized, this did not translate to women and girls accessing the justice system.[28]

Comrade Victoria or Comrade Ball-Biter during the conflict

Cholita, as a member of Shining Path and named Comrade Victoria, attested that 'so many women were raped during the war' (Isbell, 2009: 190). The stories of children born after the sexual violence experienced by their mothers show patterns of long-lasting violence and discrimination against poor Indigenous women, categorized as inferior in that society. The intersection of race, class, and gender makes it possible for Indigenous, poor, uneducated girls to undergo rape, as it was naturalized and normalized in society through the production of violent masculinities.

Juana in post-conflict

The final name used by Cholita is Juana Quispe, her mother's name.[29] Cholita became Juana in post-conflict Peru,[30] a woman who lives with regret about her life during the war. The new Juana Quispe,[31] formerly Cholita, regrets Romulo's execution;[32] she feels it was meaningless, as it did not bring back her dead mother, and she seeks forgiveness from Romulo's mother. In the dichotomic view of the conflict applied by the PTRC, Cholita was a perpetrator of violence. However, changing the focus on Cholita or Juana, not as a victim or perpetrator but rather as an adult child born of rape, she becomes disruptive to the narratives and representations of the victims of sexual violence by the PTRC. Juana existed and experience violence before the linear temporality set by the PTRC about 'the conflict violence', as her mother did. Her present and future cannot be contained and told in the narrative of sexual violence of the PTRC. Cholita's story is part of her family's story of violence, injustice, and impunity, which points to the transmission of memories that can be passed on through generations. A real-life example is an interview with Rebeca Gamboa, a child born of rape, given to Cecilia Podestá, a journalist, regarding her mother's fight for justice in Peru and outside the PTRC setting[33]: 'I think this is my story, but it is also my children's story, and that is the reason I'm telling you this. I want them to know and learn about it, this way they will know about their grandmother's plight ... look how many years have passed' (Podestá, 2015).

Rebeca, like Cholita, shows the importance of their stories as children born of violence based on their uniqueness in her present.[34] Also, Rebeca and Cholita have futures in which it becomes essential to tell their story to their children to know and learn about their family history. Their stories reflect how their identities are fluid, constantly being redefined and reimagined. They show the tension such stories have with the narratives of sexual violence from the PTRC that cannot be contained and understood, but rather have an important role for children born of violence in the peacebuilding process if further victimization, violence, and discrimination are to be dealt with.

Conclusion

This chapter demonstrates, from the Peruvian experience with children born of violence, how this kind of childhood is understood, contested, and used in global politics. The narratives and counter-narratives of children born of violence are part of the legacies of the conflict. In the case of children born of violence, the PTRC as a memorialization mechanism of transitional justice used the stories of children born of violence as political objects that were useful for defining the boundaries of belonging. However, the stories in which the children born of violence were referred to as subjects were left in the archive or outside the mechanisms of transitional justice. This particular use of children as political objects shows how children are made into meaning-making devices through which communities, or in this case the PTRC, defined victimhood. However, the counter-narratives of children born of violence left in the archive and the realm of popular culture show a complicated story, with representations of children as subjects in a space in which there are no beginnings and ends, but rather an ongoing process of comings and goings breaking with the temporalites and the binary and fixed identities of the transitional justice process (Bacon and Kaya, 2018). In this case, as shown with Lalita's birth certificate and Cholita's story, there is a shift of focus from the narrative of sexual violence to disrupt the narrative of children being objects of evidence. In this way, the counter-narratives about children born of violence in the realm of the PTRC archive and the realm of popular culture can be spaces to imagine and create different possibilities for children born of violence in post-conflict society.

Notes

1. *Informe Final.*
2. Kimberly Theidon (2004, 2012, 2015) in her research on sexual violence and children born of wartime sexual violence in Peru has mentioned that children are referred to as 'the soldier's gifts' (*los regalos de los soldados*), 'nobody's children' (*hijo de nadie*), 'what's his name' (*fulano*), and 'stray cat' (*chatarra*). However, a particular child in a Quechua-speaking community was named *Chiki*, which in Quechua means 'danger' and in daily usage refers to a warning that something bad is about to happen and should be averted (Theidon, 2012: 138).
3. For more on the importance of children's stories and identities in the peace narrative within transitional justice processes, see Caitlin Mollica's contribution in Chapter 2 of this book.
4. The data gathered for this chapter form part of a larger project on narratives about children born of violence in the Peruvian and Guatemalan Truth Commissions.
5. The data from the archive included testimonies, transcribed interviews, legal documents – for example, birth, marriage, and death certificates – emails from the personnel of the truth commission, transcriptions of focus groups, and other documents.
6. Examples include Alonso Cueto's books like *Pálido cielo* (1989), *La hora azul* (2005), *La pasajera* (2015); Santiago Rocangliolo with *Abril rojo* (2006); Claudia Salazar Jiménez with *La sangre de la aurora* (2013); Diego Trelles Paz with *Bioy* (2012); Dany Salvatierra with *Eléctrico ardor* (2014); Óscar Colchado Lucio with *Rosa Cuchillo* (1997); and Iván Thays with *Un lugar llamado Oreja de Perro* (2008).
7. These accounts rely on others speaking for children born of violence, as there is very little information about children born of violence speaking for themselves in the context of Peru.
8. It is important to highlight that the discourse could be written or verbal communication, or practices that perform, reproduce, and transmit power. Some discourses can also be narratives, as they produce knowledge in a sequential order to connect a series of events in story form with a clear beginning and end (in this case, related to the conflict experienced in Peru).
9. For more on the power of narratives and discourses, see Patricia Nabuco Martuscelli's Chapter 1 of this book, which focuses on how discourses about children shape global migration politics.
10. For instance, the Hutus that were not part of the genocide and Rwandans in ethnically mixed marriages and families.
11. This has been discussed by feminist scholars such as Cynthia Enloe, Jean Bethke Elshtain, V. Spike Peterson, Ann Tickner, Christine Sylvester, and Nira Yuval, among others, and has pointed out the gendered construction of the public and private space, in which women and children have been naturalized as apolitical and relegated to the domestic and private life.
12. The narrative structure with a clear beginning, middle, and end.
13. The name of the document is *Violencia Sexual en Huancavelica: Las bases militares de Manta y Vilca*. Unidad de investigaciones especiales de la Comisión de la Verdad y Reconciliación del Perú.
14. It is important to remark that in this chapter all the names mentioned quoting the PTRC testimonies are pseudonyms. The use of pseudonyms is a strategy to give certain degree of anonymity to the persons mentioned in the testimonies.

15   PTRC Testimony 314025 (annex 9), testimonial statement (annex 7), and birth certificate (annex 55).
16   Annex 55 from Archive-PTRC "*Violencia Sexual en Huancavelica: Las bases militares de Manta y Vilca*. Nicanor is a man that oversaw the civil registry in Manta but also provided Testimony 314025 to the PTRC. This testimony is about the rape his daughter Dora and his sister endured by two soldiers from Manta's military base.
17   PTRC Testimony 314025.
18   This is a prevalent feature in the PTRC testimonies of sexual violence.
19   For more on different mediums of popular culture to analyse the inclusion/exclusion and memorialization strategies that inform politicization and childhood, see Iuliia Hoban and Kristina Hook's Chapter 14 in this book.
20   Before the internal armed conflict, the conflict period from 1980–2000, and the post-conflict scenario.
21   From the United States.
22   Alice is Cholita's godmother.
23   Mainly mestizos.
24   Alice is Cholita's godmother; that is the reason why Romulo calls Alice *comadre*. *Alicia* is Alice in Spanish.
25   He was a mestizo from the city of Ayacucho. However, he was named director of the schools at *Pumapunku,* and he moved there. He was married to Beatriz (a respectable and decent woman), but she stayed behind in Romulo's mother's house in Ayacucho. Romulo and his wife did not have children together. Juana Quispe Cabana, a Quechua woman from *Pumapunku*, was Cholita's mother. She was studying at the school when she met Romulo. Juana had gone to the school 'for no more than six months when Romulo raped her after a drunken *fiesta* with a bunch of his chums from the city' (Isbell, 2009: 12).
26   For more on children and youth as participants in violent conflicts and justifications of their violence, see Timea Spitka's Chapter 13 in this book.
27   The judicialized cases were those considered paradigmatic, such as the Manta and Vilca Case.
28   Equally, the Peruvian Penal Code legally allowed, before and during the conflict, violent relationships in which if a rapist proposed to and married his victim, he was exempted from prosecution (Boesten, 2008; Crisóstomo, 2015). As a result, the rapist was legally protected; for the woman – and her family – honour was restored, and the illegitimate status of the children was avoided. However, the actual rape was never dealt with in the judicial system.
29   This is mentioned in chapter 14: Finding Cholita from *Finding Cholita*.
30   She left Shining Path when Abimael Guzmán was captured.
31   Juana Quispe became Christian – evangelical Protestant – and she is a schoolteacher in Paradiso, the community where she lives with her daughter, husband, and Mama Florentina.
32   And, also, other many violent actions she performed during the conflict.
33   Rebeca's testimony was not provided in the PTRC setting; instead, it was an interview in 2015 for a Peruvian newspaper. The reason for the interview was to talk about her mother's long claim for justice after being raped during the conflict.
34   There are very few children born of war talking about their experiences, at least in Peru.

References

Andrews, M. (2004) 'Opening to the original contribution: Counter-narratives and the power to oppose', in M. Bamberg and M. Andrews (eds) *Considering Counter-Narratives: Narrating, Resisting, Making Sense*, Amsterdam and Philadelphia: John Benjamins Publishing, pp 1–6.

Bacon, H.R. and Kaya, J. (2018) 'Imagined communities and identities: A spaciotemporal discourse analysis of one woman's literacy journey', *Linguistics and Education* 46: 82–90.

Bamberg, M. and Andrews, M. (eds) (2004) *Considering Counter-narratives: Narrating, Resisting, Making Sense*, Amsterdam and Philadelphia: John Benjamins Publishing.

Boesten, J. 2008. 'Marrying your rapist: Domesticating war crimes in Ayacucho, Peru', in D. Pankhurst (ed) *Gendered Peace: Women's Search for Post-war Justice and Reconciliation*, London: Routledge, pp 205–227.

Boesten, J. (2014) *Sexual Violence During War and Peace: Gender, Power, and Post-conflict Justice in Peru*, New York: Palgrave Macmillan.

Bueno-Hansen, P. (2015) *Feminist and Human Rights Struggles in Peru: Decolonising Transitional Justice*, Urbana, IL: University of Illinois Press.

Burnet, J.E. (2009) 'Whose genocide? Whose truth? Representations of victim and perpetrator in Rwanda', in A.L. Hinton and K.L. O'Neill (eds) *Genocide: Truth, Memory, and Representation*, New York: Duke University Press, pp 80–110.

Carpenter, C. (ed) (2007) *Born of War: Protecting Children of Sexual Violence Survivors in Conflict Zones*, Bloomfield, CT: Kumarian Press.

Carpenter, C. (2010) *Forgetting Children Born of War: Setting the Human Rights Agenda in Bosnia and Beyond*, New York: Columbia University Press.

Comisión de la Verdad y Reconciliación (2003) *Violencia Sexual en Huancavelica: Las Bases Militares de Manta y Vilca*, Unidad de Investigaciones Especiales de la Comisión de la Verdad y Reconciliación del Perú. Lima, Perú.

Crisóstomo, Mercedes (2015) *Mujeres y Fuerzas Armadas En Un Contexto de Violencia Política: Los Casos de Manta y Vilca En Huancavelica*, Estudios Sobre Memoria. Lima, Perú: Instituto de Estudios Peruanos, IEP.

Foucault, M. (1978) *The History of Sexuality, Volume I: An Introduction*, New York: Pantheon Books.

Isbell, B.J. (2009) *Finding Cholita*, Champaign: University of Illinois Press.

Moon, C. (2006) 'Narrating political reconciliation: Truth and reconciliation in South Africa', *Social & Legal Studies* 15(2): 257–275.

Seto, D. (2013) *No Place for a War Baby: The Global Politics of Children Born of Wartime Sexual Violence*, Farnham, UK, and Burlington, VT: Ashgate.

Silva Santisteban, R. (2008) *El Factor Asco: Basurización Simbólica y Discursos Autoritarios en el Perú Contemporáneo*, Lima, Perú: Fondo Editorial, Pontificia Universidad Católica del Perú.

Somers, M.R. (1994) 'The narrative constitution of identity: A relational and network approach', *Theory and Society* 23(5): 605–649.

Podestá, C. (2015) 'El llanto de los recién nacidos depués de los cuerpos en batalla. Testimonio de Rebeca Gamboa García', *Diario 16*, 11 January. Available at: https://dinosauriosdelaton.lamula.pe/2015/03/22/el-llanto-de-los-recien-nacidos-despues-de-los-cuerpos-en-batalla/ceciliapodesta/ [Accessed 10 May 2021].

Theidon, K. (2004) *Entre Prójimos: El Conflicto Armado Interno y La Política de La Reconciliación En El Perú*, vol 24, Lima, Peru: Instituto de Estudios Peruanos.

Theidon, K. (2012) *Intimate Enemies: Violence and Reconciliation in Peru*, Philadelphia: University of Pennsylvania Press.

Theidon, K. (2015) 'Hidden in plain sight: Children born of wartime sexual violence', *Current Anthropology* 56(S12): S191–200.

Other Sources Cited

PTRC Archive, Peru

Testimony 314025

Document: 'Investigaciones Individuales: Violación sexual en Huancavelica: Las bases de Manta y Vilca' (annex 7 and 55).

4

(Un)Recognition of Child Soldiers' Agency in UN Peacekeeping Practice

Dustin Johnson

Introduction

Peace support operations of various kinds implemented by the United Nations or other national, regional, and international actors are key forms of intervention and order making in global politics: they are some of the largest foreign deployments of military forces, are mandated to address a complex range of political problems, and are reasonably effective at reducing violence, ending civil wars, and preventing conflict recurrence (Walter et al, 2021). Since the end of the 1990s, protection has become a central focus of many peacekeeping missions, with an emphasis on the protection of civilians, the protection of children from grave violations of their rights, and the protection of women from sexual violence (Kullenberg, 2020). Children make up a substantial portion of the population of states hosting peacekeeping missions, and violations of children's rights, particularly their recruitment and use as soldiers, are considered to be particularly grave. Consequently, peace support operations provide a fruitful site for investigating how a universalized conception of childhood helps to sustain certain forms of global politics and is reproduced in doing so. International discourses on child protection primarily construct children as universally innocent, vulnerable, and dependent on adults and the state, in need of protection so that they can mature into responsible adult citizens. Deviations from this form of childhood, such as child soldiering, threaten this progression and necessitate intervention (Tabak, 2020). However, this construction of childhood does not align with children's own experiences of the specificity of their circumstances and their exercise of agency (Denov, 2012; Drumbl,

2012). Children play a range of active, political roles during armed conflict which should be considered in research on peacekeeping (Jacob, 2015).

Consequently, in this chapter, I focus on the practices of peacekeepers involved in child protection to examine both how this universal conception of childhood influences and is contradicted by peacekeeping practice, and how children actively navigate the social environment of war in ways that peacekeepers have to account for. I do so through analysing practice-oriented documents from the UN, such as training materials and manuals, and interviews with military, police, and civilian peacekeepers with experience in a range of child protection functions in several UN missions. This analysis both demonstrates one site where children play an active role in the global political world and illustrates how universalizing discourses like those on children are disrupted and contested in practice. Despite the dominance of discourses of children's lack of agency during war, child soldiering and the UN's response to it shows one way in which powerful global actors understand and implicitly acknowledge children as political actors.

Discourses on childhood and war

While children have participated in armed conflict throughout history, their involvement as soldiers and their exposure to death, injury, sexual violence, and other harms are seen as a particularly pernicious feature of post-Cold War conflicts (Machel, 1996). This has placed children on the international peace and security agenda in a way they were not before and has brought considerable media attention. However, children have been understood in limiting, decontextualized, and stereotypically gendered ways within this agenda. International law and policy on children, the communications and practices of organizations like UNICEF, and media reports on children and war tend to construct childhood as a universal experience, extending from birth until 18, that is strongly rooted in modern, Western conceptions of childhood. Children are constructed primarily as vulnerable, innocent, dependent on adults, and in the process of becoming adults who can take on political agency and become responsible citizens (Burman, 1994; Pupavac, 2001; Denov, 2012; Drumbl, 2012; Tabak, 2020; Bramwell, Chapter 7, this volume). Because of their perceived vulnerability and lack of agency, children must be protected by adults and by the state so that their developmental progress is not harmed, and failure to maintain this protection thus necessitates intervention by the international community. Jana Tabak argues that these aspects of the construction of childhood are an important feature of how the modern international system is organized and maintained (Tabak, 2020).

Child soldiering is seen as a dangerous and pathological deviation from a normal childhood and a disruption of the protection of children and their proper development (Tabak, 2020). Because of the construction of children as vulnerable and dependent, child soldiers[1] are then seen primarily as victims of the adult commanders who recruit them. When children join armed groups voluntarily, rather than through conscription or abduction, quote marks are frequently put around 'voluntary', or the term is otherwise circumscribed to denote how structural factors such as poverty, insecurity, or community pressure, or a child's presumed lack of ability to make an informed decision, are what actually causes a child to become a soldier (Denov, 2012; Drumbl, 2012; Tabak, 2020; Bramwell, Chapter 7, this volume).[2] When child soldiers are also acknowledged as a threat, they tend to be portrayed as especially dangerous due to their manipulability and lack of fear, and due to the serious moral dilemmas faced by adult soldiers who may be confronted with having to use force against a child who is supposed to also be seen as a victim in need of saving (Denov, 2012; Hoban, 2020). Myriam Denov thus argues that child soldiers are frequently understood in extreme, simplistic ways – as purely victims, as dangerous monsters who have been permanently corrupted by war, or as heroes for overcoming their experiences to become writers, advocates, or artists. These understandings build upon and reinforce colonial and racial tropes about both the need to save children from the Global South and the supposed inherent barbarism of conflicts there (Macmillan, 2009; Lee-Koo, 2011; Denov, 2012).

Despite research demonstrating the involvement of girls across all different roles that child soldiers take on, including serving as combatants (Mazurana et al, 2002; Fox, 2004; Haer and Böhmelt, 2018), child soldiers are still largely constructed in stereotypically gendered ways, with boys primarily as combatants, and girls primarily as victims of sexual violence. For instance, the UN training materials for military peacekeepers on child protection, while noting that girls may be combatants and boys may be subjected to sexual violence, primarily portray boys as combatants and girls as victims of sexual violence through various examples presented throughout these materials (United Nations, 2018). Such gendered portrayals tend to further reinforce the construction of children affected by armed conflict as primarily victims.

Social navigation and children's agency during war

In contrast to the prevalent discourse of children lacking agency and being primarily victims during war, researchers argue that children, including child soldiers, exercise meaningful capacity for political agency, informed decision-making, and deliberate choices within the many constraints imposed by war. The vulnerable, agency-less construction of the child described above relies on both a binary construction of adults versus children and of agential versus non-agential that imposes a problematic oversimplification.

This adult–child binary in agency is premised upon the 'radical voluntarism and individualism' of an 'autonomous and absolute subject' (Vigh, 2009: 432) and is a theoretical premise that has been thoroughly critiqued (for example, Edkins and Pin-Fat, 1999; Hall, 2000).

Without denying the material differences in decision-making, risk analysis, and experience across children and adults of different ages, the adult–child distinction at 18 is a social construction that demarcates a legal distinction in what agency children are allowed to exercise rather than their actual capacity for agency. In their study of soldiers who chose to join armed forces and groups as adolescents, Rachel Brett and Irma Specht highlight the importance of considering the age-related differences across children when addressing child soldiering. They note that

> [a]dolescence is a time of vulnerability with the uncertainties and turbulence of physical, mental and emotional development. It is also a time of opportunities with greater freedom, developing understanding of one's own identity and place in the community and society, and a new capacity to make choices and to take on responsibilities ... it is a time when injustice and its unacceptability are strongly felt. (Brett and Specht, 2004: 3)

The concept of social navigation provides a useful lens for understanding how children of various ages in situations of armed conflict exercise agency given the constraints imposed by both their status as children and the social environment in which they live. Drawing on the experiences of youth from Guinea-Bissau, including children as young as 16 recruited as soldiers, Henrik Vigh (2006; 2009) presents a conception of the interaction of individuals with changing social forces well suited for this task:

> Social navigation entails simultaneously moving toward a distant future location or condition (that is, movement toward future positions and possibilities), *and* making one's way across immediate and proximate oncoming changes and forces of the near future. ... our environments and futures are, in such situations, contingent upon our knowledge of the past, our experience of the here and now as well as the emergent or potential possibilities and difficulties within it, entailing that the map is never a static set of coordinates but a dense and multi-dimensional imaginary, which is constantly in the process of coming into being. (Vigh, 2009: 429; emphasis in original)

In this view of the interaction between the individual and the social world, '[w]e act, adjust and attune our strategies and tactics in relation to the way we experience and imagine and anticipate the movement and influence of social forces' (Vigh, 2009: 420). Individuals' actions and social forces both involve the exercise of power, and social navigation 'highlights the limits of the power embedded in our capacity to define and control our social worlds. In other words, no matter what the level of power, we are never completely free to move as we want' (Vigh, 2009: 432).

Children, to varying degrees, are certainly capable of 'adjusting and attuning' their 'strategies and tactics' and of exercising imagination and anticipating the future, yet these abilities are clearly constrained by their limited previous experiences (compared to adults) and developing capacities for analysis, decision-making, and determining risk. Faced with the extreme uncertainty, risk, and violence of conflict, becoming a soldier, or deciding to not escape from an armed group, presents children with one option for securing some amount of power to attempt to shape their future.

Empirical work on child soldiering reinforces the utility of this view. Summarizing a range of work, Myriam Denov states that child soldiers 'carefully and deliberately navigate the terrain of war, as well as highlighting their capacity for reflexivity, power and resilience' (Denov, 2012: 284). She also highlights that child soldiers often deliberately engage in political struggles, such as girl soldiers finding empowerment in a patriarchal society through their recruitment or Jewish children playing a significant role in the partisan resistance to the Nazis during the Second World War (Denov, 2012).

Drawing on interviews with former child soldiers in Sierra Leone, Denov highlights how they experienced a complex and simultaneous mixture of 'victimisation, participation and resistance' (Denov, 2012: 286). Children were often abducted and subjected to extreme physical and sexual violence, and perpetrating violence against others became normalized and routine. At the same time, children remained aware of the immorality of many of their acts of violence and sought various ways to resist the control of the armed group, whether through more subtle acts, such as finding private moments to cry, or seeking to escape the group (Denov, 2012; see also Shepler, 2005). Similarly, Mark Drumbl argues that child soldiers exercise agency in navigating the constraints, violence, and lack of information that define armed conflict, and that international responses to child soldiering will be more effective if they acknowledge and build upon this agency rather than viewing child soldiers as purely victims of adults (Drumbl, 2012). These authors and others advocate for more nuanced approaches to child soldiering that seek to end and prevent the many severe harms of participating in warfare without ignoring their agency or limiting responses to those framed as outsiders saving them (Tabak, 2020).

UN peacekeeping practice and the (non)agential child

Drawing on these previous analyses, I turn to how discourses on the child soldier as agency-less victim are (re)produced and disrupted in peacekeeping practice. To do so, I focus on analysis of practice-oriented peacekeeping documents, such as training materials, policies, and manuals, and interviews with military, civilian, and police peacekeepers involved in child protection in a variety of missions.[3] In UN peacekeeping missions with a child protection mandate, child protection is focused on the six grave violations of children's rights: recruitment and use as soldiers, killing and maiming, sexual violence, abduction, attacks on schools and hospitals, and denial of humanitarian access. It is conceptualized as a shared responsibility between different mission components, with distinct roles for the civilian, military, and police components, in partnership with external actors such as UNICEF and NGOs. The UN mission's responsibility is articulated primarily as the physical protection of children, dialogue and advocacy with armed forces and groups, monitoring and reporting on violations, and supporting the demobilization of child soldiers, while other actors focus on service delivery to children (United Nations, 2019, 2020).

Across UN policy, guidance, and training materials on child protection, the discourse of children's vulnerability, innocence, and lack of agency is frequently reinforced, while their agency is occasionally highlighted in ways that challenge this discourse (Johnson, 2022). For instance, the Specialised Training Materials (STMs) on child protection for military peacekeepers explicitly state that children are 'vulnerable, impressionable, frequently irrational and worthy of protection' (United Nations, 2018, §6: 16). Training materials reinforce in several places that children who are voluntarily recruited into armed groups are not truly making a voluntary decision due to limiting circumstances such as poverty or threats to their community, and note that even for children who can be legally recruited into state militaries before they turn 18, it should be assumed that conditions in a conflict zone prevent them from making what is legally considered a voluntary choice (United Nations, 2017, 2018). These framings of children's lack of agency see it in the binary manner discussed above. However, Drumbl argues that children's navigation of these constraints and challenges during war is exactly where we should analyse children exercising agency (Drumbl, 2012).

To an extent, peacekeepers themselves reproduce these views of children's lack of agency during armed conflict. Some interviewees framed the recruitment of child soldiers primarily in terms of them being 'used', 'exploited', 'abused', and 'brainwashed' by adults, no matter whether their recruitment seemed voluntary or not.[4] A peacekeeper from Sierra Leone discussing the use of child soldiers in her country during its civil war said that children 'do not think twice', have no 'self-initiative', and can be manipulated.[5] Similarly, Tabak quotes a senior advisor at UNICEF who doubted that children could ever voluntarily join an armed group, despite significant experience interacting with child soldiers (Tabak, 2020: 114).

However, there are disruptions to this discourse of vulnerability and lack of agency that appear both in UN child protection documents and in the experiences and practice of peacekeepers. This sets up a tension between different parts of the documents and between different peacekeepers' views, with implications for the effectiveness of protection. This tension is most evident in the significant discussion in the STMs on how to interact with child soldiers when they are encountered. A significant part of the sixth module of the STMs on military roles and responsibilities in child protection focuses on how to interact with armed child soldiers who may pose a threat to the peacekeeper. This section first reminds peacekeepers that their rules of engagement and principles of use of force still apply in this scenario: 'hostile act/intent, principle of self-defence, use of minimum force and only as a last resort' (United Nations, 2018, §6: 15). The STMs then go on to discuss key considerations for such encounters and present a number of potential scenarios and how to deal with them. Throughout, there are statements that reinforce the child's vulnerability, victimhood, and lack of agency, and ones that seemingly present the child as an agential soldier who needs to be dealt with as such.

For instance, they state that child soldiers might appear hostile without intending to be, indicating that the children do not think through their actions like adults do: 'It also must be stressed that when dealing with children and child soldiers, it must be understood that aggressive or hostile posturing by children may not necessarily constitute a threat. The 'aggressive' attitude of a child approaching with a weapon is not necessarily a hostile act or intent' (United Nations, 2018, §6: 15). Child soldiers' status as victims is reinforced, both in that they suffer various abuses while part of an armed group, and that their recruitment is illegal and thus they are victims of a crime: 'All children associated with armed groups are victims. They suffer from torture and other cruel treatment during their time with the group. But even the recruitment in itself is a crime ... we need to bear in mind that they are also victims for being recruited in the first place' (United Nations, 2018, §6: 17). When linked to the previous discussion of recruitment not being truly voluntary, this reinforces the child's lack of agency. However, if we accept that some recruitment is a voluntary part of how children navigate the environment of war, then this also leaves the door open to acknowledging their agency while noting the legal denial of it.

The STMs also reinforce the link between childhood and vulnerability, stating as noted above that a child 'is *still very much a child* – someone who is vulnerable, impressionable, frequently irrational and worthy of protection' (United Nations, 2018, §6: 16; emphasis in original). However, this statement is immediately followed by the admission that the child 'is *still a soldier* – and to deny this fact could be detrimental to the safety of the peacekeeper and would not be in keeping with the child's own experience' (United Nations,

2018, §6: 16; emphasis in original). Later on, when discussing encountering child soldiers at a checkpoint, the STMs note that peacekeepers should '[t]ry to reason; ... [t]reat the child with respect as though he or she was under military discipline' (United Nations, 2018, §6: 18). Together, these statements indicate that it is vital for child protection practice to in part recognize children's agency during war, or at least treat them as if they are similar in many ways to adult soldiers.

Consideration of children's agency is also apparent in discussing the need to help child soldiers who self-demobilize from armed groups. One of the scenarios used to discuss interactions is about dealing with an escaping child soldier and notes that peacekeepers should be 'aware of the ways in which a child might attempt to escape from an armed group, as well as the strategies armed groups may employ to prevent such attrition' (United Nations, 2018, §6: 20). In contrast with the discussion about how children cannot voluntarily join an armed group, there is no assumption or statement that children cannot voluntarily exit them. Myriam Denov notes that this is a form of resistance and agency exercised by child soldiers, and given the severe or deadly punishments for desertion, it seems unlikely that this is a choice a child soldier would make without some informed consideration of the risks (Denov, 2012). Consequently, this is an implicit acknowledgement that children navigate the shifting constraints and dangers imposed by both remaining with and escaping from an armed group.

Peacekeepers and others involved in child protection reproduce or challenge the prevalent discourse on children and child soldiers, and reinforce the disruptions in UN documents discussed earlier, in various ways themselves. The peacekeepers interviewed tended to have a more nuanced view of how and to what extent children are able to exercise agency during war. Their views reflect an understanding of children's capacities and the constraints of their environment that aligns with conceptualizing agency through the lens of social navigation. Even those peacekeepers mentioned above, who largely rejected the possibility of voluntary recruitment, discussed self-demobilization or joining community defence militias in ways that acknowledged some degree of agency for the child.[6] When asked about voluntary child recruitment in Mali, one of the peacekeepers who viewed children as lacking the self-initiative to be recruited voluntarily said she had not heard of it and that most recruitment was forced, but she did not deny that it was a possibility.[7]

Most other peacekeepers interviewed discussed the challenging environment children have to navigate due to insecurity, poverty, propaganda from armed groups, and community and cultural norms that encourage recruitment, while either not denying that children in these circumstances lacked agency, or arguing that they did make voluntary choices and, in some cases, found empowerment through recruitment. Three main themes related to social navigation and acknowledgements of agency in UN documents were brought up by peacekeepers. First, several peacekeepers reinforced the voluntary nature of children's self-demobilization, for reasons such as them not receiving the expected supports or reward from being a soldier or navigating tensions within the group,[8] as well as some later being re-recruited as they found the poverty of being a civilian even less appealing.[9] One stated that '[t]he children that leave, though, I think wholly do it on a voluntary basis'.[10]

Second, multiple peacekeepers viewed recruitment as sometimes taking place on a voluntary basis, with an understanding more aligned with social navigation where children made that choice faced with challenging circumstances and a lack of good options. Poverty, the normalization of violence and gun use, escaping gender-based violence, and lack of realistic information about conditions in an armed group were all cited as contributing to children's decisions to join,[11] while several also viewed that education about the reality of participating in war would change children's decisions to join.[12] One civilian peacekeeper with particularly extensive experience in child protection discussed multiple children whom he had encountered who faced complex mixtures of empowerment and victimization in their experience as soldiers, such as joining an armed group to escape forced marriage at home only to be forced to marry a commander, or simultaneously being in command of many other soldiers and being in a forced marriage with her commander.[13]

Third, several peacekeepers emphasized the role of children's trust or lack thereof in the peacekeeping mission and child protection organizations in their decision to demobilize, and that they need to be given a choice in who to interact with when being interviewed by child protection staff, particularly to avoid decisions about a child's welfare based on gender or other stereotypes. More broadly, they also discussed the importance of children's participation in child protection.[14]

Bringing together this practice-level analysis with previous work, particularly Tabak's analysis of higher-level policy and discourse, it is evident that prevalent discourses on child soldiers' vulnerability and lack of agency can be disrupted by peacekeeping practice. Some peacekeepers, and the documents analysed, reinforce in places the discourse of children's lack of agency. More detailed situational guidance in training materials, and peacekeepers themselves, understand children, particularly adolescents, as actors who are navigating a challenging, violent environment as best they can. From a social navigation perspective, both child soldiers and peacekeepers are navigating the social environment of armed conflict, drawing on their respective knowledge, experience, capacities, and power relations to do so. This should also remind us that taking a nuanced view of children's agency during wartime should extend to adults, who are also never fully under their own control, particularly in a highly militarized and violent environment. What are the practical and theoretical implications of taking such a view rather than seeing children simply as objects of protection?

Practically, some peacekeepers, based on their experience and some guidance from UN training, take this view of children's agency into account. However, it is not integrated into the wider body of policy and guidance or overarching discourses on children and armed conflict. This may miss out on ways that preventing harm to children during armed conflict can be improved by treating children as actors who have a role to play in their own protection. Such an approach may be more advanced in some NGOs that have a stronger child participation focus. Theoretically, child soldiers' interaction with UN peacekeeping demonstrates one way in which children play a role in global politics as actors. Their choices to enlist, how they interact with peacekeepers when serving, and their choices to self-demobilize all influence the conduct of armed groups and their fighting capacity, what practices peacekeepers are able to carry out where, and what information peacekeepers have access to. While many of these acts of navigating the environment of war may seem trivial, I argue that they still hold theoretical significance for their challenge to discourses of children's lack of agency, and in aggregate they likely play a significant role in armed conflict, and in peacekeeping and peacebuilding. That UN training materials contain many veiled acknowledgements of children's agency, which many peacekeepers acknowledge more or less explicitly, also indicates how global actors like the UN negotiate tensions between dominant discourses and challenges to them from below through their practices.

Conclusion

Universalizing discourses, such as those that construct children as always innocent, vulnerable, and without agency, are disrupted by the lived realities of social groups that are always far more diverse and complex. Policy draws on such universal discourses of identity to develop and justify actions that do not always work well when applied to those lived realities (Hansen, 2006). This is certainly the case in child protection and preventing the recruitment and use of child soldiers (Drumbl, 2012; Tabak, 2020). Yet practical guidance and the experiences of peacekeepers show that those responsible for developing and implementing policy do not always reproduce these same discourses and alter their practices to account for children's agency and political involvement. I argue this is an opening to take children's agency in global politics more seriously in both scholarship and practice.

Acknowledgements

Thank you to all those who provided comments on draft versions of this chapter, particularly Catherine Baillie Abidi, J. Marshall Beier, Helen Berents, Vanessa Bramwell, Caitlin Mollica, Jana Tabak, Ali Watson, and an anonymous reviewer. Funding for this research was provided by the Social Sciences and Humanities Research Council of Canada under grant 435-2019-1124.

Notes

[1] A number of terms are commonly used for child soldiers, including child combatant, children recruited and used as soldiers, and children associated with armed forces and armed groups. For simplicity, I use child soldier in this text with the understanding that it applies to children of any gender in both combat and support roles (UNICEF, 2007).

[2] For examples of this usage, see Hall, 2019; Machel, 1996; see also O'Neil, 2018. This also draws on my experience talking to colleagues and attending events in the child protection sector since 2016.

[3] Interviews were carried out as part of a research project by the author as part of his doctoral work and by his collaborators. The interview guide, consent process, and overall study design were approved by the Research Ethics Board of Dalhousie University (reference number 2020-5152).

[4] Interview with military peacekeeper, 7 January 2021 (Interview 1); interview with military peacekeeper, 8 July 2021 (Interview 2).

[5] Interview with military peacekeeper, 2 August 2021 (Interview 3).

[6] Interview 1; Interview 3.

[7] Interview 3.

[8] Interview with military peacekeeper, 6 July 2021 (Interview 4); interview with civilian peacekeeper, 24 February 2021 (Interview 5).

[9] Interview with military peacekeeper, 8 March 2021 (Interview 6).

[10] Interview 6.

[11] Interview 4; Interview 5; Interview 6; interview with police peacekeeper, 12 May 2021 (Interview 7); interview with civilian peacekeeper, 26 July 2021 (Interview 8).

[12] Interview 4; Interview 7.

[13] Interview 5.

[14] Interview 8; interview with civilian child protection worker, 10 March 2021 (Interview 9, interview conducted by project collaborator); interview with civilian child protection worker, 31 March 2021 (Interview 10).

References

Brett, R. and Specht, I. (2004) *Young Soldiers: Why They Choose to Fight*, Boulder, CO: Lynne Rienner Publishers.

Burman, E. (1994) 'Innocents abroad: Western fantasies of childhood and the iconography of emergencies', *Disasters* 18(3): 238–253.

Denov, M. (2012) 'Child soldiers and iconography: Portrayals and (mis)representations', *Children & Society* 26(4): 280–292.

Drumbl, M. (2012) *Reimagining Child Soldiers in International Law and Policy*, Oxford: Oxford University Press.

Edkins, J. and Pin-Fat, V. (1999) 'The subject of the political', in J. Edkins, N. Persram, and V. Pin-Fat (eds) *Sovereignty and Subjectivity*, Boulder, CO: Lynne Rienner Publishers, pp 1–18.

Fox, M.-J. (2004) 'Girl soldiers: Human security and gendered insecurity', *Security Dialogue* 35(4): 465–479.

Haer, R. and Böhmelt, T. (2018) 'Girl soldiering in rebel groups, 1989–2013: Introducing a new dataset', *Journal of Peace Research* 55(3): 395–403.

Hall, E. (2019) *No Choice: It Takes a World to End the Use of Child Soldiers*, Monrovia, CA: World Vision International.

Hall, S. (2000) 'Who needs identity?', in P. du Gay, J. Evans, and P. Redman (eds) *Identity: A Reader*, London: SAGE, pp 15–30.

Hansen, L. (2006) *Security as Practice: Discourse Analysis and the Bosnian War*, Abingdon, UK: Taylor & Francis.

Hoban, I. (2020) 'Objects and subjects: Strategic use of childhood in the debate over the Canadian contribution to MINUSMA', *Childhood* 27(3): 294–309.

Jacob, C. (2015) '"Children and armed conflict" and the field of security studies', *Critical Studies on Security* 3(1): 14–28.

Johnson, D. (2022) 'Women as the essential protectors of children? Gender and child protection in UN peacekeeping', *International Peacekeeping* 29(2): 282–307.

Kullenberg, J.N. (2020) 'Overlapping agendas and peacekeepers' ability to protect', *International Peacekeeping* 28(4): 661–688.

Lee-Koo, K. (2011) 'Horror and hope: (Re)Presenting militarised children in Global North–South relations', *Third World Quarterly* 32(4): 725–742.

Machel, G. (1996) *Impact of Armed Conflict on Children*, A/51/306, New York: United Nations.

Macmillan, L. (2009) 'The child soldier in North–South relations', *International Political Sociology* 3(1): 36–52.

Mazurana, D.E., McKay, S.A., Carlson, K.C., and Kasper, J.C. (2002) 'Girls in fighting forces and groups: Their recruitment, participation, demobilization, and reintegration', *Peace and Conflict: Journal of Peace Psychology* 8(2): 97–123.

O'Neil, S. (2018) 'Child recruitment and use by armed groups in contemporary conflict', in S. O'Neil and K. Van Broeckhoven (eds) *Cradled by Conflict: Child Involvement with Armed Groups in Contemporary Conflict*, Tokyo: United Nations University, pp 24–35.

Pupavac, V. (2001) 'Misanthropy without borders: The international children's rights regime', *Disasters* 25(2): 95–112.

Shepler, S. (2005) 'The rites of the child: Global discourses of youth and reintegrating child soldiers in Sierra Leone', *Journal of Human Rights* 4(2): 197–211.

Tabak, J. (2020) *The Child and the World: Child-soldiers and the Claim for Progress*, Athens, GA: The University of Georgia Press.

UNICEF (2007) *The Paris Principles: Principles and Guidelines on Children Associated with Armed Forces or Armed Groups*, New York: United Nations.

United Nations (2017) 'Lesson 2.7: Child protection', in *Core Pre-deployment Training Materials*, New York: United Nations.

United Nations (2018) *UN Military Specialised Training Materials on Child Protection*, New York: United Nations.

United Nations (2019) *Manual for Child Protection Staff in United Nations Peace Operations*, New York: United Nations.

United Nations (2020) *Policy: Child Protection in United Nations Peace Operations*, New York: United Nations.

Vigh, H. (2006) *Navigating Terrains of War: Youth and Soldiering in Guinea-Bissau*, New York: Berghahn Books.

Vigh, H. (2009) 'Motion squared: A second look at the concept of social navigation', *Anthropological Theory* 9(4): 419–438.

Walter, B.F., Howard, L.M., and Fortna, V.P. (2021) 'The extraordinary relationship between peacekeeping and peace', *British Journal of Political Science* 51(4): 1705–1722.

PART II

Governed Childhoods

5

Contested Children's and Young People's Political Representation in Global Health

Anna Holzscheiter and Laura Pantzerhielm

Introduction

Among the many invisible subjects in contemporary international politics, children and young people undoubtedly belong to those whose political agency is most strongly contested. International institutions' response to the COVID-19 pandemic acutely exposed this invisibility and the shocking extent to which children and young people are excluded from relevant sites of crisis politics and global policy making (Hettihewa and Holzscheiter, 2020). This invisibility is all the more troubling considering that children and young people were extraordinarily affected by the pandemic as they shared experiences of disrupted education, social isolation, psychological damage, and deteriorating access to essential medical services, such as routine immunizations (Human Rights Watch, 2020; International Labor Organization, 2020; Lee, 2020; The Lancet Child & Adolescent Health, 2020; United Nations, 2020; Thorisdottir et al, 2021). Not only are children and youth conspicuously absent as speakers, agents, and informants in the global pandemic response, they are also indirectly under-represented through the marginal role of ministries, experts, and scholarly disciplines dealing specifically with child- and youth-related aspects in national and international pandemic governance. Has this invisibility of children and youth as agents of global health policy making been addressed in research? The answer we give in this chapter is clearly 'no'. The overall absence of children and youth as pertinent subjects in International Relations scholarship has already been studied elsewhere. Holzscheiter (2020) highlighted the undeniable link between the low salience of young people as meaningful agents of

International Relations and their limited possibilities to shape politics and law from inside international institutions.

In this chapter, we will focus more narrowly on questions of political representation and agency of young people in global health, in itself a much-neglected issue so far, at least until the onset of the COVID-19 pandemic. The chapter starts from the observation that there is a significant discrepancy between a broad endorsement for the codified norm of child participation, on the one hand, and the actual possibilities for political representation of young people, on the other hand. While child participation as established in Article 12 of the UN Convention on the Rights of the Child (UNCRC, 'the right to be heard') enjoys wide support among international institutions, formal access rules along with further institutional, material, and performative aspects continue to limit meaningful participation of young people in salient international forums. By now, 'Children and Youth' has been established as a *major group* and thus as a separate category of stakeholders reflected in the Sustainable Development Goals (SDGs; UN DESA and UNITAR, 2020) and UN Youth has been created as a coordinating body for all youth-related activities undertaken at the United Nations. Whenever there arises the need to legitimize a stronger involvement of young people, the UNCRC figures as a normative referent to justify participation (Pincham et al, 2020). There is thus, at least at the level of international organizations' self-depictions, a strong endorsement of child and youth participation as a procedural norm in global governance (Bersaglio et al, 2015; Holzscheiter, 2018; Holzscheiter et al, 2019). At the same time, the very few studies on the practice and effects of young people's participation suggest that, from their perspective, the practice of involving them in international debates is a sobering experience (Bent, 2013; Kwon, 2019).

In the following section, we will revisit different strands of scholarly literature on global health and ask about the absence or presence of children and youth. Our systematic literature review surveys global health scholarship in pertinent academic journals, authoritative textbooks, and monographs across disciplinary (medicine and different strands of social sciences) and epistemic divides (positivist and critical global health research). It concludes that political agency and representation of children and youth in global health politics has not been systematically or comprehensively addressed. The next part of the chapter investigates the practice of international cooperation on matters of global health. We ask to what extent children and youth are recognized as relevant stakeholders in the institutions that shape global health policy making and contribute to global health governance overall. The manifold ways in which childhood and youth are defined and delimited in the policy field, though, exemplify the contestation surrounding their agency and identity. Our discussion of multiple sites of engagement for children and youth brings to light the varied forms and differing degrees of institutionalization that characterize child and youth representation in global health governance. In particular, our analysis of institutional practices of including children and youth in policy-making processes at the global level reveals a prominent place for youth, while children as independent, potentially political agents are virtually invisible inside the institutions governing global health. At the same time, though, a closer look at the justifications given for child and youth representation in global health and the ways in which appropriate child and youth representation is framed suggests that young peoples' room for manoeuvre is extraordinarily limited and that their political agency is governed by strong asymmetries between established adult policy experts, on the one hand, and promising, inexperienced young people, on the other hand. The concluding section of our chapter discusses these results and proposes new avenues for research into the political representation of children and young people in global health politics and institutions.

Children and youth in global health: presences and absences across disciplinary divides

> The limitations of any field of study are most strikingly revealed in its shared definitions of what counts as relevant.
>
> Scott, 1985: xv

In this section, we take stock and critically interrogate the state of research on childhood and youth in the politics of global health. Based on a first survey of relevant literatures, we argue that to date there is no discernible, coherent research agenda or scholarly conversation that addresses the political agency and representation of youth and children in global health politics. Instead, contributions that speak to the role, agency, or representation of young people are fragmented across disciplinary cleavages (medicine, history, sociology, anthropology), theoretical interests, and empirical foci. In order to verify our expectation that the political agency and participation of children and youth is a much under-researched field of inquiry in social science research on global health governance, we undertook an extensive literature review, starting with authoritative textbooks and monographs on global health before proceeding to the question if and how pertinent social science and interdisciplinary global health journals have published research on child and youth participation in global health. We scanned the literature for the terms 'child*' and 'youth' in combination with 'participat*' OR 'representat*' OR 'agen*'.

In pertinent academic conversations on the politics of global health institutions, the inclusion or exclusion of agents who speak either 'as' or 'on behalf of' children or youth and the performative practices that they engage in rarely receive focused analytical attention. This widespread tendency to perceive childhood and youth as peripheral to the 'real' politics of global health can be aptly illustrated by means of a systematic review of authoritative textbooks and monographs on the topic (McInnes and Lee, 2012; Coggon and Gola, 2013; Brown et al, 2014; McCracken and Phillips, 2017; Harman, 2018; Parker and Garcia, 2018; Youde, 2018; Missoni et al, 2019; Gostin and Meier, 2020). Written by acknowledged experts to introduce students to global health as a realm of study, the latter constitute an instructive genre to assess how the range of empirical phenomena that are considered to be relevant to the subject matter are delineated. Our analysis of the literature revealed that the instances in which children and youth are explicitly addressed as political agents – as in 'activism' or 'resistance' – are minimal. In our sample, only two scholarly publications address the relevance of child or youth activism for the study of global health politics directly (Harman, 2018; Sen, 2018). All other publications speaking of children and youth refer to them solely in the context of specific health policies, for example, on maternal and child health, water and sanitation, vaccinations, malnutrition, health inequality, or sexual health education. The Millennium Development Goals and, more recently, the SDGs are focal international standards frequently mentioned with regard to children and youth (Farmer et al, 2013; Poku and Whitman, 2018; Missoni et al, 2019). Child health is discussed as an integral component of global health governance, but the subjectivity and agency of children vis-à-vis these policies and the institutions that make and implement them are not addressed. In short: if textbooks tell us something about what scholars consider important in global health, youth, children, and – even more so – questions about their voice and political agency do not seem to make the mark.

If one casts a wider net in search for scholarly engagement with young people's representation and agency in global health, much academic work that explicitly addresses children and youth exhibits a strong tendency towards examining more narrowly delineated empirical settings in medical research, treatment, health policy, and legislation. In this strand of scholarship, the Committee on the Rights of the Child's General Comment No. 12 on the right of the child to be heard (UN Committee on the Rights of the Child, 2009) constitutes an important reference point. Situated at the border of social sciences and medicine, this kind of research extends our understanding of how children and adolescents can participate in the co-production of health outcomes and treatment, and it ponders how their participation in health research can contribute to improved, evidence-based treatment and increased validity of research results (D'Amico et al, 2016; Cuevas-Parra, 2020; De Pretto-Lazarova et al, 2020; Lau et al, 2020).

As an interdisciplinary scholarly field, critical global health research has long engaged with questions of marginalization and exclusion, political struggle and representation, subjectivity and power (for recent illustrative collections, see Mold and Reubi, 2013; Herrick and Reubi, 2017; O'Manique and Fourie, 2018). When we turned to critical global health journals,[1] we found that there were indeed some contributions that addressed children and youth as active agents (see for instance Elliott, 2016; Lorimer et al, 2020). However, many studies on political subjectivity and marginalization also focused on other groups, most notably women and minorities, or explored the intersections of children and youth with women, refugees, victims of war, and other marginalized groups (for illustrations, see Spini, 2018; Came et al, 2019; Newman et al, 2020; see also O'Manique and Fourie, 2018). Moreover, none of these publications studied youth and child participation in relation to salient global health institutions or decision-making processes. As a result, the absences and power assymetries that mark young people's encounters with institutionalized global health politics constitute a blind spot.

When we finally turned to a number of established health journals that regularly feature research on child and adolescent health,[2] we found that political agency, representation, and participation occupy a marginal space. Global political institutions hardly featured as research objects in these journals, even though a number of publications addressed participatory deficits of health institutions related to the SDGs (Scott et al, 2018). While the term 'participation' figured prominently, it was most commonly used in the context of clinical trials involving children and adolescents. Child and youth participation, thus, is first and foremost understood as passive participation as objects of medical research rather than active participation in the design and evaluation of these clinical trials. However, over time, there is a clear trend towards more scholarly engagement with questions of consent, with an explicit inclusion of children's and young people's perspectives on this matter (Susman et al, 1992; Joffe et al, 2006). Only a very few publications specifically dealt with small-scale questions of participatory research involving youth (Betancourt et al, 2015; Moore et al, 2016; Mogro-Wilson and Fifield, 2018). It is only very recently that explicitly medical research has also addressed political agency and participation of children, for example with regard to an initiative by the Council of Europe Action Plan on Human Rights and Technologies in Biomedicine (2020–2015) (Altavilla et al, 2021).

These strands of empirically focused research at the nexus of the social sciences and medicine hence address the agency for children and youth by acknowledging them as rights-holding agents who are capable of shaping social and medical outcomes. In doing so, they add to important conversations on best practice in research, treatment, and health policy, and highlight the rights and contributions of young people in clinical research, treatment, and as co-creators of health outcomes. However, these strands of scholarship do not systematically address the role of children and youth in the global institutional architecture of health politics. That is, they do not ask what forms of agency and subjectivity are granted to, and claimed by, children and youth in salient institutional sites and political debates at the global level. Overall, we thus found that the role of children and youth in the international institutions governing global health has not been systematically addressed. Whenever child and youth activism is mentioned, though, authors immediately highlight the missing recognition of children's agency (Fassin, 2013; Sen, 2018). There is, thus, a clear gap in the literature when it comes to the recognition and systematic study of the political agency and representation of children and youth in global health governance.

The practice of child and youth participation in global health governance

In international cooperation in global health, the health of newborns, children, and adolescents has always been an outstanding concern for policy makers. To date, there are numerous large global institutions, partnerships, and initiatives targeting child and adolescent health, most prominently GAVI (The Vaccine Alliance) or the Partnership for Maternal, Newborn and Child Health, with the World Health Organization (WHO) and UNICEF as the focal intergovernmental institutions in this area. When it comes to policy making, representation, and agency, the place of children and youth, however, is much contested. On the one hand, procedural norms on the participation of young people in global governance are widely endorsed; on the other hand, as we will show below, it is almost exclusively youth and almost never children who figure as speakers, political agents, and experts in salient sites of global health policy making.

In fact, there is an emerging institutional ecology surrounding the representation of young people in global health, reflected by the myriad events, advocacy organizations, and transnational platforms that are presented as activities for or by youth. This ecology includes international organizations (particularly from the UN family), powerful private foundations, business actors, academia, media, and, of course, youth organizations – in different constellations and varying institutional forms. The adoption of the SDGs and the Agenda 2030 in 2015 was a catalytic moment for the creation of ever more child- and youth-focused institutional spaces. As becomes obvious from our literature review above, none of these developments in the practice of global health governance has so far received adequate attention by scholars of political science, International Relations, or global health. For the purpose of this chapter, we therefore conducted a systematic study of contemporary institutionalized forms of child and youth representation in global health. Our quest to map the institutional ecology of child and youth representation in global health was informed by a systematic search for organizations, platforms, and networks targeting young people that work transnationally; child- or youth-specific sections and departments of larger intergovernmental organizations; and specific regular or one-off events (summits, conferences) at the intersection of global health with children and youth. To gain a deeper understanding of this institutional landscape, we systematically compared all entries with a view to whether they were led by young people or adult-led, what (kind of) actors they involved, their self-descriptions, and their institutional form. In a second step, we collected policy papers, self-descriptions on homepages, and mission statements from all entries in our sample. We evaluated the latter through a comparative, interpretative reading that focused on how 'young people', 'youth', and 'children' were described as a constituency and how meaningful participation and representation was understood.

Overall, we were able to distinguish six institutionalized forms: entities within international organizations (IOs) that are formally dedicated to youth representation, interorganizational forums, one-off events, recurring events, hybrid partnerships, and non-governmental platforms. Our analysis revealed that most institutions that seek to include young people are focused on youth, rather than children, as their reference group, with definitions of youth ranging between 15 and 31 years of age. Since the beginning of the COVID-19 pandemic, in particular, we could observe an acceleration of institution-building surrounding youth participation, ranging from online platforms such as 'Youth Action on COVID 19', created by the UN Major Group for Children and Youth, to formal IO advisory bodies with appointed members, such as the newly established WHO Youth Council. Children, by contrast, figure at the margins. They are rarely included alongside youth (an exception to this is the UN Major Group for Children and Youth) in institutions targeting young people in global health. In fact, our study of the manifold institutions, partnerships, events, and platforms surrounding global health revealed that international norms of child participation have so far had only minimal impact on access and voice of children in this area of global policy making. It appears, thus, that while the bodies of children are figuring as a very prominent object in knowledge production and governance in global health, the opportunities of children to be recognized as legitimate agents and to voice their opinions and interests are virtually non-existent. In the next section, we will thus narrow the focus to the evolving landscape of youth-specific organizations, partnerships, and platforms.

Youth representation in global health: types of institutions

Most of the activities on global health we found were embedded in larger organizational structures with a broader mandate than just global health, such as the UN Programme on Youth, the UN Major Group for Children and Youth, or the UN Youth Envoy. Four IOs – the UN Economic and

Social Council (ECOSOC), the WHO, the G7, and the G20 – have, by now, youth pre-summits accompanying their annual high-level summits (G7 South Summit 'Future Leaders Network'; G20 Youth Summit; Youth Pre-World Health Assembly; ECOSOC Youth Forum). In some cases, initiatives and partnerships by IOs include so-called 'youth hubs', such as the Global Health Workforce Network Youth Hub. Non-state actors and organizations representing youth on matters of global health can be, most broadly, classified alongside the adult-led/youth-led divide as well as alongside service-oriented or advocacy-oriented organizations. There are also youth-related institutional settings and activities by regional organizations, most notably the European Union and the Council of Europe, which, in 1972, had established the European Youth Foundation to 'provide financial and educational support for European youth activities' (Council of Europe, nd). In many cases, youth-led organizations active in the area of global health recruit their members from medical students or young health professionals. Most prominent among these is the International Federation of Medical Students' Associations (IFMSA), founded in 1951 and one of the oldest and largest student-run organizations in the world to date (International Federation of Medical Students' Associations, nd). It is the IFMSA that holds responsibility for organizing the annual Youth Summit accompanying the World Health Assembly in Geneva. Beyond these very large and politically active transnational youth-led organizations, there exist many issue- or disease-specific youth-led organizations, particularly on sexual and reproductive health; mental health; drugs, alcohol, and tobacco; and non-communicable diseases. In some cases, these organizations grow in scope and size and develop into more general global health youth organizations, such as the International Youth Health Organization. Originally a network of youth organizations working on the prevention and reduction of alcohol-related harm, it renamed itself in 2011 and expanded its scope towards other health issues. Such youth-led, student-run organizations can also be found in specific regions, such as Europe, Asia, and Africa; for instance, the Global Health Youth Foundation is directed by the UN Youth delegate of India, run by medical students, and active primarily in India (Global Health Youth Foundation, nd).

Images of young people in global health: representations of children and youth

In light of these diverse transnational activities at the intersection of global health and youth, we ask: to what extent are young people perceived as political actors in these institutions and initiatives, and to what extent is their own engagement and concern directed towards policy making, decision-making power, and political, institutional, and societal transformation? Again, and in parallel to our literature review, our analysis of the substance of the purpose, claims, and positions of youth-focused organizations in global health reveals that children and youth (to a lesser extent) are in many cases not perceived as political actors – particularly from the viewpoint of adult-led initiatives and organizations. Instead, a qualitative analysis of the language in which youth and youth representation are framed in speeches, websites, press releases, and other forms of meaning-making produced by global health organizations brings to light a largely homogenous vocabulary that leaves little space for political agency and risks glossing over political conflict. Notably, portrayals of children and youth as a constituency, and of young people's advocates as their representatives, to a large extent oscillate between two depictions. The first understands children and youth as vulnerable, marginalized groups exposed to a broad range of health challenges and threats. The second portrayal focuses on young peoples' potential rather than their present experiences and interests. This portrayal rarely includes children but instead describes youth as hopeful future leaders, professionals, decision-makers, local community members, and global citizens. In these narratives, young people are presented as eager to put in 'hard work' and 'extra hours', to leverage their expertise and skills for the benefit of global solutions to (public) health problems. Their agency is recognized insofar as they contribute new 'ideas', 'solutions', and 'innovations' for a more inclusive but distant global health future, particularly where it touches upon digital solutions to health issues (Wong et al, 2021). In other words, 'young people' are yet to become 'active citizens of their local, national, and international communities' and realize 'their full potential as individuals and as members of society' (The Big 6 Youth Organizations, 2021: 2, 7; see also International Federation of Medical Students' Associations, 2019; Young Leaders for Health, 2019; Bill & Melinda Gates Institute for Population and Reproductive Health, 2020).

Conclusion

In this contribution, we started by noting the troubling fact that while children and young people continue to be extraordinarily affected by global health issues, programmes, and policies, and their health constitutes a prominent item on the global health agenda, they are largely absent as speakers, agents, and informants in global health policy making. Through a systematic survey of pertinent research strands, we found that political agency and representation of children and youth in global health politics more broadly has not been systematically or comprehensively researched. As we extended our analysis to the practice of global health politics, we found that this silence in research contrasts with a proliferating ecology of (inter-)organizational entities, platforms, events, hybrid networks, and public–private partnerships formally dedicated to youth representation in global health, while children remain on the margins. By looking at one specific and very prominent area of global governance, our chapter sought to expose the contestation surrounding ideas of childhood and youth in contemporary international institutions targeting global health. We also exposed the indeterminacy of the boundaries between these two identities. While there are strong normative commitments towards child and youth participation in global (health) governance, our chapter showed that institution-building and policy discussion among hybrid coalitions of state and non-state actors has been largely focused on youth engagement. Meaningful and direct political representation of children (roughly below 14 years of age) thus remains a much-underdeveloped area of diversification and democratization of international institutions. Together, our observations point to the need for additional research and theorizing on the politics of child and youth representation in global health and beyond, particularly in the aftermath of the COVID-19 pandemic crisis. In our view, research on global health stands to profit significantly from paying systematic attention to the political agency and discursive representations of children and youth in political institutions where norms and knowledge of health and disease are constructed and acted upon on a global scale.

Notes

[1] *Social History of Medicine*; *Medical History*; *Social Science & Medicine*; *Critical Public Health*; *Medical Anthropology Quarterly*; *Globalization and Health*.

[2] *The Lancet* 'Child and Adolescent Health'; *American Journal of Public Health* 'Child and Adolescent Health'; *British Medical Journal*; *Health Policy & Planning*; *Child Development*; *Journal of Pediatrics and Child Health*; *The Journal of Pediatrics*; *Journal of Adolescent Health*.

References

Altavilla, A., Halila, R., Kostopoulou, M.-A., Lwoff, L., and Uerpmann, K. (2021) 'Strengthening children's participation in their health: The new initiative of the Council of Europe', *The Lancet Child & Adolescent Health* 5(4): 237–238.

Bent, E. (2013) 'The boundaries of girls' political participation: A critical exploration of girls' experiences as delegates to the United Nations Commission on the Status of Women (CSW)', *Global Studies of Childhood* 3(2): 173–182.

Bersaglio, B., Enns, C., and Kepe, T. (2015) 'Youth under construction: The United Nations' representations of youth in the global conversation on the post-2015 development agenda', *Canadian Journal of Development Studies* 36(1): 57–71.

Betancourt, T.S., Frounfelker, R., Mishra, T., Hussein, A., and Falzarano, R. (2015) 'Addressing health disparities in the mental health of refugee children and adolescents through community-based participatory research: A study in 2 communities', *American Journal of Public Health* 105(S3): 475–482.

Bill & Melinda Gates Institute for Population and Reproductive Health (2020) '2020 Global Health Leadership Accelerator'. Available at: https://www.gatesinstitute.org/2020-global-health-leadership-accelerator [Accessed 14 July 2021].

Brown, G.W., Yamey, G., and Wamala, S. (eds) (2014) *The Handbook of Global Health Policy*, Malden, MA: Wiley Blackwell.

Came, H.A., Herbert, S., and McCreanor, T. (2019) 'Representations of Māori in colonial health policy in Aotearoa from 2006–2016: A barrier to the pursuit of health equity', *Critical Public Health* 31(3): 338–348.

Coggon, J. and Gola, S. (eds) (2013) *Global Health and International Community: Ethical, Political and Regulatory Challenges*, London: Bloomsbury.

Council of Europe (nd) 'European Youth Foundation'. Available at: https://www.coe.int/en/web/european-youth-foundation [Accessed 7 September 2021].

Cuevas-Parra, P. (2020) 'Co-researching with children in the time of COVID-19: Shifting the narrative on methodologies to generate knowledge', *International Journal of Qualitative Methods* 19: 1–12.

D'Amico, M., Denov, M., Khan, F., Linds, W., and Akesson, B. (2016) 'Research as intervention? Exploring the health and well-being of children and youth facing global adversity through participatory visual methods', *Global Public Health* 11(5–6): 528–545.

De Pretto-Lazarova, A., Brancati-Badarau, D.O., and Burri, C. (2020) 'Informed consent approaches for clinical trial participation of infants with minor parents in sub-Saharan Africa: A systematic review', *PLOS ONE* 15(8): e0237088.

Elliott, C. (2016) 'Knowledge needs and the 'savvy' child: Teenager perspectives on banning food marketing to children', *Critical Public Health* 27(4): 430–442.

Farmer, P., Kleinman, A., Kim, J., and Basilico, M. (eds) (2013) *Reimagining Global Health: An Introduction*, Berkeley, CA: University of California Press.

Fassin, D. (2013) 'Children as victims: The moral economy of childhood in the times of AIDS', in J. Biehl and A. Petryna (eds) *When People Come First: Critical Studies in Global Health*, Princeton, NJ: Princeton University Press, pp 109–130.

Global Health Youth Foundation (nd) 'Team'. Available at: https://ghyf.org/team [Accessed 7 September 2021].

Gostin, L.O. and Meier, B.A. (eds) (2020) *Foundations of Global Health & Human Rights*, Oxford: Oxford University Press.

Harman, S. (2018) *Global Health Governance*, Abingdon: Routledge.

Herrick, C., and Reubi, D. (2017) *Global Health and Geographical Imaginaries*, London: Routledge.

Hettihewa, J.A. and Holzscheiter, A. (2020) 'Reclaiming the voice of youth: Pandemic politics and law and the invisibility of youth', *EJIL:Talk!* Available at: https://www.ejiltalk.org/reclaiming-the-voice-of-youth-pandemic-politics-and-law-and-the-invisibility-of-youth/ [Accessed 7 September 2021].

Holzscheiter, A. (2018) 'Affectedness, empowerment and norm contestation – children and young people as social agents in international politics', *Third World Thematics: A TWQ Journal* 3(5–6): 645–663.

Holzscheiter, A. (2020) 'Children as agents in international relations? Transnational activism, international norms, and the politics of age', in J.M. Beier (ed) *Discovering Childhood in International Relations*, New York: Palgrave Macmillan, pp 65–87.

Holzscheiter, A., Josefsson, J., and Sandin, B. (2019) 'Child rights governance: An introduction', *Childhood: A Global Journal of Child Research* 26(3): 271–288.

Human Rights Watch (2020) 'COVID-19 and children's rights'. Available at: https://www.hrw.org/news/2020/04/09/covid-19-and-childrens-rights [Accessed 7 September 2021].

International Federation of Medical Students' Associations (2019) Annual Report 2018–19. Copenhagen.

International Federation of Medical Students' Associations (nd) 'Who we are'. Available at: https://ifmsa.org/who-we-are/ [Accessed 7 September 2021].

International Labor Organization (2020) 'COVID-19 disrupts education of more than 70 per cent of youth'. Available at: https://www.ilo.org/global/about-the-ilo/newsroom/news/WCMS_753060/lang--en/index.htm [Accessed 31 May 2023].

Joffe, S., Fernandez, C.V., Pentz, R.D., Ungar, D.R., Ajoy Mathew, N., Turner, C.W. et al (2006) 'Involving children with cancer in decision-making about research participation', *The Journal of Pediatrics* 149(6): 862–868.

Kwon, S.A. 2019. 'The politics of global youth participation', *Journal of Youth Studies* 22(7): 926–940.

Lau, N., Parsa, A.G., Walsh, C., Yi-Frazier, J.P., Weiner, B.J., Curtis, J.R. et al (2020) 'Facilitators and barriers to utilization of psychosocial care in adolescents and young adults with advanced cancer: Integrating mobile health perspectives', *Journal of Adolescent and Young Adult Oncology* 10(4): 476–482.

Lee, J. (2020) 'Mental health effects of school closures during COVID-19', *The Lancet Child & Adolescent Health* 4(6): 421.

Lorimer, K., Knight, R., and Shoveler, J. (2020) 'Improving the health and social wellbeing of young people: Exploring the potential of and for collective agency', *Critical Public Health* 32(2): 145–152.

McCracken, K. and Phillips, D.R. (2017) *Global Health: An Introduction to Current and Future Trends*, Abingdon: Routledge.

McInnes, C. and Lee, K. (2012) *Global Health and International Relations*, Cambridge: Polity Press.

Missoni, E., Pacileo, G., and Tediosi, F. (2019) *Global Health Governance and Policy: An Introduction*, Abingdon: Routledge.

Mogro-Wilson, C. and Fifield, J. (2018) 'Engaging young minority fathers in research: Basic needs, psychological needs, culture, and therapeutic alliance', *American Journal of Public Health* 108(S1): 15–16.

Mold, A. and Reubi, D. 2013. *Assembling Rights and Health in Global Context: Genealogies and Anthropologies*, London: Routledge.

Moore, Q.L., Paul, M.E., McGuire, A.L., and Majumder, M.A. (2016) 'Legal barriers to adolescent participation in research about HIV and other sexually transmitted infections', *American Journal of Public Health* 106(S1): 40–44.

Newman, C.E., Prankumar, S.K., Cover, R., Rasmussen, M.L., Marshall, D., and Aggleton, P. (2020) 'Inclusive health care for LGBTQ+ youth: Support, belonging, and inclusivity labour', *Critical Public Health* 31(4): 441–450.

O'Manique, C., and Fourie, P. (eds) (2018) *Global Health and Security Critical Feminist Perspectives*, Abingdon: Routledge.

Parker, R. and Garcia, J. (eds) (2018) *Routledge Handbook on the Politics of Global Health*, Abingdon: Routledge.

Pincham, H.L., Harrison, J., and Collin, P. (2020) 'Successful youth participation in health research depends on the attitudes of adults', *The Lancet Child & Adolescent Health* 4(12): 857–859.

Poku, N., and Whitman, J. (2018) 'Global health challenges in the era of the Sustainable Development Goals', in R. Parker and J. Garcia (eds) *Routledge Handbook on the Politics of Global Health*, Abongdon: Routledge, pp 199–206.

Scott, J.C. (1985) *Weapons of the Weak: Everyday Forms of Peasant Resistance*, New Haven, CT: Yale University Press.

Scott, K, Jessani, N., Qiu, M., and Bennett, S. (2018) 'Developing more participatory and accountable institutions for health: Identifying health system research priorities for the Sustainable Development Goal-era', *Health Policy and Planning* 33(9): 975–987.

Sen, G. (2018) 'Fault-lines in global health: Intersecting inequalities, human rights, and the SDGs', in R. Parker and J. Garcia (eds) *Routledge Handbook on the Politics of Global Health*, Abingdon: Routledge, pp 17–23.

Spini, L. (2018) 'Ethics-based global health research for all, including women, children, indigenous people, LGBTQI, people with disabilities, refugees and other relevant stakeholders, especially in least developing countries and small island developing states in the Global South', *Social Science & Medicine* 214: 167–170.

Susman, E.J., Dorn, L.D., and Fletcher, J.C. (1992) 'Participation in biomedical research: The consent process as viewed by children, adolescents, young adults, and physicians', *The Journal of Pediatrics* 121(4): 547–552.

The Big 6 Youth Organizations (2021) 'Joint Position on Non-Formal Education'. Available at: https://globalyouthmobilization.org/wp-content/uploads/2021/03/Joint-Position-on-Non-Formal-Education-.pdf [Accessed 19 May 2021].

The Lancet Child & Adolescent Health (2020) 'Growing up in the shadow of COVID-19 [editorial]', *The Lancet Child & Adolescent Health* 4(12): 853.

Thorisdottir, I.E., Asgeirsdottir, B.B., Kristjansson, A.L., Valdimarsdottir, H.B., Jonsdottir Tolgyes, E.M., Sigfusson, J. et al (2021) 'Depressive symptoms, mental wellbeing, and substance use among adolescents before and during the COVID-19 pandemic in Iceland: A longitudinal, population-based study', *Lancet Psychiatry* 8: 663–672.

UN Committee on the Rights of the Child (2009) General comment No. 12 (2009): The right of the child to be heard. CRC/C/GC/12. Available at: https://www.refworld.org/docid/4ae562c52.html [Accessed 31 May 2023].

UN DESA and UNITAR (2020) Stakeholder Engagement and the 2030 Agenda. United Nations.

United Nations (2020) 'Special issue on COVID-19 and youth', *United Nations Youth Flash*.

Wong, B.L.H., Gray, W., and Holly, L. (2021) 'The future of health governance needs youth voices at the forefront', *The Lancet* 398(10312): 1669–1670.

Youde, J. (2018) *Global Health Governance in International Society*, Oxford: Oxford University Press.

Young Leaders for Health (2019) 'YLH Social Entrepreneurship Challenge on eHealth 2019'. Available at: https://eb30886c-03df-4001-a310-bdf2218ab3f7.filesusr.com/ugd/14e8ef_0ad9b7ec49db49c0be38d59b423d1e2a.pdf [Accessed 19 May 2021].

6

The Representative Breakthrough? Children and Youth Representation in the Global Governance of Migration

Jonathan Josefsson

Introduction

Recent decades have demonstrated an unprecedented institutionalization and mainstreaming of children and youth participation in international decision-making processes (Holzscheiter et al, 2019; Kwon, 2019; Knappe and Smith, 2021). In the UN system, children and youth have been identified as one of the 'major groups' (United Nations, 1992) whose participation is critical for effective and just global governance of sustainable development. As a result, we have witnessed a significant growth in the organization of youth constituencies, working groups for children and youth, child rights strategies, and youth forums in a wide range of areas such as climate, peace and security, health, and migration (UNICEF, 2014; United Nations, 2018; Holzscheiter and Pantzerhielm, 2023). The development follows a broader shift in international politics, from nation-state-centred negotiations to the opening up of global institutions to include actors such as NGOs, philanthropies, cities, businesses, and experts to tackle some of the most pressing global issues of our time (Tallberg et al, 2013). This is also the case in the global governance of migration (Schierup et al, 2018). In a time when global migration is reaching unprecedented heights and states of the Global North are trending towards restrictive border regimes, international organizations like the UN and the International Organization for Migration are seeking to find durable solutions to 'safe, orderly and regular' migration through the inclusion of new stakeholders.

However, while the inclusion of children and youth as political actors in international politics has certainly enabled new inclusionary forms of global political representation, the institutionalization of young people's participation remains contested. Scholars have critically noted that the mainstreaming and implementation of children's rights and their participation do not necessarily mean that the life situation of children and youth is becoming better or that young people's experiences of injustices are being recognized (Reynaert et al, 2012; Josefsson and Wall, 2020). It has been pointed to how the institutionalization of young people's rights and voices in decision-making processes has also become an instrument to govern, regulate, and control children and youth (Prout, 2003; James, 2007; Holzscheiter et al, 2019; Kwon, 2019). Further, the massive mobilizations of children and youth against global injustices of racism, climate change, labour, oppressive policing, and restrictive migration policy seriously contest the ways in which they are politically represented at local, national, and global levels (Cummings, 2020; Josefsson and Wall, 2020; Bessant, 2021; Josefsson et al, 2023). This gives rise to a set of questions: What kinds of political representations are made possible in the current regime of child and youth participation in the global governance of pressing transboundary issues, such as migration? Who claims to speak and act on behalf of the constituency of children and youth, in what sites, and what are the limits and transforming effects of such representations?

In this chapter, policy documents, social media posts, and interviews from the Global Forum on Migration and Development (GFMD) and Global Compact for Safe, Orderly and Regular Migration (GCM) are used to examine recent developments in child and youth representation in global migration governance. I demonstrate how the global governance of migration in the last two decades has experienced a major shift in the expansion, formalization, and institutionalization of children and youth representation. Yet, while we can note a significant growth in the number, presence, and formalization of young delegates in the global governance of migration, this has developed along certain discursive, material, and institutional trajectories that clearly limit what kinds of child and youth representations are made possible, which complicates the story about 'the representative breakthrough'.

Children and youth representation in global politics: historization and conceptualization

The drive to include children and youth in global decision-making processes has run in parallel with political activism by, and behalf of, children and youth within, outside, and in contestation with these institutions for decades (Holzscheiter, 2016; Ansell, 2017; Holzscheiter et al, 2019; Beier, 2020; Josefsson and Wall, 2020; Bessant, 2021; de Moor et al, 2021; Sandin et al,

2023). In the 1960s and 1970s, the 'discovering' of children and youth as right subjects (Margolin, 1978) provided a historical backdrop to the global diffusion of children's rights norms and the implementation of legislations, policies, and institutions following the adoption of the United Nation Convention on the Rights of the Child in 1989 (Holzscheiter et al, 2019). This development forced governments not only to be morally responsible for the protection of the rights of children and youth in vulnerable situations but also to be legally and politically responsive to the rights, interests, and participation of young citizens (Prout, 2003; James, 2007; Bessant, 2021; Josefsson, 2023). This was accompanied by the establishment of new organizations and institutions with the purpose of representing children and youth in national and international politics, such as national children's ombudspersons, The UN Committee on the Rights of the Child and the UN Major Group for Children and Youth (UNMGCY). As an outcome of Agenda 2021, in 1992, The UNMGCY was founded as the 'United Nations General Assembly mandated, official, formal and self-organized space for children and youth' (UNMGCY, 2018–2021: 2021 homepage). The UNMGCY institutionalized a bridge between young people and the UN system aiming to ensure meaningful participation. This development was later strengthened by, for example, the establishment of the UN Secretary-General's Envoy on Youth in 2013, the priority of children and youth participation in Agenda 2030 (United Nations, 2015) and the UN adoption in 2018 of the 'Youth Strategy 2030' that sought to 'significantly strengthen the UN's capacity to engage young people and benefit from their views, insights and ideas' (United Nations, 2018: 5).

From a conceptual point of view, while a discourse of *participation* has been particularly salient in the scholarly conversations about the inclusion of children and youth in decision-making processes (Prout, 2003; Lundy, 2018; Twum Danso and Okyere, 2020), with some exceptions, less attention has been paid to the *political representation* of children and youth (Anandini and Wall, 2011; Holzscheiter, 2016; Bessant, 2021; Knappe and Smith, 2021; Josefsson, 2023; Josefsson et al, 2023). In recent years we can note a revitalized debate within political theory, which I suggest offers important conceptual resources for the analysis of political representation in relation to children and youth. What is referred to as the 'constructive turn' (Disch, 2019) has rejected a traditional understanding of political representation as a 'transmission of pre-constituted interests' from a constituency via elections to a representative where the represented is logically prior to the representative (Saward, 2020). Instead, political representation has primarily been regarded as a constitutive and mobilizing force that also 'facilitates the formation of political groups and identities' (Urbinati, 2006: 37). The representative is thus contributing to the identity of what is represented by making representative claims on behalf of an imagined constituency in a wide range of political spaces (Saward, 2020; Knappe and Smith, 2021). And as Lisa Disch has indicated, this challenges traditional conceptions that the core mechanism of authorization and accountability primarily take place through elections and within the territorial borders of the nation state and institutions of representative democracies (Disch, 2019).

When a new landscape of actor constellations and global systems of child and youth representation emerged at the turn of the 21st century, this resulted in what can be described as 'new defining features' of the linkage between the representative and the represented (Josefsson, 2023). The political representation of children and youth developed, not as a traditional reciprocal relationship between the elected and the electorate, but through a complex playing field involving professionals, NGOs, international organizations, corporations, a plurality of state agencies, families, and young people themselves. The opening up of global governance institutions made possible new forms of representing children and youth, while at the same time becoming a productive tool for governance and the advancement of different political interests (Holzscheiter, 2016; Holzscheiter et al, 2019; Kwon, 2019; Beier, 2020; Josefsson et al, 2023). If, as constructivists suggest, one regards representation as 'a space between the representative and the represented', it is in these global spaces of governance that children and youth disrupt as well as feed into dominant forms of political representation through the making of representative claims (Saward, 2020).

The representation of children and youth in the GFMD and GCM

The GFMD was launched in 2007 as 'a state-led, nonbinding and informal process' and the 'most comprehensive arena for continuous intergovernmental deliberations between sending, receiving and transit states on emerging standards for the global governance of migration' (GFMD, 2022). The GFMD still provides a platform to enable dialogues between a plethora of international organizations, multilateral global and regional bodies, business actors, and civil society (Schierup et al, 2018). In recent years the GFMD has been increasingly integrated with frameworks for the Sustainable Development Goals (SDGs), adopted in 2015, and the GCM, which in 2018 was adopted by 164 states under the auspices of the UN (Pecoud, 2021). In the following sub-section, focus is put on the historical development of the GFMD and GCM as sites of global migration governance and how young people and other actors have made claims to represent children and youth.

The analysis is based on the official documents that have been produced in conjunction with the annual meetings of the GFMD from 2007–2021 together with Facebook posts, blog posts, and webpages by youth delegates from 2014 onwards. Finally, participant observations of approximately 120 hours and 16 interviews with delegates have been conducted before, under, and after the GFMD in Dubai in January 2021 and the International Migration Review Forum (IMRF) in New York in May 2022. While the official records of the GFMD and GCM offer an overview of general discourses, themes, issues, and participating actors, youth organizations' Facebook and blog posts, homepages, and interviews provide a richer source about experiences, priorities, and actor constellations that have represented children and youth during the period.

Representing the child as the 'vulnerable other'

In the first and formative period of the GFMD, 2007–2012, children and youth were almost exclusively represented by other actors, primarily from civil society, and their interests and rights were primarily framed in terms of their need of protection in particularly vulnerable situations. In the GFMD meetings 2007–2012, there were no formal mechanisms, procedures, or invitations to involve young delegates in their capacity of being a child or youth. Participant lists for the Civil Society Days indicate that some young delegates were sporadically present and that influential NGOs, such as the UNICEF and Save the Children UK, had delegates in place. Yet, there was no formalized child or youth constituency at the time.

While *youth* as a particular group of concern was hardly mentioned at all in the formal documentation in the first years, *children* were paid at least some attention. A quantitative analysis of the final reports of the GFMD 2007–2012 (each report approximately 50–150 pages) shows that 'youth★' occurs, on average, twice per report 2007–2009 and 'child★' 16 times. Strikingly, about a decade later, the picture had changed radically to the opposite, namely that the figure of youth dominated over a declining attention to children as a category, a development we will return to later in the chapter. During these formative years of the GFMD, children were primarily mentioned in a context of child protection and in conjunction with other groups in irregular and vulnerable situations. Not least, civil society organizations emphasized how restrictive migration laws had detrimental impacts on families with children and how children and women experienced particular risks of being detained or abused along migration routes. The discussions around child migrants fed into the general focus of the GFMD on labour migration and that migrants must be regarded not as commodities but as humans, and who also often have families and children that were left behind or in need of support systems to protect children's access to education, health, psychological support, and integration into host societies (GFMD, nd: 2011:3). From 2011 onwards, the protection of unaccompanied and separated minors became a salient issue on its own (GFMD, nd: 2011:42, 2012:44). Largely, the discussions mirrored a broader trend in public and scholarly conversations where migrant children were considered appendages to parents and families escaping war and poverty (Bhabha, 2014; Brittle and Desmet, 2020).

Children and youth making claims to represent themselves

In the period 2013–2017, the first steps were taken by children and youth to represent themselves. At the GFMD meeting in Stockholm in 2014, a group of 10–20 youth aged 16–25 were invited by the Swedish secretariat to participate in the forum (UNICEF, 2014; GFMD, nd: 2014:38). A Swedish government official described this as an active attempt to increase the participation of children and youth into the GFMD structure (interview 5 April 2021), and in the GFMD final report it was noted that the invitation of the youth group was part of a broader effort to create a more dynamic forum by seeking input from a diverse set of private and civil society actors (GFMD, nd: 2014:10). The group of youth highlighted how barriers such as racism and xenophobia, absence of state responsibility, and exploitation have resulted in asylum seekers being distrusted and locked into exclusionary systems. On the webpage of the Swedish National Youth Council, they stated that it is 'all too common that integration projects are focused on differences' and called for integration projects where people can meet and where similarities of people can be in focus (LSU, 2014). In the upcoming years, youth delegates from the meeting in Stockholm organized under the name of 'One Third' and participated regularly in the GFMD meetings with the ambition to increase the opportunity of children and youth to participate (One Third Facebook, 2014–2019). The group prioritized issues like the protection of young migrants' rights in crisis and transit, as well as the need to fight xenophobia and make possible the social inclusion of migrants and diaspora. As an accredited organization, they worked towards 'bringing a youth perspective' to the GFMD and pushed for 'a permanent seat for a youth representative on all of the GFMDs to come' (One Third Facebook, 2014–2019; 13 October 2014, 8 December 2016).

At the GFMD and GCM meeting in Marrakesh in 2018, a new era of children and youth representation began. Until then, the actual presence of youth delegates had been somewhat limited in number, and the agenda of the group had been focused on moving from temporary and volatile participation to obtaining a permanent status. In the time leading up to Marrakesh, the group had increasingly joined forces with the UNMGCY to organize the work of youth participation. In a Facebook post, One Third symbolically handed over the torch to UNMGCY: 'We have grown from a local group into an international movement – of youth. .... Within the GFMD there is now a permanent seat at the decision-making table for young people, which was our goal. Youth are now valued and recognized as a significant, key stakeholder' (One Third Facebook, 2014–2019, 2 January 2019).

It is at this point that a major shift can be noted about how and by whom children and youth as a group were represented. Firstly, there was a move from young people primarily *being represented by others* to them being formally recognized as a stakeholder group that *represent themselves*. Secondly, and as has been marked even more strongly after 2018, there was a shift in emphasis from representing young migrants primarily as *children* in a particularly vulnerable situation in need of protection to representing them as *youth* with agency to act as credible stakeholder partners. Obviously, the inclusion of youth delegates fitted well with the GFMD and GCM agenda to build partnership with a diverse set of actors to tackle the global challenges of migration as well as with the broader development of institutionalizing and mainstreaming youth participation and representation in international institutions and global governance processes (United Nations, 2015; Kwon, 2019).

Institutionalizing space for children and youth representation

The period 2018–2021 can be portrayed as a phase of expansion, formalization, and institutionalization of the children and youth constituency in the global governance of migration. The institutionalization of children and youth representation continued under the auspices of the UNMGCY. In 2021 they re-established themselves as the Migration Youth and Children Platform (MYCP) to constitute the official children and youth constituency of the GFMD and as a member of the UN Migration Network (GFMD, 2022; MYCP, 2022a). With that came experience of organizing youth involvement from other areas in the UN system and, as it turned out, better financial support (at least temporarily) and other resources to make possible a considerably larger and more organized participation by children and youth (UNMGCY, 2018). The establishment of selection procedures for the admission of delegates, systematic regional and global consultations to set priorities, and expanding participation in thematic roundtables, together with the production of policy briefs and annual impact reports, have constituted some of the key components to strengthen the capacity of the constituency. The growth in capacity is illustrated by the preparations to the GFMD in Dubai 2021 and IMRF in New York 2022, when the MYCP organized extensive regional and global consultations, according to their reports, including up to 381 youth-led organizations representing and serving over 556,000 youth across 79 countries (GFMD, 2021; UNMGCY, 2021; MYCP, 2022b).

In this process of expansion, formalization, and institutionalization of children and youth as an official constituency, we can observe some changes in how young migrants are 'imagined' as a group. On one hand, from 2018 onwards there was a considerable increase in the mentioning, recognition, and inclusion of *youth* as a key stakeholder and group of particular concern in the GFMD and GCM processes. This is made evident in terms of the number of youth participating in the negotiations, their obtaining of key speaking positions, the organization of entire sessions focusing on youth, closer cooperation with secretariats, the visibility of youth priorities, and a distinctive recognition and change in official discourse around youth (GFMD, 2018–2021; UNMGCY, 2018–2021; IMRF, 2022). For example, while the GFMD meetings during the period 2013–2017 gathered around 5–10 young delegates each year and 'youth*' was mentioned, on average, 10 times in the final reports of 2007–2017, in the period 2018–2021 the meetings gathered 90–200 young delegates each year and 'youth*' was mentioned, on average, 48 times in the final reports (GFMD, 2007–2021; UNMGCY, 2018–2021; One Third Facebook, 2014–2019). As a new constituency, the youth have put effort into building capacity and demonstrating their credibility and competence as stakeholders by putting 'even more solutions to the table' and getting 'young people to present innovative initiatives' and highlight youth priorities in relation to the focus areas of the GFMD and GCM (GFMD, 2007–2021: 2018, 2019/2020 2020/2021; UNMGCY, 2018–2021; MYCP, 2022a).

On the other hand, and what appears somewhat paradoxical, during this formative period of strengthening the representation of children and youth, *as a unity*, the representation of *children as a separate category* has not followed the same trajectories as youth and seems rather to have been weakened. As an illustration, while the final reports of the GFMD during the period 2007–2017 mention the word 'child*' an average of 34 times, during the period 2018–2021 'child*' is mentioned an average of 21 times and in 2020 and 2021 only 7 and 8 times, respectively. Hence, at same time as the figure of 'youth' has fed into discourses on young migrants as 'innovators' and 'future leaders' in the GFMD and GCM, the space for representing young migrants as children of lower age, with less capabilities, or as targets of restrictive border regimes, seems to have shrunk. In addition, a range of formal and informal norms have in practice made impossible the in-person participation of younger delegates under the age of 18 years old. A picture is thus emerging where the mainstreaming and participation of children and youth as a group has actually implied little progress, or even less presence on the part of the youngest migrants as a separate category.

This speaks also to other and more general barriers to meaningful participation for children and youth in the global governance of migration. In conjunction with the IMRF in New York 2022, the critique against shrinking space and systematic exclusion of civil society was harsh (The Civil Society Action Committee, 2022). For the youth constituency, this meant in concrete terms that out of the 381 youth-led organizations and 556,000 youth in 39 countries that participated in their global consultations proceeding the meeting (MYCP, 2022b), only 5 official youth delegates made it to the New York meeting. Some of the main barriers were difficulties in obtaining accreditation, lack of financial resources, and hindrances to achieving visas. This has, not least, been hitting groups of undocumented migrants, and under-aged and young delegates from the Global South.

Openings, barriers, and non-performatives

As I have described this chapter, the global governance of migration has over the last two decades experienced a major expansion, formalization, and institutionalization of children and youth representation. What can be referred to as a representative breakthrough of children and youth in the global governance of migration appears to be the result of both political mobilization by young people themselves, which has 'facilitated the identity formation' of children and youth as a group by making representative claims (Urbinati, 2006: 37; Saward, 2020), and long-term historical developments and institutional change in global politics (Tallberg et al, 2013; Kwon, 2019). Yet, even though this 'breakthrough' certainly has enabled new openings for child and youth representation, it has also come with limitations and has been conditioned by the very specific institutional legacies, contexts, and discourses of the GFMD and GCM. Firstly, the recent focus on involving youth as credible partners, future leaders, and innovators feeds into, and is confined by, dominant discourses and institutional conditions of neoliberal internationalism and developmentalism that have characterized the 'invited spaces' of contemporary global governance processes like the GFMD and GCM for a long time (Schierup et al, 2018; Kwon, 2019). And while the trajectories of competence, innovation, and leadership has encouraged and largely required the participation and representation of highly skilled, well-educated, and professionalized youth, it has made little room for children and youth of lower ages, with weaker educational background, with less communicative skills, or who more radically contest the very legitimacy of state authorities and current migration regimes (see also Wise, 2018; Pecoud, 2021), as has been salient in pro-migrant protest movements at national and local levels (Tyler and Marcianack, 2013; Ataç et al, 2016; Josefsson, 2023). In this sense, the opening up to child and youth representation in global governance of migration has crowded out other possibilities regarding the ways in which issues are being addressed, what actors that can make it to these sites, and what kinds of roles young delegates can play.

This brings us to a second point. Recurrently, delegates bear witness to a wide range of structural and practical barriers to gaining a place at the GFMD and IMRF and the difficulties of exercising meaningful participation once on site. Some of the most common barriers are related to impediments to obtain accreditation, lack of financial resources for travel and housing, as well as various obstacles to being granted visas.

On site, the limited access to government-dominated negotiation spaces, formal and informal speaking rules, and limited English language skills are some of the barriers that young delegates face. This particularly affects representatives with undocumented status, those who come from areas of lower income, and those who face high formal and bureaucratic thresholds to receive visas. These kinds of barriers to meaningful participation in global governance processes is certainly not a new phenomenon, but they highlight some of the global inequalities in access and uneven power relations that have characterized the structure of international society, international institutions, and migration regimes for decades, not least from a post-colonial perspective (Mayblin, 2017; Zeynep, 2017; Getachew, 2019).

Thirdly, at the same time as the child and youth constituency has taken significant steps to towards recognition and participation in the GFMD and GCM, this has simultaneously, and somewhat paradoxically, resulted in even less 'presence' of younger child migrants as a separate category. The practical impossibility of the in-person participation of children and youth under the age of 18 years makes apparent the structural age ordering of international institutions. And the recent discursive decline in the visibility of the young child migrant illustrates that representative progress for a constituency can actually imply less attention and performance for particular groups, interests, or values. In her article 'Nonperformativity of antiracism', Sara Ahmed examines how and why mainstreaming and institutional speech acts in the context of antiracism and equality policy at UK universities fails to do what it sets out to do. In her analysis, the failure of institutional speech acts (for example, about antiracism or, in this case, youth inclusion) is not a failure of intent or circumstance, but rather that the mainstreaming of policies 'work' precisely 'by not bringing about the effects they name' (Ahmed, 2006). Drawing on her concept of non-performativity, we may theorize these kinds of (lack of) effects on children and youth representation in terms of *non-performatives of child and youth representation*. The mainstreaming and institutionalization of children and youth representation seem to work precisely because they do not bring about the effects that they name. Along the same line, the inclusion of young people in global governance on matters affecting them has not only led to recognition and the advancement of their rights and interests, but has also become a technology of government that results in an actual non-performance (Ahmed, 2006; Holzscheiter et al, 2019; Beier, 2020). However, these technologies of government, in recent years often discussed in terms of 'youth tokenism' or 'youth washing', have not gone unnoticed or without contestation by young people. Instead, the representative claim to speak on behalf of young people continues to be a matter of contention and a source of political action. Given the apparent dearth of empirical knowledge and theorizing on these issues, the political representation of children and youth in global governance processes appears to open up a critical research agenda for many years to come.

Acknowledgements
The research for this article has been financed by Riksbankens Jubileumsfond and the project 'Youth Representation in Global Politics: Climate, Migration and Health Governance Compared' (https://liu.se/en/research/youth-representation-in-global-politics, P19–0845:1) based at the Department of Thematic Studies – Child Studies, Linköping University. A special thanks to Joel Löw, Linköping University, who assisted with parts of the data collection in conjunction with the GFMD 2021.

References
Ahmed, S. (2006) 'The nonperformativity of antiracism', *Meridians* 7(1): 104–126.
Ansell, N. (2017) *Children, Youth, and Development*, 2nd edn, Abingdon: Routledge.
Ataç, I., Rygiel, K., and Stierl, M. (2016) 'Introduction: The contentious politics of refugee and migrant protest and solidarity movements: Remaking citizenship from the margins', *Citizenship Studies* 20(5): 527–544.
Beier, J.M. (ed) (2020) Discovering Childhood in International Relations, Cham: Palgrave Macmillan.
Bessant, J. (2021) *Making-up People: Youth, Truth and Politics*, Abingdon: Routledge.
Bhabha, J. (2014) *Child Migration and Human Rights in a Global Age*, Princeton: Princeton University Press.
Brittle, R. and Desmet, E. (2020) 'Thirty years of research on children's rights in the context of migration', *International Journal of Children's Rights* 28(1): 36–65.
Capan, Z.G. (2017) 'Decolonising International Relations?' *Third World Quarterly* 38(1): 1–15.
Cummings, M. (2020) *Children's Voices in Politics*, Oxford: Peter Lang.
Dar, A. and Wall, J. (2011) 'Children's political representation: The right to make a difference', *The International Journal of Children's Rights* 19(4): 595–612.
de Moor J., De Vydt, M., Uba, K., and Wahlström, M. (2021) 'New kids on the block: Taking stock of the recent cycle of climate activism', *Social Movement Studies* 20(5): 619–25.
Disch, L. (2019) 'Introduction: The end of representative politics?' in L. Disch, M. van de Sande, and N. Urbinati (eds) *The Constructive Turn in Political Representation*, Edinburgh: Edinburgh University Press.

Getachew, A. (2019) *Worldmaking after Empire: The Rise and Fall of Self-determination*, Princeton: Princeton University Press.

GFMD (nd) 'Final Reports 2007–2021'. Available at: https://www.gfmd.org/docs [Accessed 2 April 2022].

GFMD (2022) 'Background', homepage. Available at: http://www.gfmd.org/ [Accessed 21 June 2023].

Holzscheiter, A. (2016) 'Representation as power and performative practice: Global civil society advocacy for working children', *Review of International Studies* 42(2): 205–226.

Holzscheiter, A. and Pantzerhielm, L. (2023) 'Contested childhood and young people's political representation in global health', in J.M. Beier and H. Berents (eds) *Children, Childhoods, and Global Politics*, Bristol: Bristol University Press.

Holzscheiter, A., Josefsson, J., and Sandin, B. (2019) 'Child rights governance: An introduction', *Childhood* 26(3): 271–88.

IMRF (2022) 'International Migration Review Forum 2022', homepage. Available at: https://migrationnetwork.un.org/international-migration-review-forum-2022 [Accessed 21 June 2023].

James, A. (2007) 'Giving voice to children's voices: Practices and problems, pitfalls and potentials', *American Anthropologist* 109(2): 261–72.

Josefsson, J. (2023) 'Political strategies of self-representation: The case of young Afghan migrants in Sweden', in B. Sandin, J. Josefsson, K. Hanson, and S. Balagopalan (eds) *The Politics of Children's Rights and Representation*, New York: Palgrave Macmillan, pp 275–298.

Josefsson, J. and Wall J. (2020) 'Empowered inclusion: Theorizing global justice for children and youth', *Globalizations* 17(6): 1043–1060.

Josefsson, J., Sandin, B., Hanson, K., and Balagopalan, S. (2023) 'Representing children', in B. Sandin, J. Josefsson, K. Hanson, and S. Balagopalan (eds) *The Politics of Children's Rights and Representation*, New York: Palgrave Macmillan, pp 1–28.

Knappe, H. and Schmidt, O. (2021) 'Making representations: The SDG process and major groups' images of the future', *Global Environmental Politics* 21(2): 23–43.

Kwon, S.A. (2019) 'The politics of global youth participation', *Journal of Youth Studies* 22(7): 926–940.

LSU (2014) 9 April blog post. Available at: https://lsurepresentanter.wordpress.com/2014/04/09/migration-ar-ett-viktigt-medel-for-utveckling-och-utveckling-ar-ett-viktigt-medel-for-migration/

Lundy, L. (2018) 'In defense of tokenism? Implementing children's right to participate in collective decision-making', *Childhood* 25(3): 340–54.

Margolin, C.S. (1978) 'Salvation versus liberation: The movement for children's rights in a historical context', *Social Problems* 25(4): 441–452.

Mayblin, L. (2017) *Asylum after Empire: Colonial Legacies in the Politics of Asylum Seeking*, London: Rowman and Littlefield.

Migration Youth and Children Platform (MYCP) (2022a) Available at: https://migrationyouthchildrenplatform.org/ [Accessed 21 June 2023].

MYCP (2022b) Global Compact for Migration Regional Reviews, Youth Consultations – Global Overview. Available at: https://migrationyouthchildrenplatform.org/wp-content/uploads/2023/02/MYCP_consultations_Global_Overview.docx.pdf [Accessed 21 June 2023].

One Third Facebook (2014–2019) Available at: https://www.facebook.com/One-Third-1478229142458372/

Pécoud, A. (2021) 'Narrating an ideal migration world? An analysis of the Global Compact for Safe, Orderly and Regular Migration', *Third World Quarterly* 42(1): 16–33.

Prout, A. (2003) 'Participation, policy and the changing conditions of childhood', in C. Hallet and A. Prout (eds) *Hearing the Voices of Children: Social Policy for a New Century*, London: Routledge, pp 11–25.

Reynaert, D., Bouverne-De Bie, M., and Vandevelde, S. (2012) 'Between "believers" and "opponents": Critical discussions on children's rights', *International Journal of Children's Rights* 20(1): 155–168.

Sandin, B., Josefsson, J., Hanson, K., and Balagopalan, S. (eds) (2023) *The Politics of Children's Rights and Representation*, Cham: Palgrave Macmillan.

Saward, M. (2020) *Making Representations: Claim, Counterclaim and the Politics of Acting for Others*, Lanham: Rowman & Littlefield.

Schierup, C.U., Likić-Brborić, B., Wise, R.D., and Gülay T. (2018) 'Migration, civil society and global governance: An introduction to the special issue', *Globalization* 15(6): 733–745.

Tallberg J., Sommerer, T., Squatrito, T., and Jönsson, C. (2013) *The Opening Up of International Organizations: Transnational Access in Global Governance*, Cambridge: Cambridge University Press.

The Civil Society Action Committee (2022) 'Re: Closing Space for Civil Society: A Call for meaningful participation of all relevant stakeholders in the entire IMRF', Open letter to Amb. Abdulla Shahid, President of the General Assembly, United Nations. Available at: https://csactioncommittee.org/wp-content/uploads/2022/03/Open-Letter.pdf [Accessed 31 June 2023].

Twum-Danso I.A. and Okyere, S. (2020) 'Towards a more holistic understanding of child participation: Foregrounding the experiences of children in Ghana and Nigeria', *Children and Youth Services Review* 112: 1–7.

Tyler, I. and Marciniak, K. (2013) 'Immigrant protest: An introduction', *Citizenship Studies* 17(2): 143–156.

UNICEF (2014) 24 April blog post. Available at: https://blog.unicef.se/2014/04/24/unicef-lsu-och-fryshuset-i-gemensam-satsning-for-att-lyfta-ungas-roster-om-migration/?fb_action_ids=712692938753666&fb_action_types=og.likes&fb_source=aggregation&fb_aggregation_id=288381481237582&fbclid=IwAR27egrk_QQtqfTsAeGzn7iZAoAdXWPmg5K4oRBgOq6_vDFPuSNo8LEdwu [Accessed 21 June 2023].

United Nations (1992) *Agenda 21, United Nations Conference on Environment and Development*, Rio de Janeiro, Brazil. Available at: https://sustainabledevelopment.un.org/content/documents/Agenda21.pdf [Accessed 21 June 2023].

United Nations (2015) Transforming our world: The 2030 Agenda for Sustainable Development, General Assembly, A/RES/70/1. Available at: https://www.un.org/en/development/desa/population/migration/generalassembly/docs/globalcompact/A_RES_70_1_E.pdf [Accessed 21 June 2023].

United Nations (2018) UN Youth Strategy 2030. Available at: https://www.un.org/youthenvoy/wp-content/uploads/2018/09/18-00080_UN-Youth-Strategy_Web.pdf [Accessed 21 June 2023].

UNMGCY (2018–2021) Youth Forum Impact Reports 2018–2021. Available at: https://migrationyouthchildrenplatform.org/resources/ [Accessed 21 June 2023].

Urbinati, N. (2006) *Representative Democracy: Principles and Genealogy*, Chicago: University of Chicago Press.

Wise, R.D. (2018) 'Is there a space for counterhegemonic participation? Civil society in the global governance of migration', *Globalizations* 15(6): 746–761.

7

The Office of the Special Representative of the Secretary-General for Children and Armed Conflict: A Normative Agenda and Children's Agency in Armed Conflict

Vanessa Bramwell

Introduction

Children are ever-present in arenas of armed conflict. In contemporary consciousness, pictures of suffering children are almost synonymous with 'new wars'. When we interrogate our mental image-bank, we struggle to identify the child in these pictures as one with agency, the capacity to enter freely into conflict without coercion or compulsion. Plenty has been said about the political utility of constructing the conflict-affected child in this way, which will be elaborated on below; states, regional actors, NGOs, and international organizations (IOs) of varying mandates make use of this norm of children lacking agency. This chapter examines the presence of this norm in annual reports of the Special Representative of the Secretary-General for Children and Armed Conflict (OSRSG-CaAC), based on a wider textual analysis project conducted by the author. Mark Laffey and Jutta Weldes' (1997) concept of symbolic technologies is introduced through a discussion of the non-agentic child soldier as a norm, and then utilized to explain the way norms are afforded common phrases in these reports, which allows the reader to analyse their frequency and spread as well as gain insight into how the presence of this norm may be impacting the perception of child protection at a high policy level in the United Nations.

The non-agentic child in conflict: contemporary discussion

Scholars in anthropology, critical security studies, International Relations (IR) and broader studies of childhood have all discussed the normative assumption that conflict-affected children lack agency. For example, David M. Rosen (2005) has written on the agency of children during the Warsaw Uprising in World War II and examined how this is ignored by contemporary narratives of the event. Such discussions of conflict-affected children's agency typically engage across two central points. The first is the question of who, exactly, is a child – when 'adulthood' is or should be reached, and what the relative difference in autonomy is between adult and child. The second is the representation of childhood itself as a condition in which agency is assumed to be inherently absent because adulthood and agency are considered synonymous. Both points of this discussion are engaged with in post-colonial arguments relevant to the analysis in this chapter.

Often the question of whether conflict-affected children's agency exists has centred around the definition of childhood itself, and whether it should be applied to children affected by a given conflict. Post-colonial arguments in IR and security studies engage with the idea that definitions of childhood – or the implied parameters of childhood – are applied in inconsistent ways to children in the Global North and Global South through the reproduction of phrases or images (Lee Koo, 2011; Berents, 2016). David J. Francis (2007) makes the argument that the official United Nations conception of a child as anyone under the age of 18 (commonly referred to as the 'Straight 18' position, based in the Convention on the Rights of the Child) is inappropriate for many localities, where young people may attain the age of majority much earlier. The result is that a lack of agency is at times assumed on the part of anyone younger than 18 years old. However, in many of the developed nations that make up the 'Global North', young people may enlist in armed forces before they are 18, though they may not be permitted to engage in combat. Francis' argument speaks to the assumption that agency is, in a way, synonymous with adulthood. Helen Berents (2016) makes a post-colonial argument in her analysis of social media campaigns which construct narratives of Global South girlhood; the construction of childhoods in the Global South creates an implicit dichotomy with Global North childhoods, which may be at least somewhat agentic. Katrina Lee-Koo (2011) usefully illustrates this contrast by comparing the Australian Defence Force's 2009 'Gap Year Challenge' with the work of the Coalition to Stop the Use of Child Soldiers, focused on the Global South. In each case, children of the Global South, or of particular conflicts associated with the Global South, are represented (by normative language itself, or perhaps by images like photographs) as more child-like, or more strictly and quintessentially children, than those of the Global North. While Australian minors are not permitted to engage in combat in accordance with the Optional Protocol on the Involvement of Children in Armed Conflict, they are considered capable of consenting to being militarized to a significant degree. Images of these smiling Australian minors in military gear can be compared to images of militarized children of the Global South, which are imbued with threat (Lee Koo, 2011; Berents, 2020). In UN agencies such as UNICEF and others under the wider umbrella of the Economic and Social Council, a nominal category of 'youth' also exists, though the age parameters vary depending on the agency (this is expanded upon below). Partly in connection to the 'Youth, Peace and Security' agenda, and partly a function of the requirement for needs-based categorization on the part of development-focused agencies, this category is generally associated with agency only when peacebuilding or consultation on proposed conflict or development solutions are concerned (certainly not in active conflict).

While the definition of childhood itself has been debated in IR and security studies as a determinant of agency, scholars have also engaged with the assumption that childhood itself inherently lacks agency by virtue of not being adulthood. Berents (2020: 57) critically assesses the framing of childhood in images used to illustrate journalistic coverage of conflict, noting that these images play a role in characterizing the conflict-affected child as 'innocent, dependent, and in need of protection'; the state of childhood itself is a constructed one in which a lack of agency is central – although conflict-affected children may, in reality, exercise agency on their own terms as children (Huynh, 2015; Brocklehurst, 2020; Holzscheiter, 2020; Lee-Koo, 2020). Jana Tabak (2020) has explored the utility of such a conception of children as lacking agency (particularly in the Global South) for the function of producing, or reproducing, stable and secure societies. The child is a site for investment, with the end goal of societal return. This child is the one that was surely envisaged by drafters as an ideal product of the Convention on the Rights of the Child – psychologically secure, protected, and non-political; a citizen in training. The vast global humanitarian infrastructure, comprising the UN as well as NGOs and IOs, has been considered both a contributing and reinforcing agent for this norm of childhood; Tabak (2020: 2) terms this archetype the 'world child'. In this sense, the world child plays a role not just as the kind of child 'we' aim to produce in the Global North as the inheritor of 'our' supposedly stable and enlightened systems of governance, but also as a civilizing agent in peacebuilding in the Global South. The ideal child in the post-conflict society is rehabilitated, politically involved in peace processes, and a stabilizing actor for their future state.

Discussions around children's agency in IR and security studies historically addressed the question of agency through conceptualizations of the child soldier. This is a well-worn topic in IR literature which has been assessed more critically in 21st century work (Rosen, 2005; Lee-Koo, 2011). The child soldier has functioned as a theoretical device for discussing the agency of children more broadly, and various tropes have been assigned to the concept in the course of these discussions; threatening and hypermasculine identities have generally been assigned to child soldiers. The hypermasculine child soldier is a thuggish threat to wider society, the very antithesis to the 'world child'. He is driven by a masculinity constructed by military commanders and inculcated by the essentially 'masculine' conflict environment. This is not to deny that the deconstructing of certain masculinities as a part of Disarmament, Demobilization and Integration (DDR) programmes is not important; on the contrary, strong cases have been made for the necessity of recognizing and addressing such cultural issues (Ni Aolain et al, 2011). However, the popular trope of the indoctrinated, hypermasculine young combatant is a definite facet of child soldiers' representation as non-agentic. Scholarship now notes an over-emphasis on child soldiers, as a characterization of conflict-affected children's experiences, in the late 20th and early 21st centuries in the humanitarian sphere (Bramwell, 2021; Lee-Koo, 2011), and in the OSRSG-CaAC report set discussed below, this over-emphasis is certainly clear. Nonetheless – and even because of its ubiquity – the symbolic technology of recruitment language regarding the child soldier is a very useful focal point in this report set for examining inherent ideas of agency. As John Baylis, Steve Smith, and Patricia Owens (2017: 1) argued, 'the agency of child soldiers is a site of knowledge in understanding international relations', though I make the case that this site of understanding is relevant to norm diffusion at a high policy level in the UN.

The following section of the chapter first outlines and situates the role of the OSRSG-CaAC in the wider child protection infrastructure – UN bodies and policy streams. It then briefly introduces some existing work around the movement of norms between different UN workstreams and offices for scene-setting purposes before explaining Laffey and Weldes' concept of symbolic technologies and applying this theoretical frame to recruitment language in the report set. The aim of the next section is to use the symbolic technology of the child soldier as a vehicle for elucidating how norms of children's agency are reproduced and maintained at a high policy level within the UN (the OSRSG-CaAC).

Norm presence in the UN CaAC infrastructure: examining reports of the OSRSG

In terms of the United Nations mandate for conflict-affected children specifically, there is a large and complicated infrastructure of different bodies which are involved in both policy production and field operations. This comprises the specific tool for measuring the six 'grave violations' of children in armed conflict, the Monitoring and Reporting Mechanism (MRM), and its associated office, the OSRSG-CaAC, as well as offices such as UNICEF, the United Nations High Commissioner for Refugees, and the Department of Peace Operations, at both a policy and field level.

Work has been done on examining the transfer of norms between different UN workstreams; for example Jeremy Shusterman and Michelle Godwin (2019) examine norm transfer between the Responsibility to Protect (R2P) and CaAC mandates. The authors find that normative language native to the R2P workstream is duplicated in the CaAC workstream. Cited by the authors is Alex J. Bellamy (2013), who found that the frequency of normative language relevant to a particular workstream in the discourse of state leaders, NGOs, and UN offices is related to the likelihood of the Security Council passing a related resolution. With this in mind, one wonders how normative language specifically about children's agency presents itself in high-level policy that interacts directly with the Security Council. Clearly, this normative language has an impact on Council decisions and agendas. As discussed above, other scholars have thoroughly established the presence of norms relating to conflict-affected children elsewhere in the protection infrastructure; what requires more examination is the lateral movement of such norms. From what points do they enter the CaAC mandate? What offices are they travelling between within the mandate itself?

This was a subset of the question I posed in a research project examining norms regarding conflict-affected children in the UN CaAC mandate. The research involved a close textual analysis of 22 annual reports of the OSRSG-CaAC, covering the period from its inception to the present: 1998 to 2021. The OSRSG-CaAC was chosen as a focal point for the project because it is the centre of the CaAC mandate at the highest policy level; the Security Council seeks advice from this office yearly. This office therefore represents the embodiment of norm transfer between the mandate itself and the Security Council, who decide on resolutions. The OSRSG's annual reports are presented in the same format as Security Council reports, with a preamble, introduction, sequentially numbered paragraphs, and then final recommendations. In examining these reports, an analysis of discourse used, as well as the frequency of certain phrases, allowed the author to identify norms about children's agency in conflict and to chart their presence and frequency across the set of reports.

In theorizing the transfer of norms – and seeking to identify them in a body of text – it is necessary to have a discursive tool with which to communicate the idea of a 'unit' of norm transfer. To this end, Laffey and Weldes' (1997) concept of symbolic technologies is useful. As constructivist scholars in IR, Laffey and Weldes (1997: 210) argue that conceptualizing ideas as technologies, which can be represented by tools such as phrases or photographs, recognizes the discursive function of those ideas and therefore, also, their relation to power: '... symbolic technologies are themselves forms of power through their capacities to produce representations'. As an example, the authors discuss the norm of 'development' as it was contemporarily understood. The promulgation of the norm, or symbolic technology, of 'development' had the inevitable effect of creating power relations through its ideological associations. The concept of 'development' created the dichotomy of 'advanced' and 'backward' societies, 'First' and 'Third' World countries, and so on. In this way, symbolic technologies such as phrases representing norms (like 'development') can be conceived of as units of norm creation and transfer which have effects relating to power.

R. Charli Carpenter (2005) has applied this idea in post-colonial security studies to her investigation of the gendered discourse of civilians. Carpenter conceived of the idea of 'women and children' (as a homogenous group of non-agentic victims in conflict) as a symbolic technology which has the ideological effect of characterizing women and children in conflict in a certain way that ascribes little or no agency. Taking guidance from Carpenter's analysis, my examination of the annual reports of the OSRSG-CaAC made use of several phrases that represented symbolic technologies – norms – in the reports themselves, about children's agency in conflict. These symbolic technologies were identified in the literature about the wider CaAC mandate; my goal was to examine whether and to what degree they were present in this particular office, which works closely with the Security Council. A close reading allowed examination of the context of each symbolic technology. From these observations, a discussion was constructed on the normative function of ideas of children's agency in the report set.

The diffusion of norms relating to conflict, in particular, has been examined in IR following the constructivist literature around norms in IR and international law more broadly; Martha Finnemore and Kathryn Sikkink's (1998) theory of norm generation and diffusion has been adapted and discussed in relation to such norms as the banning of cluster munitions (Rosert, 2019) and the outlawing of the child death penalty (Linde, 2014). Each of these topics provides a useful case study to examine the movement and entrenchment of norms in the IR space. A particular symbolic technology which demonstrated interesting patterns of presence and frequency across the report set in this study was the norm of the child soldier, in particular, discussions of child recruitment and an implied lack of agency in this regard. The next section will engage with the idea of children's lack of agency in the report set through the lens of recruitment language, to clearly illustrate the role of symbolic technologies in the promulgation of such norms. It is hoped that this will add to the body of existing examples of norm diffusion in the conflict subject area.

The 'non-agentic' children norm in annual reports of the OSRSG-CaAC: norm diffusion and the language of recruitment

Starting from the annual report from the year 2000, the 'era of application' of norms is announced (United Nations, 2000: para. 29). This is described as an agenda of normative spread, an effort to disseminate norms about conflict-affected children with the aim of raising awareness with the general public, as well as mainstreaming the subject throughout the UN mandate. It is not surprising, then, that such norms have been bouncing around in the wider child protection workstream. This office is intended to be the authority on everything in the sphere of conflict-affected children, at once (supposedly) informed by field work and directing its priorities in a reciprocal policy relationship. Media outreach is discussed at length in this report. Moving into 2006, the language of norm spread is more formalized, still with reference to the broad 'era of application', but also referring to 'destinations for action' (United Nations, 2006: para. 43) in the context of mainstreaming said norms in other UN workstreams (here, the Human Rights Council). Reports from here on refer to partnerships with various celebrities with the goal of raising awareness of the supposed universal plight of the non-political child soldier. It is clear that the era of application is synonymous with the popularization of a certain conception of the conflict-affected child, and particularly the child soldier – a symbolic technology.

The frequency of references to a lack of agency, particularly in this context of child soldier recruitment, is very high throughout the 22-year period spanned by the report set. Much emotive language is used to discuss the issue of recruitment, and initially this only makes reference to abductions and violence as the means of recruitment, with agency completely denied: 'Children simply have no role in warfare' (United Nations, 1998: para 18).

Reports after the year 2000 increasingly acknowledge that some children may *perceive* that they have agency in becoming involved with armed groups: 'In many devastated, impoverished, highly polarised or ideologically charged environments, children are lured into joining in hostilities for reasons other than forced recruitment' (United Nations, 2001: para 79). It is perhaps difficult to argue that a starving child engaging with armed groups to achieve food security, for example, is truly agentic. However, it is maintained that even when a child has an ideological motivation for engaging in conflict, this is imposed on them by coercive actors. Any political or personal motivation must be purely extrinsic, a product of 'polarized' or 'ideologically charged' environments. The logical extension of this argument is that children are expected to be purely non-political. After all, it is usually considered justified for adults to enter into conflict on the basis of grave political concerns; such opposing perspectives between two warring parties would probably be described as polarized. Here we can see one dimension of Tabak's 'world child' – although expected to be a site of future political cohesion and stability, the child must not engage in politics.

Overall, a trend in the discussion of recruitment – and agency in the process – is evident. The incidences of associated symbolic technologies (phrases) are very high in the earliest reports but steadily drop to a low point in 2005. They remain low until 2010, at which point the frequency increases quite rapidly until its highest point in the 2015 report. It then drops off almost as rapidly, reaching a mid-point in the 2020 report.

It is possible to make an educated guess about the reasons for this pattern. Interestingly, 2005 was the year of the landmark Resolution 1612, establishing the MRM for grave violations against children in armed conflict. In this sense, the trend reflects a growing conceptualization prior to 2005 of a six-part characterization of the experience of the conflict-affected child. The relative absence of the norm between 2005 and 2010 may reflect its new role as part of this wider characterization. Interestingly, even though the prominence of recruitment as the salient problem is reduced by this change in the OSRSG-CaAC reports, it was still apparently considered the most significant violation; until Resolution 1882 (United Nations Security Council, 2009), it was the only violation that could result in an armed group or state party being listed in the annexes of the Secretary-General's annual report on children and armed conflict.

The rapid increase in discussion around recruitment and agency after 2010 can partially be attributed to the growing inclusion of the Syrian civil war; aside from issues of recruitment, the use of children for terrorist activities such as suicide bombing begins to enter the report set. In the 2012 report, some further theorizing on children's agency is apparent:

> [The SRSG] argued therein [in front of the ICC (International Criminal Court)] that there was in fact no distinction between voluntary enlistment and forced recruitment, pointing out that children were not always recruited through abduction or the brute use of force. (United Nations, 2012: para 9)

> [C]hildren could not give 'informed' consent because they possessed limited understanding of the short-term and long-term consequences of their choices and actions and did not control or fully comprehend the structures and forces with which they were faced. (United Nations, 2012: para 11)

This discourse presents an absolute binary answer to the question of whether conflict-affected children have agency. In this document set, norms clearly prescribe agency only to people over 18 years. By virtue of the 'Straight 18' position, any person below 18 years of age is not capable of political agency in conflict as they do not fully comprehend the political context. Yet, harking back to Lee-Koo's discussion of the Australian Defence Force's 'Gap Year Challenge' campaign, it is clear that children of the Global North are disaggregated to a degree that children who are the subject of OSRSG-CaAC reports are not. Children of the Global North enjoy a third category of being: there is a period somewhere in the couple of years preceding their eighteenth birthday in which they are judged to have at least some degree of agency. It may not be agency enough to enter combat, but it is agency enough to consent to being militarized. The analysis of this report set establishes that the norm identified by Lee-Koo, among others, exists and fluctuates in the highest level of policy representation of the CaAC mandate.

The reason for the climax of frequency in 2015, and subsequent decline, can also be guessed at. That was the year that Resolution 2250 on Youth, Peace and Security was passed. According to the official website of this mandate, maintained by the UN Development Program and the UN Inter-agency Network on Youth Development, this new normative agenda seeks to upend commonly held misconceptions about young people in conflict: 'In countries affected by conflict and violence, young people are commonly perceived as either perpetrators or victims. ... In reality, the role of young people in relation to peace and security is poorly understood and much more complex than these stereotypes suggest' (United Nations Security Council, 2015).

These stereotypes appear to be very much in line with the norms discussed throughout this chapter as conceptualizations of conflict-affected children. However, Resolution 2250 is clear that it defines a 'young person' as aged between 18 and 29 years. This is not analogous with the meaning of 'youth' as defined by other, non-conflict-specific UN organizations (also acknowledged in the resolution), which apply the term to people aged 15–24, thus constructing the 'third category' that, in discussions of conflict, is generally reserved for children of the Global North. In this sense, the Youth, Peace and Security (YPS) agenda is an attempt at mainstreaming the same norm about age and agency as is present in the CaAC mandate rather than a conception of youth as including people under 18. However, as demonstrated in the quote above, this strong focus on the agency and participation of youth contrasts strongly with previous normative conceptualization of youth in conflict, which were centred in victimhood. The construction of this agenda is therefore a conscious attempt at reimagining youth in conflict discourse within the UN.

While it does not apply to people under 18, awareness of this normative change may have caused a discursive adaptation in mandates related to other groups traditionally conceived of as victims in conflict – like children. It is possible that this new norm transferred into the OSRSG-CaAC report set as a result of lateral movement from another office, as well as collaborative work between different 'Special Representatives'. This may have resulted in less willingness to characterize the agency of children, a 'vulnerable group' as youth once were in UN parlance, in such reductive terms.

The question of how intentional this discursive shift was in the OSRSG-CaAC reports, and whether it was an attempt to reduce scrutiny of the norm of the non-agentic child, would require further research to answer. However, Ole Elgström (2000) provides a useful argument for the ways that norms (or symbolic technologies) can be redefined multiple times through their process of spread and diffusion, arguing that things like text negotiation can alter their meanings and then affect the way they influence power relations. Such a perspective conceives of this evolution as an inherent aspect of the life cycle of norms and does not contextualize it necessarily in the context of post-colonialism. Barbara K. Trojanowska (2019: 30) specifically terms this process 'norm negotiation' and applies it to their analysis of Australia's National Action Plan for the implementation of the Women, Peace and Security (WPS) agenda, this agenda being another site of the eventual move away from discursive norms of victimhood and a lack of agency. Norm negotiation between different UN sites of interaction may be a useful way to conceptualize the process by which norms about conflict-affected children are being acted upon.

Norm negotiation certainly makes sense in the context of colonialisms and related power relations in these mandates. As Tabak's idea of the 'world child' demonstrates, the evolution of norms about young people or children from ascribing complete victimhood to allowing for agency under certain prescribed conditions (that is, in peacebuilding processes, as promulgators of peace and stability – as opposed to in conflict, where agency is denied) can be argued to be a negotiation acted upon by colonialism. Overall, though – whether an attempt to move towards categorizing children as 'world children' responsible for maintaining stability in conflict areas of the Global South or simply an unconscious evolution of symbolic technologies – the language in SRSG-CaAC reports from 2015 onwards reflects a muted focus on a lack of agency, and this may reflect such changes in the WPS and YPS agenda.

Conclusion

A textual analysis of annual reports produced by the OSRSG-CaAC provides insight into the presence and frequency of the norm of the non-agentic child in armed conflict. The concept of symbolic technologies (Laffey and Weldes, 1997) was used to examine the presence of the norm of the non-agentic child through the use of language relating to the recruitment of child soldiers as a focal point. This analysis can complement the work already carried out by scholars such as Carpenter (2005), Lee-Koo (2011), Bellamy (2013), Berents (2016), and others towards the goal of establishing a complete picture of the lateral transfer of norms regarding conflict-affected children in the wider child protection mandate. The OSRSG-CaAC is the highest policy focal point for the CaAC mandate, receiving reporting from field actors and local, national, and regional policy offices and presenting a normative summary of the situation of conflict-affected children to the Security Council via its report to the Secretary-General. The interaction between these two bodies is therefore a kind of 'norm highway' along which large volumes of norm 'traffic' can expect to be travelling – both upwards and downwards along the chain of command, and laterally out to other offices through collaboration in the child protection cluster. It is clear that the norm of the non-agentic child in conflict is not applied equally in popular discourse – nor perhaps in wider UN mandates – to children of the Global North and of the Global South; post-colonial theories may aid in explaining the presence of this norm in the annual reports of the OSRSG-CaAC as well as other UN literature. Further research could examine in more depth the influences on the fluctuation of this norm within annual reports of the OSRSG-CaAC with the aim of theorizing wider norm transfer into, within, and out of this office.

References

Baylis, J., Smith, S., and Owens, P. (2017) *The Globalization of World Politics: An Introduction to International Relations*, New York: Oxford University Press.

Bellamy, A.J. (2013) 'The responsibility to protect: Added value or hot air?', *Cooperation and Conflict* 48(3): 333–357.

Berents, H. (2016) 'Hashtagging girlhood: #IAmMalala, #BringBackOurGirls and gendering representations of global politics', *International Feminist Journal of Global Politics* 18(4): 513–27.

Berents, H. (2020) 'Politics, policy-making and the presence of images of suffering children, *International Affairs* 96(3): 593–608.

Bramwell, V. (2021) 'Protecting children in armed conflict', in D. Rogers (ed) *Human Rights in War*, Singapore: Springer, pp 1–15.

Brocklehurst, H. (2020) 'Doing IR: Securing children', in: J.M. Beier (ed) *Discovering Childhood in International Relations*, Cham: Palgrave Macmillan, pp 89–113.

Carpenter, C.R. (2005) '"Women, children and other vulnerable groups": Gender, strategic frames and the protection of civilians as a transnational issue', *International Studies Quarterly* 49(2): 295–334.

Elgström, O. (2000) 'Norm negotiations: The construction of new norms regarding gender and development in EU foreign aid policy', *Journal of European Public Policy* 7(3): 457–476.

Finnemore, M. and Sikkink, K. (1998) 'International norm dynamics and political change', *International Organization* 52(4): 887–917.

Francis, D.J. (2007) '"Paper protection" mechanisms: Child soldiers and the international protection of children in Africa's conflict zones', *The Journal of Modern African Studies* 45(2): 207–31.

Holzscheiter, A. (2020) 'Children as agents in international relations? Transnational activism, international norms, and the politics of age', in J.M. Beier (ed) *Discovering Childhood in International Relations*, Cham: Palgrave Macmillan, pp 65–87.

Huynh, K., D'Costa, B., and Lee-Koo, K. (2015) *Children and Global Conflict*, Cambridge: Cambridge University Press.

Laffey, M. and Weldes, J. (1997) 'Beyond belief: Ideas and symbolic technologies in the study of international relations', *European Journal of International Relations* 3(2): 193–237.

Lee-Koo, K. (2011) 'Horror and hope: (Re)presenting militarised children in Global North–South relations', *Third World Quarterly* 32(4): 725–742.

Lee-Koo, K. (2020) 'Decolonizing childhood in international relations', in J.M. Beier (ed) *Discovering Childhood in International Relations*, Cham: Palgrave Macmillan, pp 21–40.

Linde, R. (2014) 'The globalization of childhood: The international diffusion of norms and law against the child death penalty', *European Journal of International Relations* 20(2): 544–568.

Ni Aolain, F., Haynes, D.F., and Cahn, N. (2011) 'Disarmament, demobilization and reintegration programs', in *On the Frontlines: Gender, War, and the Post-Conflict Process* [online], Oxford University Press, pp 131–151.

Rosen, D.M. (2005) *Armies of the Young: Child Soldiers and the War on Terrorism*, New Jersey: Rutgers University Press.

Rosert, E. (2019) 'Norm emergence as agenda diffusion: Failure and success in the regulation of cluster munitions', *European Journal of International Relations* 25(4): 1103–1131.

Shusterman, J. and Godwin, M. (2019) '"Children heard, half-heard?": A practitioner's look for children in the responsibility to protect and normative agendas on protection in armed conflict', in B. D'Costa and L. Glanville (eds) *Children and the Responsibility to Protect*, Leiden: Brill, pp 1–13.

Tabak, J. (2020) *The Child and the World: Child-soldiers and the Claim for Progress*, Georgia: University of Georgia Press.

Trojanowska, B.K. (2019) 'Norm negotiation in the Australian Government's implementation of UNSCR 1325', *Australian Journal of International Affairs* 73(1): 29–44.

United Nations (1998) 'Protection of children affected by armed conflict: Report of the Secretary-General for children and Armed Conflict' A/53/482.

United Nations (2000) 'Protection of children affected by armed conflict: Report of the Secretary-General for children and Armed Conflict' A/55/442.

United Nations (2001) 'Protection of children affected by armed conflict: Report of the Secretary-General for children and Armed Conflict' A/56/453.

United Nations (2006) 'Protection of children affected by armed conflict: Report of the Secretary-General for children and Armed Conflict' A/61/275.

United Nations (2012) 'Protection of children affected by armed conflict: Report of the Secretary-General for children and Armed Conflict' A/67/256.

United Nations Security Council (2009) Resolution 1882 [Children and Armed Conflict]. S/RES/1882. Available at: http://unscr.com/en/resolutions/1882 [Accessed 1 June 2023].

United Nations Security Council (2015) Resolution 2250 [Youth, Peace and Security]. S/RES/2250. Available at: https://undocs.org/S/RES/2250(2015) [Accessed 1 June 2023].

8

In/visible Subjects: Global Migration Management and the Integration of Refugee Children into Schools in Addis Ababa, Ethiopia

Alebachew K. Haybano and Jennifer Riggan[1]

Introduction

What agency do refugee children have in the face of policies and practices that emerge from global migration management paradigms? The critical literature on migration, asylum seeking, and refugees makes the key point that, due to securitized borders around destination countries, child migrants will encounter walls, detention, forced deportation, and other harsh measures which deprive them of freedoms (Bhabha, 2014; see also Chapter 9, this volume). Children sit in an uncomfortable relationship with the increasingly bifurcated categories of 'criminal alien' and 'deserving refugee' (Heidbrink, 2014; Herz, 2019; Wernesjö, 2020). Meanwhile, a corollary migration management paradigm in refugee hosting states in the Global South incentivizes and encourages would-be migrants to stay in the South. While countries in the North seek to curtail the number of refugees entering their borders, states in the Global South, close to refugees' home countries, work with donors to reconfigure how they host and discourage secondary migration (Crawford and O'Callaghan, 2019; Nigusie and Carver, 2019; Graham and Miller, 2021). These host countries are situated to engage in a form of humanitarian borderwork on behalf of countries in the North (Rumford, 2008; Pallister-Wilkins, 2015; Little and Vaughn-Williams, 2017).

Care for children is key to this humanitarian borderwork. We focus on one component of that care – integration into local schools. This process has come to be accepted as the best practice for large hosting states in the Global South, as adopted by the United Nations High Commissioner for Refugees (UNHCR, 2019). It is a key component of broader policies aimed at curtailing migrant flows northward by locally integrating refugees into local economies and institutions (Crawford and O'Callaghan, 2019). However, local integration policy neglects the salience of long-standing regional political histories which belie the goals of welcoming and integrating refugees as they play out in refugee's everyday personal lives.

In this chapter, we examine the diverse experiences of Somali and Eritrean refugee students as they experienced local integration into government schools in Addis Ababa, the capital of Ethiopia. Focusing on the agency of refugee children and their families, we explore how refugees navigate interconnected axes of global policy, regional politics, and relationships with local actors.

Work on children's agency in global politics draws on feminist International Relations theories which emphasize the importance of the everyday sphere illuminating the ways that the personal is both political and embodied (Kallio, 2008). Flipping this around, we show that the political is also personal – specific regional political histories shape refugee children's subjectivity when they integrate into local schools. These are embodied in the ways young people move through space, behave, and form relationships. This embodied experience frames their overall sense of belonging, precariousness, and marginalization.

We draw on ethnographic data collected separately in schools in Addis Ababa by the co-authors. Between 2015 and 2017, Haybano conducted interviews and focus groups with students (grades 5–8), parents, teachers, and host community representatives in six primary schools that hosted large refugee populations (three Eritrean, three Somali). As part of a study of Eritrean refugees in Ethiopia, Riggan conducted interviews, focus groups, and participant observation in three schools with significant numbers of Eritrean refugees.

Global migration management and integration into local schools

Ethiopia has hosted a substantial number of refugees for five decades. Most live in camps managed by the UNHCR and the Administration for Refugee and Returnee Affairs (ARRA), a semi-autonomous government agency responsible for refugee management. Most refugee students attend primary schools managed by ARRA and funded by the UNHCR in camps. Refugee children in urban areas and those at the secondary and tertiary levels of education attend integrated national schools.

In 2010, Ethiopia began moving away from long-standing policies of encampment by introducing the Out of Camp policy. This policy initially extended only to Eritrean refugees, due to their historic ties with Ethiopia, and was meant to allow refugees to reside outside camps if they could survive without UNHCR support. In 2016, Ethiopia took additional steps towards a more progressive refugee policy, signed the September 2016 New York Declaration for Refugees and Migrants, and announced nine pledges, which were signed into law in 2019. The pledges included, among other things, access to education.[2] Ethiopia's pledges and the 2019 law gave the country a central role in several model international initiatives, placing it at the forefront of rethinking refugee and migration management worldwide (BBC News, 2016; Department for International Development, 2017; UNHCR, 2018, 2017; World Bank, 2017).

The Comprehensive Refugee Response Framework, formulated during the 2016 New York Summit, and the Global Compact on Refugees, a non-binding global framework developed in 2018, put forth a more positive tone for the mechanism to 'govern mobility' by 'easing pressure' on host states in the Global South. This management arrangement is 'a simple bargain between refugee hosting states and donor countries: you host, we fund' (Crawford and O'Callaghan, 2019: 3). Ethiopia immediately aligned its refugee policy with the global shift and partnered with the UNHCR and the donor community (Nigusie and Carver, 2019; Graham and Miller, 2021). These policy shifts created a role for hosting states to engage in a particular kind of humanitarian borderwork (Rumford, 2008; Pallister-Wilkins, 2015; Little and Vaughn-Williams, 2017).

The care of refugee children is central to Ethiopia's role in humanitarian borderwork. Large numbers of unaccompanied minors from Eritrea (reaching 150–200 per month in 2014; US Committee for Refugees and Immigrants (USCRI), 2015) have illuminated the Ethiopian state's caretaking role. Secondary migration particularly impacts children: of the 300–400 Eritrean children who arrived in refugee camps in Ethiopia each month in 2014, approximately 200 left (USCRI, 2015). Similarly, over half (59 per cent) of the refugee population in Somali refugee camps in the Jijiga area of Ethiopia are under the age of 18, and 10 per cent of these are unaccompanied minors. The intention to migrate to Europe is high, with 31 per cent of refugees intending to move onward from Jijiga (UNHCR and DRC, 2016). These children are the focus of programmes intent on slowing the secondary migration of refugees.

Education, thus, took on a new policy salience as Ethiopia participated in these global initiatives; however, the use of education to locally integrate refugees failed to consider that these populations of refugees already had long-standing relationships with host communities. The political histories undergirding these relationships manifested in prejudices and discrimination at the local level. Regional politics and conflicts play out in schools, and students developed strategies to navigate through this complex political field.

Brothering and othering: Ethiopian imaginaries of Eritreans and Somalis

The relationships between Somali and Eritrean refugees and Ethiopians have been formed by decades of war, disputed borders, and migrations. The legal status of each population in Ethiopia is complex and fluid due to ongoing, interstate political volatility. Each population is imagined by the host population in Ethiopia as belonging to or not belonging to the Ethiopian nation. These imaginaries frame assumptions, stereotypes, and prejudices about refugees among community members and teachers in schools.

Over the last 60 years, Eritreans in Ethiopia have been regarded as citizens, enemy combatants, and refugees as the relationship between Eritrea and Ethiopia has oscillated between war, peace, and frozen conflict. Eritrea was annexed to Ethiopia in 1961 and became independent in 1991 (official in 1993). In 1998 a war broke out over a border dispute. Although fighting stopped in 2000, the conflict remained frozen until peace was declared in 2018.

Many Ethiopians still imagine Eritrea and Eritreans as a part of Ethiopia, despite Eritrea's formal secession 30 years ago, positing a cultural, historical, and religious connection between the people. An Ethiopian in a focus group commented: 'We sympathize with Eritrean people because they are our brothers, they are our blood.' The separation of the two nations is seen as an aberration.

Eritreans chafe at this assertion of sameness, which negates cultural and religious diversity in both Eritrea and Ethiopia. An Eritrean national identity, independent from that of Ethiopia, was forged in the country's 30-year 'struggle' for liberation and firmly established through 30 years as an independent state. Eritrean refugees report that Ethiopians have a complex reaction to their assertions of having an identity that is distinct. One of our interlocutors stated that half of the Ethiopians they met were welcoming and warm to them, while the other half were hostile. Some Ethiopians stigmatize Eritreans as citizens of an enemy nation, at times even referring to them as 'Shaebia', the nickname of the ruling party in Eritrea, the party that, ironically, Eritreans fled from, but a nickname that is often synonymous with being warlike or belligerent. Others suggest Eritrean refugees are opportunistic migrants from a wayward enemy nation who are just using Ethiopia and draining its resources.

The relationship between Somalia and Ethiopia was also forged in a history of war over shared boundaries. For the early part of the 20th century, the boundary between Ethiopia and Somalia was imprecise, porous, and fluid. The attempt to establish precise borders in the 1930s sparked conflicts. Tensions continued even after Somalia became independent, erupting into a war in 1977–1978, which remains unresolved. Additionally, since the dissolution of the Somali state in 1991, large numbers of Somali refugees have entered Ethiopia. Finally, there are many Somalis living in Ethiopia with neither citizenship nor refugee status as permanent legal residents. All of this means that Somalis occupy several different statuses in Ethiopia. Some are citizens of Ethiopia, some are refugees, and some are permanent legal residents.

Historically, notions of Ethiopianness pivot around a highland, Christian 'Habesha' identity.[3] Many Ethiopians regard those who do not fit into these categories as 'other'. But Somalis are not only religiously, geographically, linguistically, and culturally other; because of the history of war and the regional security situation, they are seen as a threat. A local community representative's attitudes reveal the prejudice that derives from this political situation: 'They are aggressive, impolite, and disobedient.'

The relationship between Somali and Eritrean refugee populations and the Ethiopian host community have been forged by war and shifting, fluid categories of belonging, but this looks very different for the two populations. Eritreans feel safer blending in, while Somalis are highly visible and feel safer in community.

The residential choices of Somali and Eritrean refugees reflect these different political histories. The Somali population is concentrated in the Bole Michael area of Addis Ababa, which is referred to by some as 'little Mogadishu'. This community enclave is visible to the host community, with many refugees opening guesthouses, shops, and restaurants as a means of livelihood. In contrast, Eritrean refugees live dispersed all over the city, including in the peripheries and the new expansion sites of the city, and as a result remain invisible. Some research participants explained that the dispersed settlement of Eritrean refugees is rooted in mistrust towards the local host community and among the refugees themselves. The point we hope to make with this brief history of these two refugee populations in Ethiopia is that the experiences of local integration policies are different and shaped in specific ways by regional political histories. Below, we show how this dynamic shapes children's agency in schools.

Strategies of in/visibility in schools

Where are the refugees? Eritrean student invisibility in Addis Ababa schools

When I (Riggan) began field work in schools identified as having Eritrean refugees, I was surprised how hard it was to find the refugees. As is often the protocol when doing research in Ethiopia, school directors selected students for my interviews and focus groups. In one school, the director produced an interviewee who immediately told me that she was not Eritrean. In another school, the director walked into a classroom and, to my shock, asked for Eritrean volunteers to present themselves. (Before anyone volunteered, I quickly stopped this approach, explaining that calling out students could endanger them.) What is notable here is both that the school directors had no ready means to identify which students were refugees and the sense that students avoided being identified as such. Even successful interviews and focus groups were short, and the students' slightly recoiled posture and barely audible tone of voice reflected a hesitance to talk. Although interviews gave me little information in terms of what these students *said*, their embodied response to being identified as a refugee and an Eritrean spoke loudly.

An Eritrean refugee parent articulated how the politics can disturb the invisible existence of children in the schools:

> 'My fear is if schools promote Eritrean identity the current relationship of children with local students can be affected. Children are exposed to the media message regarding the conflicting relationship between Ethiopian and Eritrean governments. Currently you cannot distinguish Eritrean refugee students from the local students. They are extremely integrated with the local students.' (Parent, May 2015)

Eritrean refugees and refugee students are wary of their positioning within the volatile politics of Ethiopian–Eritrean relations, which has already changed their status many times. They feel their best strategy is to remain invisible and blend in as much as possible. This enables them to take advantage of educational opportunities and avoid being singled out.

Invisibility in Addis Ababa extends from the landlords with whom Eritreans often share the same compound to the neighbourhood in which they live and to their school. A 17-year-old Eritrean student who attends grade 7 noted, "My teachers don't know that I am an Eritrean refugee. In fact, I do not also know who is Eritrean among the students in this school. We don't know each other". A 15-year-old grade 6 student noted, "Nobody knows that I am Eritrean. I don't think our landlords with whom we share the same compound know that we are Eritreans. But we have a good relationship with them".

Students have several strategies to safeguard their invisibility. Students only associate with people from their immediate family or with local students and avoid associating with other Eritreans. One refugee student noted, "My best friends are Ethiopians. They don't speak Tigrigna. They speak only Amharic". Teachers also commented that Eritrean refugee students avoided close friendships, especially with Eritrean refugee students who were not related to them. A principal of one school noted that: "They [Eritreans] do not trust people around them. Those from the same family, wherever they go, they travel together as a convoy. They even do not trust other Eritreans from their neighbourhood. They are extremely attached with their family members only" (Principal, May 2015). The idea of keeping Eritrean identity invisible was connected to staying alone and only being friends with close friends or family members.

A related strategy to make themselves invisible was to avoid sitting in the same place, or to sit alone, a strategy that teachers thought was connected to mistrust and a desire for physical security for their property. As another student explained, "I sit alone in the classroom". A teacher participant at one school observed the following behaviour of Eritrean refugee students in her classroom:

'They change their desk every time. They do not like sitting in permanent place. Of course [name of the student] prefers being alone. He never trusts leaving his school bag on the desk. Wherever he goes in the school compound he carries his school bag with himself. He has a big lock for his bag. ... In my class there are three Eritrean refugee students. I have not seen the three of them as friends.' (Teacher, May 2015)

Another strategy to remain invisible is attempting to be organized and careful, to be a sort of model student who would not call attention to him or herself:

'I have one Eritrean student in grade two. She is little bit aggressive. She does not like a permanent seat. Sometimes she prefers to be alone. She withdraws herself from her classmates sometimes. She is so organized and careful beyond her age. When I give task to students, she is extremely committed to accomplish the task on time and to my expectation. I mean she is little bit different. Other students always avoid her during play.' (Teacher, May 2015)

Ironically, while blending in may allow Eritreans to avoid calling attention to their refugee status, it also reinforces a common Ethiopian attitude: that Eritreans, who speak the Tigrinya language, are the same as Ethiopian Tigrinya-speakers (Tigreans). School personnel identify Eritrean refugee students with Ethiopian ethnic Tigreans and consider them as insiders. A school principal noted, "[F]irst of all, I do not understand the difference. For me Eritreans are Tigreans and Tigreans are Eritreans. Therefore, both are Ethiopians!.

Given the history of being targeted in Ethiopia as Eritreans, the long history of animosity between the two countries, and the facility Eritreans have with blending in, it is no surprise that Eritreans opt for a strategy of invisibility. We repeatedly heard from teachers that they sometimes did not even know who the Eritrean students were in their classes. Students seemed to avoid being singled out as Eritreans, not speaking until they had mastered Amharic and sometimes physically shrinking themselves so as not to be noticed. Interestingly, children did not articulate an awareness of the political histories that we have recounted here, but they intuited or were instructed that they should not call attention to themselves. This embodied practice, whether it was done knowingly or unknowingly, references the particular political history of Eritreans in Ethiopia and, therefore, becomes Eritreans' particular approach to integrating locally. But blending in and integration are not the same thing, and in fact becoming invisible can conceal a silent marginalization. Blending in is not the only option, as we will see below.

"Local students call us Al Shabab": Somali refugee stigmatization and hyper-visibility

The Somali urban refugee parents sat in a large circle on the floor, talking animatedly, upset at a change in policy. Previously, they had received tuition funding which enabled them to send their children to private schools in the Somali community. These schools, Somalis thought, would better enable them to stay close to and protect their community. The Amharic Schools, as the Somali refugees refer to the public primary schools, are 'difficult and alien' for them. They cannot find their identity markers. As a result, a refugee parent commented, "mostly, half of us [Somali parents] do not send our children to [government] schools". He added, "instead, we send children to Quran schools and language schools with Somali and Arabic languages".

According to the local integration policy, they were no longer eligible for that funding. They would now have to send their children to government schools. They explained to us that going to a government school was not a viable option. Their children would either have to drop out or they would have to, somehow, raise funds to attend private schools. Why was it so important for Somali parents that their children not attend Ethiopian schools?

Unlike Eritreans, due to linguistic, cultural, and religious differences from the majority population in Addis Ababa, Somalis are already visible as a community. As noted above, members of the local community believed that Somali refugees were not positive towards the local culture, citing the inability to speak Amharic. In a focus group, an Ethiopian community representative highlighted Somali refugees' attitude towards the local language and culture: 'They are very much biased towards their own culture. Even those Somali refugee children who were born in Addis Ababa, they cannot speak Amharic properly. They are not positive towards our culture' (Local community representative, June 2015). The refusal to integrate was a common theme in interviews with local community members and teachers. The concentration of refugees in a small geographic area has promoted a notion of the Somali as the other, both among refugees themselves and the host community. This contributes to the preservation of Somali identity but also enables negative stereotypes to emerge.

Many Somali refugee students noted that they were separated from the host population. They did not have Habesha (Amharic-speaking) friends at school and seldom interacted with Habesha neighbours. As one student said: "All our neighbours are Habesha. I do not speak with them. Because there is no Somalian. They are all Habesha. We do not share anything with them. I do not have friend in the neighbourhood. I go to other neighbourhood to my Somali friends and play." This is a key component of becoming a visible other and, in many respects, is the opposite of the Eritrean choice to remain invisible.

In schools, Somali students became visible in new ways and were exposed to prejudices. The following comments by a teacher on Somali students are common:

> 'The most difficult issue with Somali students is their behaviour. They disturb the class. They do not respect teachers. Usually they are ready for conflict. They are extremely sensitive. All Somalis cooperate during conflict. They are unfairly biased towards each other. They always want to instigate conflict and inflict damage on local students. If a single Somali student quarrels with a local student, all Somalis from all grade levels gather together and attempt to attack all the other Ethiopian students. They do not work on their homework. I think there is no one at home that checks their progress in education.' (Teacher, June 2015)

Somali visibility in schools brings on stereotypes, prejudices, and othering of the Somali community in schools. A 15-year-old grade 7 student explained her experience of being othered: "Local students say to us, 'You terrorists, Al Shabab'." Some refugee students dropped out from school due to such insults. One student dropped out from school because he did not want to fight with local students and go to jail due to constant insults' (student, May 2015). A school principal also noted the link between Somali students visibility – their tendency to stick together – and their rejection of the school and tendency to fight with other students: "The behaviour of Somali students is different from local students. They are careless. They do not know school discipline. They are aggressive."

Whereas Eritrean students could blend in and the political history of oscillating relations between Eritrea and Ethiopia made them feel it was safer to remain invisible, Somali students were the target of prejudices that singled them out and made them visible, so that they effectively leaned into this strategy of visibility. As with Eritrean students, regional politics informed relations with Ethiopian students and impacted their everyday choices about how to act and who to socialize with. The mandate to locally integrate refugees into schools, which was born from global initiatives, brought prejudices and attitudes which came from decades of political history into the classroom. Children and families responded with strategies of making themselves visible and invisible.

Conclusion

There are a number of ways to make sense of children's political agency, many of which are discussed in the other chapters of this volume. As other chapters have noted, children are often objects of policy and the requisite epistemologies that undergird policies. Children are often assumed to be lacking in agency, particularly in policy spheres that regard them as victims. Improving the lives of children is often the rationale for policies (Berents 2020; Martuscelli, Chapter 1, this volume). Assumptions may even be made that they are malleable and that policy can shape their life outcomes. And yet, as we have seen throughout this chapter, all of this is complex.

Policies which are global in reach and design, like the local integration policies in schools, often target children. Local integration is a manifestation of global politics, which seeks to curtail the onward migration of large refugee populations hosted in Ethiopia and was rationalized as being good for children, but local integration, at the level of everyday experience, was a fraught space for children to navigate. As schools integrate locally, long-standing regional politics play out. Thus, bringing understandings of how regional political histories are embodied in children's agency is essential.

Consideration of children's agency brings examinations of everyday politics into the sphere of Childhood Studies (Kallio, 2008). Examinations of everyday politics include exploring how the political is embedded in ordinary and everyday activity, for example, children's play (Chapter 11, this volume). In the process of exploring quotidian politics, it is also important not to lose sight of the way formal politics manifests in the quotidian realm. Children act and react in response to a number of elements which include but are not limited to the experience of being displaced or the decision to migrate onwards. But as Global South host states are increasingly incentivized to integrate refugees for the long term in order to encourage them to stay, refugee children must navigate not only the stigma of being a refugee but also the interaction of their specific regional political histories with the stigma of being a refugee.

For refugee children attending these schools, their experience of regional political tensions was embodied in their everyday experience of schools. Somalis clustered together with other Somalis in order to push back against being called names or singled out as different. Meanwhile, Eritreans developed strategies to shrink and remain silent and not be noticed. In both cases, children's agency took the form of an embodied reaction which reflected a local politics.

Children's bodies, in schools, communities, or families, are the object – the targets – of policy. Policies that mandated that children be locally integrated into local schools were rationalized as being better for children, but what was not considered here was the way in which the school would function as a microcosm of the broader political situation and that children would be treated in a way that reflected these regional politics. For Eritrean young people, the policies of local integration in many ways enabled them to remain invisible. But for Somali refugees who would have preferred to attend their own schools and live in their own visible, but distinct, communities, local integration made them vulnerable to being stereotyped and targeted. Blending in was not a choice for them, and so they chose, at times, to be belligerent, having no choice but to defend themselves.

From the vantage point of refugee students, integration is problematic. Somalis are actively othered, and the stigma against them prevents them from fully integrating or being accepted into the school community. Meanwhile, Eritrean strategies of blending in and remaining invisible may lead to better school performance, but it reinforces beliefs that Eritreans are the same as Ethiopians and may inhibit their receiving necessary supports. Both visibility and invisibility are challenges and responses to local politics and the long history of relations between these countries and the host country.

Notes

[1] Both authors played an equal role in producing this paper. Names are therefore listed in alphabetical order.
[2] The pledges include the following: making work permits available to some refugees, allocating industrial park jobs to refugees, expanding the provision of education, making land available, and enabling a path to permanent legal status for refugees who have been in Ethiopia for more than 20 years. Pledges also promise to enhance social services, facilitate the opening of bank accounts, and provide documentation such as birth certificates, driving licences, and marriage certificates.
[3] *Habesha* is a fluid and controversial term that typically refers to Ethiopians of Semitic origin and includes Tigrinya- and Amharic-speaking ethnic groups, among others.

References

BBC News (2016) 'Refugee crisis: Plan to create 100,000 jobs in Ethiopia', 21 September. Available at: http://www.bbc.com/news/world-africa-37433085 [Accessed 12 January 2017].

Berents, H. (2020) 'Politics, policy-making and the presence of images of suffering children', *International Affairs* 96(3): 593–608.

Bhabha, J. (2014) *Child Migration and Human Rights in a Global Age*, Princeton: Princeton University Press.

Crawford, N. and O'Callaghan, S. (2019) *The Comprehensive Refugee Response Framework: Responsibility-sharing and Self-reliance in East Africa*, Humanitarian Policy Group Working Paper. Available at: https://cdn.odi.org/media/documents/12935.pdf

Department for International Development (2017) 'Ethiopia Profile', July. Available at: https://www.gov.uk/government/uploads/system/uploads/attachment_data/file/630866/Ethiopia.pdf [Accessed 26 July 2017].

Graham, J. and Miller, S. (2021) 'From displacement to development: How Ethiopia can create shared growth by facilitating economic inclusion for refugees', Center for Global Development and Refugee International case study. Available at: https://static1.squarespace.com/static/506c8ea1e4b01d9450dd53f5/t/60c7959f83c9e30424d56695/1623692708140/Displacement-to-Development-How-Ethiopia-Can-Create-Shared-Growth.pdf [Accessed 1 June 2023].

Heidbrink, L. (2014) *Migrant Youth, Transnational Families, and the State. Care and Contested Interests*, Philadelphia: University of Pennsylvania Press.

Herz, M. (2019) '"Becoming" a possible threat: Masculinity, culture and questioning among unaccompanied young men in Sweden', *Identities: Global Studies in Culture and Power* 26(4): 431–449.

Kallio, K. (2008) 'The body as battlefield: Approaching children's politics', *Geografiska Annaler: Series B, Human Geography* 90(3): 285–297.

Little, A. and Vaughn-Williams, N. (2017) 'Stopping boats, saving lives, securing subjects: Humanitarian borders in Europe and Australia', *European Journal of International Relations* 23(3): 533–556.

Nigusie, A. and Carver, F. (2019) 'The comprehensive refugee response framework: progress in four East African countries', Humanitarian Policy Group Working Paper. Available at: https://odi.org/en/publications/the-comprehensive-refugee-response-framework-progress-in-four-east-african-countries/ [Accessed 1 June 2023].

Pallister-Wilkins, P. (2015) 'The humanitarian politics of European border policing: Frontex and border police in Evros', *International Political Sociology* 9(1): 53–69. [https://doi.org/10.1111/ips.12076]

Rumford, C. (2008) 'Introduction: Citizenship and borderwork in Europe', *Space and Polity* 12(1): 1–12.

UNHCR (2017) 'Oral Update on the Comprehensive Refugee Response', 16 March. Available at: http://www.unhcr.org/58cfa1d97.pdf [Accessed 25 July 2017].

UNHCR (2018) 'Briefing Note: CRRF Ethiopia: Applying the Comprehensive Refugee Response Framework (CRRF)'. Available at: https://data2.unhcr.org/en/documents/download/65916 [Accessed 15 June 2023].

UNHCR (2019) 'Refugee education 2030: A strategy for refugee inclusion', Copenhagen. Available at: https://www.unhcr.org/5d651da88d7.pdf [Accessed 1 June 2023].

UNHCR and DRC (2016) Study on the Onward Movement of Refugees and Asylum-Seekers from Ethiopia. Addis Ababa, Ethiopia: Author. Available at: https://www.refworld.org/docid/58c287224.html

UNHCR and PRM (2012) 'Report of a Joint UNHCR-PRM Mission to Review Urban Refugee Issues in Uganda and Ethiopia'. Available at: https://2009-2017.state.gov/j/prm/releases/releases/2012/208926.htm]

US Committee for Refugees and Immigrants (USCRI) (2015) 'Forgotten Refugees: Eritrean Children in Northern Ethiopia, Findings and Recommendations'. Available at: http://refugees.org/wp-content/uploads/2016/02/USCRI-Report-Forgotten-Refugees.pdf [Accessed 13 January 2017].

World Bank (2017) 'Africa takes the lead to support refugees and their hosts with long-term solutions', 7 June. Available at: http://www.worldbank.org/en/news/feature/2017/06/08/africa-takes-the-lead-to-support-refugees-and-their-hosts-with-long-term-solutions [Accessed 25 July 2017].

World Bank (2020) 'Impact of refugees on host communities in Ethiopia: A social analysis', Washington, DC. Available at: https://openknowledge.worldbank.org/handle/10986/34267 [Accessed 1 June 2023].

Wernesjö, U. (2020) 'Across the threshold: Negotiations of deservingness among unaccompanied young refugees in Sweden', *Journal of Ethnic and Migration Studies* 46(2): 389–404.

9

Alone and on the Move: Unaccompanied Children in UK Parliamentary Debates 2015–2016

Lesley Pruitt and Antje Missbach

Introduction

In recent years, unaccompanied children on the move have featured prominently in global politics, with significant implications for the children themselves, but also for the potential host countries. The number of first-time child asylum applicants (both unaccompanied and with their families) in the EU rose from 64,330 in 2011 to 386,415 in 2016 (Eurostat, 2021). The number of unaccompanied child asylum applications in the EU also increased, from 11,690 in 2011 to 63,250 in 2016, with a 2015 peak of 95,205 unaccompanied children applying for asylum in the EU, including 3,255 in the UK (Eurostat, 2021b). In Europe in 2016, around one third (390,770) of asylum applications lodged were for children, with the UK receiving a relatively small number (9,200) of those applications compared to Germany, where two thirds (261,300) of the children applied (UNHCR et al, 2017). However, while in other European countries the 2015 peak has not been superseded, the UK saw higher numbers in 2019, when it received 3,755 asylum applications for unaccompanied children, suggesting that action to address these children's needs remains significant there. With the Russian invasion of Ukraine in February 2022, numbers of unaccompanied child refugees once again began to rise in the UK, even more so in Poland and Germany.

Although the presence of independently migrating children is not an entirely new phenomenon, their increased presence has challenged accepted ideas about children and childhood held by policy makers. Moreover, the growing visibility of unaccompanied children and awareness of their specific needs pose significant questions for policy makers and wider host societies alike. This has been particularly notable in the UK, where questions of migration were politically leveraged throughout the Brexit decision process with significant implications for policy making and people's everyday lives in the UK, Europe, and beyond.

During the so-called 'refugee crisis' of 2015–2016, public concerns relating to children on the move increased concurrently with major related political debates in Europe, including the Brexit vote in mid-2016 – a particularly prominent example of a broader political decision widely linked to ideas about immigration. Drawing on data gathered through a wider study considering political representations of young people on the move, in this chapter we consider the particular salience of representations of unaccompanied children, who are often highlighted as the children seen as most at risk or causing most concern.

Specifically, we apply discourse analysis to Hansard records to examine how unaccompanied children were represented in formal parliamentary debates in the UK during 2015–2016. While analysing Hansard records limits the study to elite views, we note that our intent is not to situate these as the most important views. Rather, we aim to recognize they are some vital views among many and have particular salience for this study as they directly impact formal political decision-making. Parliamentary debates are an important, relevant arena in which discourses of state interests are constructed and positioned hierarchically in specific national settings (Wagnsson et al, 2010).

Critically analysing data accessed via Hansard, we pay attention to central discourses and the ways they overlap and clash. This includes discourses centred on state duties for protecting unaccompanied children by allowing them to apply for and receive protection in the UK. In contrast, others suggest that the best way for the state to protect these unaccompanied children is to refuse their entry to the UK. In this chapter, we identify and critically reflect on two key related themes uncovered in our examination. First, we find that unaccompanied children are painted as inherently and particularly vulnerable. Moreover, we relatedly find that the UK state is commonly constructed as needing to step in as their 'substitute' parent, which is at times linked with depictions of 'bad' biological parents elsewhere.

To support our argument, this chapter is structured as follows. First, we provide contextual background and analyse literature concerning migration in UK politics and key scholarly insights and debates concerning child migration to demonstrate why and how our case study contributes an important piece of the research puzzle. Next, we explain the research methods utilized. From there, we present our findings of how unaccompanied children on the move were constructed in formal political discourse in the UK in the timeframe considered. We then discuss the wider relevance and implications of these constructions, including how they may contribute to understandings of unaccompanied children, perceptions of childhood, political agency, and the role of these concepts in political decision-making, which has local and global ramifications. We conclude by summarizing key points.

Contextual background and relevant scholarship

In 2014 conflict-related forced displacement reached a global peak not seen since World War II (UNHCR, 2015), and it has since remained exceptional. Up to 2012 the EU saw a gradual increase in asylum applications from non-member country citizens, and the numbers then increased more rapidly, with notable growth in 2015 and 2016. Specifically, while first-time applications for asylum in 2014 totalled 627,000, 2015 and 2016 saw 1.3 million per year lodged (Eurostat, 2017).

This increase in migration was referenced in several contentious and highly politicized debates across European countries (Pruitt et al, 2018). The increase was particularly politically salient in the UK, where a growth of both regular and irregular immigration had long been linked with frustrations regarding EU membership (Goodwin and Millazzo, 2017) and its asylum and migration policies. From 2015 this opposition to EU migration and asylum approaches increased (Goodwin and Millazzo, 2017). Notably, research suggests that concerns regarding both regular and irregular migration played a central role in the June 2016 Brexit referendum resulting in the UK decision to leave the EU (Goodwin and Millazzo, 2017; Tammes, 2017; Wincott et al, 2017). In the lead-up to the Brexit vote, the dominant discourse in popular news outlets in the UK painted migrants as causing a crisis rather than themselves facing or fleeing crises (Pruitt, 2019).

These existing studies offer important elements for understanding the specific context in the UK, yet further analysis is needed to fully understand the political dynamics that will continue to play out now that the UK has officially left the EU. In this regard, exploring the role of unaccompanied children, including the ways childhood and children may be framed in relation to politicization of migration and the advancing securitization of the UK borders, is ripe for further investigation.

Historically, migration has often been deemed an adult activity, and primarily an adult male domain, but over the last 50 years migration has become increasingly feminized (Kofman, 2019). Moreover, age and age-related factors in migration have started to receive more scholarly attention, expanding the focus to minors and elderly migrants (Ensor and Goździak, 2010). Likewise, rather than treating children as appendages to adults, migration scholars have increasingly recognized that many children migrate independently and make their own migratory decisions or at least have a say in their migratory decision-making (Bhabha, 2014).

Children's reasons for leaving their home countries are similar to those of adult migrants and refugees. UNHCR et al, (2017) reported that in 2016 children departing home via the Eastern Mediterranean Route gave the following reasons for leaving: 'war, conflict or political reasons (84 per cent)', 'economic reasons (14 per cent) and limited access to basic services or other reasons (2 per cent)', while 'on the Central Mediterranean Route, reported reasons were war and conflict (63 per cent), economic reasons (20 per cent) and limited access to basic services (14 per cent)'. Yet the challenges that children encounter along the route can be very different from those faced by adults, depending of course on the constellation of their fellow travellers, the routes, and the financial opportunities they can afford. Likewise, girls' and boys' experiences may differ, with UNHCR et al (2017) reporting that in 2016, three boys arrived for every two girls.

During their journeys unaccompanied children not only have to overcome dangerous terrains and long distances, but they also encounter highly guarded and militarized borders. The latter may come as a particular shock to them, not least because these 'young migrants aspire to a future that is more secure and rights respecting than the past they left behind' (Bhabha, 2014: 10). Yet the growing dominance of security concerns and protectionism in the wider political climate makes overcoming the dilemmas unaccompanied children face increasingly challenging. Ambivalence thus arises in the policy making context as demands for protection of the state from outsiders meet obligations around protecting children.

Existing research considers discourses about refugee journeys and irregular border crossings in general and gives special attention to the experiences of unaccompanied minors along the frequently used migration routes and in host or final destination countries. For example, Heidbrink's (2014) work in the US and Herz's (2019) and Wernesjö's (2020) work in Sweden have highlighted the conflicting perceptions of minors as either 'criminal alien' or 'deserving refugee', and the self-positioning of minors within those discourses. While many scholars have deeply engaged with the societal perceptions surrounding the increased presence of unaccompanied children at large, there are only a few analyses that have studied formal political discourse regarding unaccompanied children and migration.

Some research has looked at how policy makers perceive children and migration. For example, Allsopp and Chase have examined policy discourses in Europe to see how best interests, durable solutions and notions of belonging are taken into consideration. In their study, they noted 'tension between policy assumptions and what we know of the lived experiences and aspirations of these young people' (2017: 293). A study by Hedlund and Cederborg (2015), who interviewed Swedish legislators, found legislators tended to not consider unaccompanied minors as having their own agency and aspirations, and that biological age tended to be seen as the most important criterion to have one's rights acknowledged. In order to make their claims legitimate, unaccompanied children had to draw on their value and rights 'as children' first, and 'as refugees' later. From these findings, Hedlund and Cederborg (2015) concluded that childhood has become increasingly politicized in discourses around refugees and the right to asylum.

Nevertheless, it is important not to assume that this politicization of childhood would appear in universal ways across different settings. Indeed, Lidén and Vitus's (2010) research examining political discourses and practice in Denmark and Norway shows that children seeking asylum were perceived differently between the two countries, with Denmark primarily seeing them as asylum seekers, whereas Norway also saw them as children.

Previous research looking at the time of increased asylum applications in Europe during 2015–2016 has suggested this period can be seen as a possible watershed moment in how children are understood as refugees (Pruitt et al, 2018), with 2015 proposed as a crucial time in which discourses relating to child refugees entered the public arena in ways that were unprecedented (Lems et al, 2020). Notably, research demonstrates 'how public representations of young people ... can be deeply influenced by stereotypes and assumptions', which can hinder the ability of these young people to access more secure living conditions (Pruitt et al, 2018: 688). Indeed, scholars considering this period have thus shown how a range of identity factors, such as race, gender, and age, can significantly affect understandings of migrants and the ways they are securitized in public discourses (Gray and Franck, 2019). Moreover, contrasting with previous widely accepted depictions of migrant and refugee children as victims, McLaughlin's research on one political debate around unaccompanied children in the UK in this period suggests that their childhood was sometimes deemed 'no longer a stable category which guarantees protection, but is subject to scrutiny and suspicion and can, ultimately, be disproved' (2018: 1757).

Likewise, our research contributes to understanding how children and childhood are represented in migration-related debates in the UK. Up until now, limited analysis exists around how, if at all, policy makers construct unaccompanied children in related formal debates. Our focus in the UK enables us to shed light on how these discourses may coalesce at times, while competing discourses may also be used to support varied political responses or agendas.

Methods

In this chapter we analyse discourses in the UK Parliament relating to migration to ask whether and how parliamentarians across the political spectrum represent unaccompanied children. Through employing discourse analysis, we consider how different actors speak in order to critically analyse how discourses 'coalesce, clash, or compete with one another' (Wagnsson et al, 2010: 12). Whether people can identify with or feel for the trauma of another is influenced by how that trauma is represented (Hutchison, 2016). Therefore, applying discourse analysis is especially enlightening for considering political debates relating to asylum seekers or refugees fleeing violent settings, which includes many of the young people in question here.

Data for the wider study was gathered through searching Hansard online (https://hansard.parliament.uk/) to collect transcripts of parliamentary debates during the height of the 'refugee crisis', and to include any connections to the lead-up to and conduct of the Brexit referendum, which coincided with the increase in asylum applications in Europe. The search was restricted to 13 months, from 10 June 2015 to 10 July 2016. These dates covered relevant key news reporting periods on the topics of Brexit and the 'refugee crisis' widely reported in Europe. Those reports were therefore seen as potentially influencing public perceptions of migrants, particularly refugees and asylum seekers in the UK, thus potentially affecting political decision-making regarding migration policy.[1]

Search terms included: migra, immi, asylum, refuge, unaccompanied, displaced, asylum seekers, refugees, migrants, and Calais. While this purposive sample aided in limiting the scope of the data for analysis, the sample was still sizeable, with 184 results returned, which stitched into a single pdf made up of 2,627 A4 pages. The analysis started with reading the full data set to identify key themes for further analysis and review. Meanwhile, for this chapter we returned to this body of data to analyse constructions of unaccompanied children. Specifically, we look to the data to ask how unaccompanied children on the move were constructed in UK parliamentary debates relating to migration and what the wider political implications of these representations are.

Findings

Within the parliamentary debates examined, the topic of unaccompanied children occupied significant space. Indeed, in the data analysed, the word 'unaccompanied' appeared 668 times, while the related word 'alone' appeared 209 times. For example, several Labour party policy makers referred to 'unaccompanied minors' (Tolhurst, 2015a) speaking of 'children making such treacherous journeys on their own' (Keir Starmer, 2016b: vol 608) 'children on their own in refugee camps' (Cooper, 2015: vol 603) and 'orphaned and abandoned children' (McCabe, 2015: vol 600). Stephen Twigg (2016: vol 608) of Labour Co-op noted that '[t]hose children are facing harsh conditions and they are facing them on their own'.

Our analysis uncovered related but sometimes divergent framings. From these depictions, here we highlight two prominent themes identified: the construction of unaccompanied children as particularly and inherently vulnerable and the construction of the UK state as the 'substitute' parent for these children, noting this theme is often linked with constructions of 'bad' parents putting the children at risk.

Alone and vulnerable

While a broader study of this data has found migrant children in general were typically characterized as innocent victims needing protection (Pruitt, 2021), this analysis suggests that framing is particularly magnified when it comes to unaccompanied children, who are held up as representations of vulnerability, or indeed as those situated atop a presumed vulnerability hierarchy. Indeed, unaccompanied children are often deemed among the most vulnerable and challenging figures for policy makers to consider, with their status as children on their own posing particular complexities in political decision-making.

For policy makers, the status of being unaccompanied was explicitly linked to increased vulnerability. For example, Keir Starmer (Labour) (2016c: vol 608, col. 1209) stated, 'I think that any child alone, fleeing across a border having made a treacherous journey, is vulnerable wherever they have found themselves'. Others made similar suggestions, such as Baroness Butler-Sloss' (CB) who spoke of 'children in great danger in different parts of Europe [where there is] ... no shortage of children who are unaccompanied and alone and need help' (2016: vol 771) and Stephen Phillips (2016: vol 608) (Conservative) speaking of children who 'are alone, far from their families. They are cold, frightened, hungry and frequently without help or access to those who might help or protect them'. Baroness Sheehan (2016: vol 769) (Liberal Democrat) likewise stated that these children are 'without adult protection – some left home on their own ... fending for themselves'.

The focus on unaccompanied children as particularly vulnerable was commonly explained to be due to perceived heightened risks of being exploited or going missing. As one Labour Member of Parliament (MP) put it, 'I am concerned about the number of unaccompanied children in Europe. It is not only about the number, but the fact that more than 1,000 have disappeared. They are particularly vulnerable, so I urge the Government to do more for unaccompanied children' (Keir Starmer, 2016a: vol 605). Likewise, Tim Farron (2016: vol 608) (Liberal Democrat) claimed that 'something like a third of those unaccompanied children in Europe go missing. They are now in the hands of child traffickers who exploit them and use them in child prostitution'. Meanwhile, others noted these unaccompanied children need to be 'protected from traffickers' (Brokenshire [Conservative] 2016: vol 608).

The state as substitute parent

Relatedly to the vulnerability framing, policy makers speak of unaccompanied children as in need of parental protection and specifically needing to rely on the UK state 'as though we are their parents' (Baroness Kennedy of the Shaws [Labour] 2016: vol 769). Likewise, connecting this to the protection imperative, Thangham Debbonaire (Labour) suggests the state needs to act as parents 'to protect other people's children' (2016: vol 608), while Byron Davies (Conservative) insists Parliament needs to make efforts 'to ensuring that children are not left unaccompanied and in danger' (2016: vol 608).

Several MPs made statements by calling on their own status 'as parents' (Robert Buckland [Conservative] 2015: col 393) and/or 'grandparents' (Lord Roberts of Llandudno [Liberal Democrat] 2016: vol 769), a position they claimed provided them with a more empathic stance (from which to call for state assistance) for unaccompanied migrant children. These parliamentarians also critically highlighted the differences between what would be expected for 'our' children, that is, UK citizens, and what care should therefore be shown to migrant children.

Although many parliamentarians were sympathetic with unaccompanied minors and other migrant children and deemed it the duty of the state to provide adequate support, there were also parliamentarians who opposed such calls. For example, speakers sceptical of the UK admitting unaccompanied minors cited fears that 'bad' parents overseas want to take advantage of the UK and endanger their children by sending them ahead to secure a place for their other family members.[2] Moreover, we find that some MPs spoke of these children not as vulnerable people needing and deserving protection, but rather focused more on them as claimants putting 'pressure on the resources and services' (Tolhurst [Conservative] 2015a: vol 600), and relatedly arguing that '[w]e simply will not be able to cope with the vast number of people who could legitimately claim that they come from a country where there is a certain amount of instability' (Holloway, 2015: vol 599) (Conservative).

Overall, a certain level of empathy for the extraordinary hardship these minors faced in their journeys and after arrival in Europe appeared fairly regularly. However, clearly this recognition of hardship has not been enough to subdue fears or political panics around questions of security and border control.

Broader implications

At first sight, our findings seem to confirm previous studies highlighting that migrant children have been constructed as vulnerable victims in many contexts and yet may also be leveraged in other ways for political purposes. However, these findings also offer an important snapshot of a crucial time, which set the political course for post-Brexit immigration and asylum policy making in the UK. Likewise, our findings offer an important contribution to showing – in this particular state in this particular time – how these constructions of unaccompanied children entered formal political discourse and were deployed by policy makers across the political spectrum to advance their political goals.

Many politicians suggested a relation between vulnerability and victimization without relying on any evidence, but rather on assumptions, for example, that children who go missing automatically end up exploited. Future research is needed to scrutinize the relations between vulnerability and exploitation assumed by politicians. Only by critically interrogating such assumptions can the wider debates around unaccompanied children be translated into effective decision-making. After all, Lemberg-Pedersen (2021) finds that discourses painting children as vulnerable and European countries as caring rescuers have actually facilitated deportations of children, even in the absence of any family members being located to look after the child once returned to the country of origin. In short, some policy makers at times construct children in ways that may appear to support the idea of the state as 'substitute' parent yet in fact lead to greater vulnerabilities for the children in question, who are left without actual or substitute parents. Hence, critical attention is needed both to the range of ways policy makers construct children and the related outcomes of the policies affecting these children.

Even where policy makers could come to some agreement on assisting unaccompanied children, implementation has stagnated. For example, the Dubs Scheme, referred to as Section 67, became effective in April of 2016 through the 2016 amendment to the Immigration Act. The Scheme set out how the Home Secretary was to admit to the UK a set number of unaccompanied refugee children following approval by local authorities. The Scheme's namesake, Lord Dubs, and other supporters advocated for the UK assisting 3,000 unaccompanied minors deemed most vulnerable, yet by 2017 only 480 children had arrived in the UK via this Scheme, leading to critics suggesting the UK has shirked its responsibilities to these children (Iusmen, 2019).

In addition, unaccompanied children who managed to enter the UK despite barriers to doing so face challenges within the country. For example, non-medical age assessment procedures, which use non-child-friendly, intrusive practices to assess migrants' real age, are applied to make applying for protection harder (Iusmen, 2019). Furthermore, until the real age is determined, these young people continue to be treated as adults and likewise exposed to further risks, such as greater likelihood of deportation (Iusmen, 2019).

Last but not least, under current immigration rules children under the age of 18 still do not have a right to sponsor family members to come to the UK.[3] Meanwhile, in January 2020 *The Guardian* reported that in debates around the bill for the EU withdrawal agreement, proposals to maintain child refugee protections were rejected in redrafts of the document; indeed, 'MPs voted 348 to 252 against the amendment, which had previously been accepted by Theresa May's government and which would have guaranteed the right of unaccompanied child refugees to be reunited with family members living in the UK after Brexit' (Gentlemen et al, 2020).

Conclusion

In this chapter we have used discourse analysis to consider formal political debates in the UK during 2015–2016 relating to unaccompanied children on the move. To do so, we collected parliamentary records through Hansard, noting that the views of these policy makers hold particular weight as they directly inform political decisions that affect the children in question.

Through looking at how these discourses share similarities and divergences, we have shown how policy makers across parties tend to share the framing of unaccompanied children as vulnerable people needing special protections, and many therefore construct unaccompanied children as in need of the UK state to act as a 'substitute parent'. However, this framing was also subject to ongoing contestations and scepticism among some speakers, who instead sought to highlight perceived potential vulnerabilities the UK may face in terms of resources and capacity that may be required in taking up these parental duties. In light of the Brexit decision and decreasing opportunities that followed for unaccompanied children seeking refuge in the UK, ongoing observation and analysis of constructions of children remain crucial to understanding political dynamics and material conditions for unaccompanied children in this novel and continuously changing context. Paying attention to the creation and maintenance of certain framings of 'ideal childhoods' and the assumed responsibilities of host countries for unaccompanied refugee children as 'substitute parents' will help broaden our understanding of the relational positioning of adults and children in global politics.

Notes
[1] For more on the wider study event selection, see Pruitt (2021).
[2] For more on this theme, see Pruitt (2021).
[3] See: https://researchbriefings.files.parliament.uk/documents/CBP-7511/CBP-7511.pdf

References

Allsopp, J. and Chase, E. (2017) 'Best interests, durable solutions and belonging: Policy discourses shaping the futures of unaccompanied migrant and refugee minors coming of age in Europe', *Journal of Ethnic and Migration Studies* 45(2): 293–311.

Bhabha, J. (2014) *Child Migration and Human Rights in a Global Age,* Princeton, NJ: Princeton University Press.

Ensor, M.O. and Goździak, E.M. (2010) *Children and Migration: At the Crossroads of Resiliency and Vulnerability,* New York: Palgrave Macmillan.

Eurostat (2017) 'Annual asylum statistics', Eurostat Asylum and Managed Migration Database. Available at: https://ec.europa.eu/eurostat/statistics-explained/index.php?title=Asylum_statistics&oldid=558181 [Accessed 19 March 2021].

Eurostat (2021) 'Asylum and first-time asylum applicants by citizenship, age and sex – annual aggregated data (rounded)', Eurostat Asylum and Managed Migration Database. Available at: https://ec.europa.eu/eurostat/statistics-explained/index.php?title=Children_in_migration_-_asylum_app licants [Accessed 18 June 2023].

Eurostat (2021b) 'Asylum applicants considered to be unaccompanied minors by citizenship, age and sex – annual data (rounded)', *Eurostat Asylum and Managed Migration Database.* Available at: https://ec.europa.eu/eurostat/databrowser/view/migr_asyunaa/default/table?lang=en [Accessed 19 March 2021].

Gentlemen, A., O'Carroll, L., Walker, P., and Brookes, L. (2020) 'MPs vote to drop child refugee protections from Brexit Bill', *The Guardian,* 9 January.

Goodwin, M. and Milazzo, C. (2017) 'Taking back control? Investigating the role of immigration in the 2016 vote for Brexit', *British Journal of Politics and International Relations* 19(3): 450–464.

Gray, H. and Franck, A.K. (2019) 'Refugees as/at risk: The gendered and racialized underpinnings of securitization in British media narratives', *Security Dialogue* 50(3): 275–291.

Hedlund, D. and Cederborg, A. (2015) 'Legislators' perceptions of unaccompanied children seeking asylum', *International Journal of Migration, Health and Social Care* 11(4): 239–252.

Heidbrink, L. (2014) *Migrant Youth, Transnational Families, and the State: Care and Contested Interests,* Philadelphia: University of Pennsylvania Press.

Herz, M. (2019) '"Becoming" a possible threat: Masculinity, culture and questioning among unaccompanied young men in Sweden', *Identities: Global Studies in Culture and Power* 26(4): 431–449.

Hutchison, E. (2016) *Affective Communities in World Politics: Collective Emotions after Trauma,* Cambridge: Cambridge University Press.

Iusmen, I. (2019) 'Unaccompanied migrant children and the implications of Brexit', in M. Dustin, N. Ferreira, and S. Millns (eds) *Gender and Queer Perspectives on Brexit,* New York: Springer International Publishing, pp 185–208.

Kofman, E. (2019) 'Gender and the feminisation of migration', in C. Inglis, W. Li, and B. Khadria (eds) *The SAGE Handbook of International Migration,* London: SAGE, pp 216–231.

Lemberg-Pedersen, M. (2021) 'The humanitarianization of child deportation politics', *Journal of Borderlands Studies* 36(2): 239–258.

Lems, A., Oester, K., and Strasser, S. (2020) 'Children of the crisis: Ethnographic perspectives on unaccompanied refugee youth in and en route to Europe', *Journal of Ethnic and Migration Studies* 46(2): 315–335.

Lidén, H. and Vitus, K. (2010) 'The status of the asylum-seeking child in Norway and Denmark: Comparing discourses, politics and practices', *Journal of Refugee Studies* 23(1): 62–81.

McLaughlin, C. (2018) '"They don't look like children": Child asylum-seekers, the Dubs amendment and the politics of childhood', *Journal of Ethnic and Migration Studies* 44(11): 1757–1773.

Pruitt, L. (2019) 'Closed due to "flooding"? UK Media representations of refugees and migrants in 2015–16 – Creating a crisis of borders', *British Journal of Politics and International Relations* 21(2): 383–402.

Pruitt, L. (2021) 'Children and migration: Political constructions and contestations', *Global Policy* 12(5): 592–602.

Pruitt, L., Berents, H., and Munro, G. (2018) 'Gender and age in the construction of male youth in the European "migration crisis"', *Signs: Journal of Women and Culture in Society* 43(3): 687–709.

Tammes, P. (2017) 'Investigating differences in Brexit-vote among local authorities in the UK: An ecological study on migration- and economy-related issues', *Sociological Research Online* 22(3): 143–164.

UNHCR (2015) *World at War: UNHCR Global Trends Forced Displacement 2014*, Geneva: United Nations.

UNHCR, UNICEF, and IOM: The United Nations Migration Agency (2017) *Refugee and Migrant Children – Including Unaccompanied and Separated Children – in Europe: Overview of Trends in 2016*. Geneva: United Nations.

Wagnsson, C., Hellman, M., and Holmberg, A. (2010) 'The centrality of non-traditional groups for security in the globalized era: The case of children', *International Political Sociology* 4(1): 1–14.

Wernesjö, U. (2020) 'Across the threshold: Negotiations of deservingness among unaccompanied young refugees in Sweden', *Journal of Ethnic and Migration Studies* 46(2): 389–404.

Wincott, D., Peterson, J., and Convery, A. (2017) 'Introduction: Studying Brexit's causes and consequences', *British Journal of Politics and International Relations* 19(3): 429–433.

Hansard (House of Commons = HC; House of Lords = HL)

Brokenshire, James. 25 April, 2016. 'Immigration Bill', London: HC. Vol 608. Col 1203.

Buckland, Robert. 5 November, 2015. 'Immigration Bill (Eleventh Sitting)', London: HC. Col 393.

Butler-Sloss, Baroness. 26 April, 2016. 'Immigration Bill', London: HL. Vol 771. Col 1113.

Cooper, Yvette. 1 December, 2015. 'Immigration Bill', London: HC. Vol 603. Col 240.

Davies, Byron. 25 April, 2016. 'Immigration Bill', London: HC. Vol 608. Col 1237.

Debbonaire, Thangham. 25 April, 2016. 'Immigration Bill', London: HC. Vol 608. Col 1213.

Farron, Tim. 25 April, 2016. 'Immigration Bill', London: HC. Vol 608. Col 1232.

Holloway, Adam. 8 September, 2015. 'Refugee Crisis in Europe', London: HC. Vol 599. Col 268.

Llandudno, Lord Roberts of. 26 March, 2016. 'Immigration Bill', London: HL. Vol 769. Col 2097.

McCabe, Steve. 19 October, 2015. 'Immigration', London: HC. Vol 600. Col 233WH.

Phillips, Stephen. 25 April, 2016. 'Immigration Bill', London: HC. Vol 608. Col 1212.

Shaws, Baroness Kennedy of the. 15 March, 2016. 'Immigration Bill', London: HL. Vol 769. Col 1784.

Sheehan, Baroness. 21 March, 2016. 'Immigration Bill', London: HL. Vol 769. Col 2099.

Starmer, Keir. 10 February, 2016a. 'Migration into the EU', London: HC. Vol 605. Col 645WH.

Starmer, Keir. 25 April, 2016b. 'Immigration Bill', London: HC. Vol 608. Col 1206.

Starmer, Keir. 25 April, 2016c. 'Immigration Bill', London: HC. Vol 608. Col 1209.

Tolhurst, Kelly. 13 October, 2015a. 'Immigration Bill', London: HC. Vol 600. Col 243.

Tolhurst, Kelly. 5 November, 2015b. 'Immigration Bill (Twelfth Sitting)', Vol 601, London: HC. Vol 601. Col 430.

Twigg, Stephen. 25 April, 2016. 'Immigration Bill', London: HC. Vol 608. Col 1230.

10

Pathologies of Child Governance: Safe Harbor Laws and Children Involved in the Sex Trade in the United States

Robyn Linde

Introduction

The protection of children under the age of 18 by the state has been so firmly embedded within United States law, practice, and policy that it regulates nearly every aspect of childhood. Collectively, these laws and practices create a shared expectation of children's experiences and development that, in their ideal form, should produce adult citizens in service of the state in terms of their health, intellect, morality, and abilities. Certain deviations from the norms of childhood – sexual exploitation, abuse, and even some forms of juvenile sexual activity – have historically been addressed with new policy, law, education, and adjudication. In some cases, however, a disconnect exists between the expectations of childhood and the actual lived experiences of diverse groups of children, leading to *pathologies of child governance*, defined here as unintended consequences or outcomes from laws and policies that exacerbate the abuse, delinquency, criminalization, and exploitation of children. While this chapter examines the US case, pathologies of child governance can be found throughout the international system, including within key institutions of the children's rights regime (see Chapters 1, 4, and 9 in this volume).

I examine here one such pathology – the exclusion of a cohort of children, a significant percentage of children involved in the sex trade, from treatment as victims under the law and the subsequent protections afforded other children involved in the sex trade in the United States.[1] Precise numbers of children involved in the sex trade in the United States are difficult to come by, unsurprisingly, but studies have put the number between 5,000 and 21,000 (NCSL, 2017; Hounmenou and O'Grady, 2019). The protections studied here are Safe Harbor laws, a patchwork of US laws that seek to protect some children from criminal penalties associated with involvement in the sex trade. Boys, as well as lesbian, gay, bisexual, transgender, and queer (LGBTQIA+) children, and those children with LGBTQIA+ clients make up the majority of children excluded from Safe Harbor protections. Of these groups, Black and Latino children are overrepresented. The common connection among these excluded children is twofold. First, children in this cohort tend to deviate from the expectation of what a 'victim' should be, usually a white, cisgender female child naively derailed from her prescribed path to adulthood (Baker, 2013; Austin and Farrell, 2017). Second, they tend to operate in the sex trade without a third party (commonly known as a pimp).[2] I argue in this chapter that through an examination of this pathology – the exclusion of children in the sex trade from Safe Harbor protections – as well as a consideration of other pathologies of child governance, we can better understand how a singular narrative of childhood, with its oversimplified conceptions of gender and agency, produces outcomes antithetical to the intention of child protection efforts by the state. The outcome of this pathology is that in attempting to separate victims from perpetrators, governance related to children involved in the sex trade misidentifies child sexual agency, conflates it with consent and culpability, and further traumatizes and exploits already marginalized children.

Modern governance efforts related to child sexuality

In response to the sexual liberation movement of the 1960s and 1970s, both conservatives and radical feminists grew increasingly preoccupied by the spectre of child sexuality and sexual abuse, although for completely different reasons. Feminist campaigns against familial violence, originally brought on by concerns about incest, expanded to include concerns about children's sexual abuse more broadly (Adler, 2001). Religious conservatives were motivated by their perception of rampant cultural sexuality, a preoccupation that came to include child sexuality.

During the moral panics of the 1980s and 1990s, radical feminists increasingly defined women's global identity as marked by male violence. Much of this violence was identified as the targeting of girls in the home. In response, public policy championed by these advocates in the late 20th and early 21st centuries focused on pornography, child abuse and sexual assault laws, and sex trafficking. Calling these phenomena *moral panics* is not to say that there are not (and have not been) serious problems of child sexual abuse and trafficking in the United States and elsewhere. It is only to suggest that the response – the degree of public fear – was out of proportion to the actual threat (Evans, 1994; Angelides, 2004; Robinson, 2013). In their advocacy, radical feminists found common cause with Christian conservatives who opposed 'moral crimes', including sex work, homosexuality, premarital or extramarital sex, and sex trafficking. This common ground on trafficking resulted in the passage of the 2000 Trafficking and Victims Protection Act (TVPA), legislation that would protect trafficking victims by granting them and their families special visas and access to social services usually reserved for citizens. The passage of the TVPA was accomplished in the context of emerging international law on trafficking, via the Convention on the Rights of the Child's Optional Protocol on the Sale of Children, Child Prostitution and Child Pornography and the Protocol to Prevent, Suppress and Punish Trafficking in Persons, Especially Women and Children (Trafficking Protocol), which came into force in 2002 and 2003, respectively.

In the context of these laws, the victim narrative is rigid, coarsely constructed, and oversimplified. It is preoccupied with the trafficker, also crudely constructed through racialized and gendered narratives. Given its cultural importance, however, police and state institutions are highly invested in the victim–perpetrator narrative and use it to govern policy and practice (Marcus et al, 2014: 225: Sano, 2016). Not surprisingly, there is great disparity in the treatment of children involved in the sex trade in the United States. In some US states, children can be arrested and prosecuted as sex workers, while in others, they are channelled into welfare services and treated as victims.

Safe Harbor laws

The US Safe Harbor laws have emerged as one answer to child trafficking. In an ideal form, these laws express the idea that criminal penalties should not be extended to children (those under the age of 18) who are involved in the sex trade because they are unable to consent to commercial sex (Shared Hope, 2017). According to international law, children involved in the sex trade should be considered victims and protected as such. The international community's consensus on the issue is seen across a spectrum of human rights instruments, including the Convention on the Rights of the Child and its protocols, the International Labour Organization's Worst Forms of Child Labour Convention, and the Trafficking Protocol, mentioned above. National laws emerging from these instruments construct the sex trade (coerced or not) as a criminal justice issue and one that should be regulated by the police and the judicial arm of states. Globally, it is not surprising that most states focus on the arrest and prosecution of traffickers and less on the social and economic conditions of children involved in the sex trade. The United States is no exception.

There is great variety in the implementation of Safe Harbor across the US states that have passed these laws. Thirty states and the District of Columbia (DC) have to some degree enacted protections for children under the age of 18 (Shared Hope, 2020), with 19 states requiring control by a third party to merit protections (Shared Hope, 2019a). These protections vary from diversion programmes, where juveniles are diverted from punishment after they have admitted guilt or been charged with a crime, to immunity provisions that prohibit children from being charged with specific crimes, such as prostitution (Williams, 2017). Twenty-one states and DC prohibit the criminalization of minors for prostitution, while nine states require a designation of trafficking to merit protections (Shared Hope, 2019b). Thirty-one states also distinguish between child prostitution and child sex trafficking (Shared Hope, 2019a), with most requiring a demonstration of 'force, fraud or coercion' (Shared Hope, 2015: 2), a violation of the TVPA (Section 103, 8). Non-governmental organizations (NGOs), such as Shared Hope, Polaris, and End Child Prostitution and Trafficking in the US, advocate for the provision of child welfare services in addition to decriminalization (Shared Hope, 2017). These NGOs want states to stop charges altogether but not arrests, because arrests bring these children under the purview of state child welfare services (Shared Hope, 2017) and assist the police in prosecuting third parties.

Disparities in state practice towards children involved in the sex trade underscore the arbitrary nature of victimhood (Marcus et al, 2014; Sano, 2016). The age of eligibility for legal protection ranges from 13 to 17 (Mehlman-Orozco, 2015), with eligibility for protection often contingent upon evidence of coercion. Yet children who become involved in the sex trade, like adults, do so for many complicated reasons that do not lend themselves to simple explanations of coercion. Violence at home, discrimination against LGBTQIA+ youth, survival sex, abuse, poverty, and street violence complicate notions of free choice (Cray et al, 2013). Dustin Johnson, in Chapter 4 of this volume on UN peacekeeping, observes that UN training materials challenge children's agency when their actions, such as joining an armed group, contradict norms of innocence and victimization, but accept children's agency when they choose to leave such groups. A similar observation can be made regarding children in the sex trade: agency is denied only to those children who choose to work in the trade, not those attempting to leave it. The examples here and elsewhere in this volume indicate that narratives of children's victimization traverse borders, cultures, and issue areas.

As first responders, police also choose how to treat children involved in the sex trade, and some officers entertain misinformed or prejudiced opinions that shape how the penal system will process children (Fichtelman, 2014; Fahy, 2015; Mehlman-Orozco, 2015). These initial judgements are complicated by assumptions about race, culture, class, and sexual and gender identity. Judges and prosecutors possess discretion as well, and rulings confirming or denying penalties are informed by these biases (Fahy, 2015; Gezinski, 2021). Some states that have Safe Harbor laws do not extend protections to children who are second or third 'offenders' (Polaris, 2015; Hounmenou and O'Grady, 2019). Additionally, children who assist third parties or who exploit, recruit, or punish other children at the behest of a third party (Fernandez, 2013; Butler, 2015) are not protected under Safe Harbor laws in many states (Dysart, 2014). Patricia Martuscelli (in Chapter 1 of this volume) and Lesley Pruitt and Antje Missbach (in Chapter 9) argue that denying agency is a tool both for protecting children and for carrying out state policies that may otherwise be seen to harm them, for example, deporting children in the name of family reunification. Martuscelli also examines the ways in which some children who migrate alone are labelled 'imposter children' by the state and, via their presumed agency, denied protections based on unreliable determinations of age. One marker of alleged 'imposters' among children in the sex trade is authority over other children, or assistance to third parties in the trade. As discussed below, the children most likely to considered imposters are those without a third party at all, those children who have entered the sex trade without recruitment.

Gender and racial dynamics also play a role in the application of Safe Harbor: girls are assumed to be the dominant demographic in the sex trade, but more recent research suggests that the number of boys 'may be equal to (or even exceeding) that of girls' (Hasselbarth, 2014: 414). Estimates of boys range from 45 to 60 per cent of children involved in the sex trade in the United States (Conner, 2016; Murphy, 2016; Hounmenou and O'Grady, 2019). Studies have also found that more than 80 per cent of children involved in the trade are Black or Latino, children who are less likely to trust and cooperate with the police based on past interaction (Clayton et al, 2013; Murphy, 2016; Gezinski, 2021). A smaller percentage of children (2 to 8 per cent) identified as transgender or gender non-conforming in studies (Conner, 2016; Murphy, 2016; Hounmenou and O'Grady, 2019).

In some states, protections are extended by prosecutorial discretion only to those children who help to prosecute third parties and clients (Bergman, 2012; Fernandez, 2013; Fichtelman, 2014; Fahy, 2015; Gezinski, 2021). Children operating without a third party also may not be considered victims, the aforementioned 'imposters' (Adelson, 2008; Dysart, 2014).[3] Statistics regarding children involved in the sex trade without third parties range from 42 to 92 per cent (Dennis, 2008; Conner, 2016; Murphy, 2016; Swaner et al, 2016; Hounmenou and O'Grady, 2019; Gezinski, 2021). Of those children who do not have third parties, boys and LGBTQIA+ children are overrepresented, making them less likely to be considered victims than cisgender girls in the sex trade (Adelson, 2008; Dennis, 2008; Conner, 2016; Murphy, 2016; Polaris 2016; Swaner et al, 2016; Hounmenou and O'Grady,

2019). Multiple studies have linked homelessness to the sex trade (Conner, 2016; Murphy, 2016; Swaner et al, 2016; Hounmenou and O'Grady, 2019; Gezinski, 2021), and findings indicate that LGBTQIA+ homeless children are three to seven times more likely to engage in survival sex than their non-LGBTQIA+ peers (Cray et al, 2013; Martinez and Kelle, 2013; Hounmenou and O'Grady, 2019). Of LGBTQIA+ homeless children, there is evidence that Black and Latino children are disproportionately represented by as much as 70 per cent, with roughly 11 per cent of these youths identifying as transgender (Cray et al, 2013). Polaris has also found that of those detained for being involved in the sex trade, LGBTQIA+ children are overrepresented (2016). Since boys involved the sex trade tend to have male clients and are less likely to work with third parties, they tend to be viewed less sympathetically by law enforcement.

In short, the status of victim accorded to children involved in the sex trade is far from assured under the law. Rather, it hinges on conformity with gendered, racialized, and entrenched notions of victimhood and culpability, notions that find legal expression through Safe Harbor. In most states, laws regarding children involved in the sex trade do not give due consideration to the complexities of street survival. The exclusion of some children from protective policies shines a revealing light on the narrative of victimhood that resonates with police officers, prosecutors, judges, civil society, and the global children's rights regime. Measurements of victimhood are also shaped by the racial, gender, and class prejudices present in wider society and global norms of childhood.

Discussion

Safe Harbor laws exclude children whose identity, presentation, experience, or resistance to engaging with law enforcement diverges from the traditional narrative of victimhood. As a result, Safe Harbor laws produce a pathology of child governance that criminalizes the very children these laws should protect and rehabilitate. All children involved in the sex trade challenge shared social expectations and norms of childhood, but those excluded from protections such as Safe Harbor laws also challenge social expectations of child victims. The shared characteristics of those denied protections help to reveal the objectives of these laws, those who advocate for them, and the difficulty of assessing consent, culpability, and agency.

In this discussion, I will present three arguments. First, Safe Harbor laws fail to protect children who deviate from the rigid narrative of victimhood, those who are both victims and perpetrators, and those who act without a third party. Second, Safe Harbor laws misidentify children's sexual agency and, as a result, further endanger, exploit, and abuse already vulnerable children. Safe Harbor's focus on the identification of 'good victims' results in a pathology of governance that misidentifies a high percentage of child victims, mislabels victims as perpetrators, denies them legal protection, and criminalizes them. Third, Safe Harbor laws reveal a preoccupation with traffickers at the expense of child protection. This preoccupation with traffickers can be traced to the moral panics of the 1980s and 1990s about child sexual abuse and to the growing concern in the late 20th century about trafficking and violence against women and girls. Each of these is taken in turn below.

Rigid narratives

The rigid narrative of victimhood is evident when children involved in the sex trade are denied victim status because of their independence from third parties or because they function within a stratified system of abuse. These children inhabit a liminal space in the narrative, exhibiting some markers of victim, some markers of perpetrator, and some markers of agent. The simplistic binary cannot accommodate the complexities of the sex trade and the harsh realities of street survival. Children involved in the sex trade have had widely ranging experiences, and their causal path is rarely linear.

Likewise, the child who acts alone challenges the narrative of victimhood because victims require a perpetrator. Children acting without a third party – who make up a large portion of children involved in the sex trade – are also more likely to be denied victim status, and thus, protection under law (Clayton et al, 2013: 206). The law as applied fails to acknowledge or recognize the relative independence or interdependence of these children. These imposter children, those who fall outside of the rigid narrative of victimhood, are often seen as prematurely sexualized by 'choice', since there is no third party to blame for recruitment. Drawing on the work of Nadera Shalhoub-Kevorkian, we can say they are *unchilded*, first by a society that does not ensure their safety, nutrition, shelter, or education, and second, by state violence that arrests them for survival work in the sex trade (2019).

Comparative responses to pathologies

Pathologies of child governance are not uncommon, as many unintended consequences emerge from the interaction among macro-level policies, the diverse lived experiences of children, and changes in norms. Solutions (albeit imperfect ones) to two other types of pathologies in child governance are useful in exploring the rigid narrative that Safe Harbor laws embody: First, the prosecution of statutory rape cases – based on laws that prohibit sexual relations with children under the age of consent – is designed to protect children from abuse and exploitation but may produce a pathology of child governance when those prosecuted are children close in age to the alleged victim (James, 2009; Kern, 2013). These laws are highly gendered – men are almost always the ones charged – and the penalties can be draconian, including long sentences and lifelong registration as a sex offender. Beginning in the 1970s, advocates sought to correct this pathology by advocating for age-gap provisions and Romeo and Juliet laws, which carve out exceptions to the stark penalties of statutory rape by excluding cases where the age discrepancy between the couple is within two to six years, even if one member is a legal adult (Smith and Kercher, 2011; Flynn, 2013, Kern, 2013). Through these laws and policies, consensual sexual interaction between teenagers close in age is not a crime at all in many states, and, in others, it is reduced from a felony to a misdemeanour (Flynn, 2013: 687).

Second, sexting by teens – the self-production and dissemination of explicit images – has resulted in a pathology of child governance when criminal statutes intended to target paedophiles were used against children who photographed or videotaped themselves (Levick and Moon, 2010; McLaughlin, 2010). In response to some very public prosecutions, states began to seek ways to address sexting among children beginning in 2008, primarily by amending statutes to reduce penalties and offer diversion programmes and other non-punitive alternatives (Levick and Moon, 2010; Strasburger et al, 2019).

Efforts to remedy these pathologies – in the form of Romeo and Juliet laws, age-gap provisions, and sexting laws – demonstrate the sometimes successful incorporation of children's sexual agency within existing legal protections. While law and policy governing statutory rape and sexting have been re-examined to allow for children's sexual agency and to reflect realities on the ground, few modifications have been made to Safe Harbor laws. The examples of statutory rape and sexting show that pathologies of child governance can be remedied by challenging assumptions and acknowledging lived realities, clearing the way for the alignment of child law and policy with the goal of child protection.

A preoccupation with traffickers

Unlike in sexting and statutory rape – where the lack of an adult mitigates or eliminates the criminality of the act – children involved in the sex trade who are not trafficked and do not have a third party face an increased chance of being arrested and charged with a crime. Why the disparity? One possible reason is that Safe Harbor legislation has less to do with child victims and more to do with the third party. Safe Harbor is a product of its creators, formed from their assumptions and objectives of social change. The attempt to implement law and policy to protect children involved in the sex industry through a joint social conservative and radical feminist lens resulted in Safe Harbor laws that direct some children into social services while prosecuting traffickers. The consequence of this bifurcated approach was the creation of strict, mutually exclusive categories that do not overlap: children in the trade are understood to be exclusively either victims or perpetrators. Moreover, the binary construct of agency and victimhood that Safe Harbor laws codify is highly gendered, racialized, decidedly ideological, and rooted in a preoccupation with guilt and innocence that has little to do with children's diverse, lived experiences. Yet the consequences of these laws are all too real, resulting in the denial of protection to large numbers of the very children these laws were intended to help. The pathology of Safe Harbor is that it excludes and exacerbates the victimization of the sex trade's most marginalized and vulnerable children, mainly children of colour and LGBTQIA+ children, those who would benefit most from legal protections and social services.

Conclusion

I argue in this chapter that through an examination of one particular pathology of child governance we can better understand how a rigid narrative of childhood produces outcomes antithetical to the intention of child protection efforts by the state. In the case of Safe Harbor, the protections exclude some children, the result of a preoccupation with the trafficker and the uncritical adoption of a narrative of victimhood that does not allow for diverse lived experiences and ambiguity in the designation of both victim and perpetrator. Consent and culpability are measured by the presence of an adult as a third party, whose absence is used to assess criminality. Assessments of consent and culpability among children in the sex trade underscore a phenomenon seen in many other chapters in this volume, namely, that children who depart from narratives of childhood innocence and vulnerability are denied protections afforded others who conform with norms and expectations. Such children become sites of contestation of state authority and violence, carceral policies, and cultural preoccupations, resulting in pathologies of child governance that can further harm children.

Notes

[1] I use the expression *children involved in the sex trade* or *sex industry* as a neutral description, regardless of whether the state considers them victims or criminals, and regardless of whether they work with a *third party* (colloquially known as a pimp) – someone other than the worker or the client – or operate alone. I employ the term *third party* because it avoids the classed and racialized stereotypes inherent in (or attached to) pimp and because it better denotes the range of roles and services provided (STELLA,

2013). I further choose the term *sex trade* as opposed to prostitution because of its greater neutrality.
2   Individuals that work in the sex trade without a third party will arrange connections on their own or with the help of others in the trade, others in the informal economy, or via the internet (apps, websites).
3   Five states require third-party control: Mississippi, North Dakota, Rhode Island, West Virginia, and Wyoming. Other states may be biased towards it by hinging protections on trafficking victim status: Alabama, Montana, New Hampshire, South Carolina, and Vermont (Shared Hope, 2017).

References

Adelson, W. (2008) 'Child prostitute or victim of trafficking?' *University of St. Thomas Law Journal* 6(1): 96–128.

Adler, A. (2001) 'The perverse law of child pornography', *Columbia Law Review* 101(2): 209–273.

Angelides, S. (2004) 'Feminism, child sexual abuse, and the erasure of child sexuality', *GLQ: A Journal of Lesbian and Gay Studies* 10(2): 141–177.

Austin, R. and Farrell, A. (2017) 'Human trafficking and the media in the United States', in *Oxford Research Encyclopedia of Criminology*, London: Oxford University Press.

Baker, C.N. (2013) 'Moving beyond "slaves, sinners, and saviors": An Intersectional feminist analysis of US sex-trafficking discourses, law and policy', *Study of Women and Gender: Faculty Publications*, Northampton, MA: Smith College.

Bergman, A.L. (2012) 'For their own good? Exploring legislative responses to the commercial sexual exploitation of children and the Illinois Safe Children Act', *Vanderbilt Law Review* 65(5): 1361–1400.

Butler, C.N. (2015) 'Bridge over troubled water: Safe Harbor laws for sexually exploited minors', *North Carolina Law Review* 93(5): 1281–1338.

Clayton, E.W., Krugman, R.D., and Simon, P. (2013) 'Confronting commercial sexual exploitation and sex trafficking of minors in the United States', Institute of Medicine and National Research Council of the National Academies, Washington, DC: The National Academies Press, pp 1–439.

Conner, B.M. (2016) 'In loco aequitatis: The dangers of "Safe Harbor" laws for youth in the sex trades,' *Stanford Journal of Civil Rights & Civil Liberties* 12(1): 43–120.

Cray, A., Miller, K., and Durso, L.E. (2013) 'Seeking shelter: The Experiences and unmet needs of LGBT homeless youth', Center for American Progress.

Dennis, J.P. (2008) 'Women are victims, men make choices: The invisibility of men and boys in the global sex trade', *Gender Issues* 25:11–25.

Dysart, T. (2014) 'Child, victim, or prostitute? Justice through Immunity for prostituted children', *Duke Journal of Gender Law & Policy* 21(255): 255–288.

Evans, D.T. (1994) 'Falling angels? The material construction of children as sexual citizens', *The International Journal of Children's Rights* 2(1): 1–33.

Fahy, S.R. (2015) 'Safe Harbor of minors involved in prostitution: Understanding how criminal justice officials perceive and respond to minors involved in prostitution in a state with a safe Harbor law', PhD thesis, Boston, MA: Northeastern University.

Fernandez, K. (2013) 'Victims or criminals? The intricacies of dealing with juvenile victims of sex trafficking and why the distinction matters', *Arizona State Law Journal* 45(859): 859–890.

Fichtelman, E.B. (2014) 'The double entendre of juvenile prostitution: Victim versus delinquent and the necessity of state uniformity', *Juvenile & Family Court Journal* 65(3–4): 27–46.

Flynn, D. (2013) 'All the kids are doing it: The unconstitutionality of enforcing statutory rape laws against children and teenagers', *New England Law Review* 47(3): 681–714.

Gezinski, L.B. (2021) '(De)criminalization of survivors of domestic minor sex trafficking: A social work call to action,' *Social Work* 66(3): 236–244.

Hasselbarth, N. (2014) 'Emerging victimhood: Moving towards the protection of domestic juveniles involved in prostitution', *Duke Journal of Gender Law & Policy* 21(Spring): 401–416.

Hounmenou, C. and O'Grady, C. (2019) 'A review and critique of the U.S. responses to the commercial sexual exploitation of children', *Children and Youth Services Review* 98: 188–198.

James, S. (2009) 'Romeo and Juliet were sex offenders: An analysis of the age of consent and a call for reform', *UMKC Law Review* 78(1): 241–262.

Kern, J.L. (2013) 'Trends in teen sex are changing, but are Minnesota's Romeo and Juliet laws?', *William Mitchell Law Review* 39(5): 1607–1622.

Levick, M. and Moon, K. (2010) 'Prosecuting sexting as child pornography: A critique', *Valparaiso University Law Review* 44(4): 1035–1054.

Marcus, A., Horning, A., Curtis, R., Sanson, J., and Thompson, E. (2014) 'Conflict and agency among sex workers and pimps: A closer look at domestic minor sex trafficking', *The Annals of the American Academy* 653(1): 225–246.

Martinez, O. and Kelle, G. (2013) 'Sex trafficking of LGBT individuals: A call for service provision, research, and action', *International Law News* 42(4): 21–24.

McLaughlin, J.H. (2010) 'Crime and punishment: Teen sexting in context', *Penn State Law Review* 115(1): 135–182.

Mehlman-Orozco, K. (2015) 'Safe Harbor policies for juvenile victims of sex trafficking: A myopic view of improvements in practice', *Social Inclusion* 3(1): 52–86.

Murphy, L.T. (2016) 'Labor and sex trafficking among homeless youth: A ten-city study executive summary', Modern Slavery Research Project, Loyola University New Orleans.

National Conference of State Legislatures (NCSL) (2017) 'Safe Harbor: State efforts to combat child trafficking'. Available at: https://www.ojp.gov/ncjrs/virtual-library/abstracts/safe-harbor-state-efforts-combat-child-trafficking [Accessed 21 June 2023].

Polaris (2015) 'Human trafficking issue brief: Safe Harbor'. Available at: https://polarisproject.org/wp-content/uploads/2019/09/2015-Safe-Harbor-Issue-Brief.pdf [Accessed 5 June 2022].

Polaris (2016) 'Sex trafficking and LGBTQ youth'. Available at: https://polarisproject.org/resources/sex-trafficking-and-lgbtq-youth/ [Accessed 5 June 2022].

Robinson, K.H. (2013) *Innocence, Knowledge and the Construction of Childhood*, New York, NY: Routledge.

Sano, A. (2016) 'Victimhood and agency in the sex trade: Experiences and perceptions of teenage girls in rural West Java', PhD thesis, Utrecht, Netherlands: University of Utrecht.

Shalhoub-Kevorkian, N. (2019) *Incarcerated Childhood and the Politics of Unchilding*, Cambridge: Cambridge University Press.

Shared Hope (2015) 'Eliminating the third party control barrier to identifying juvenile sextrafficking victims'. Available at: https://sharedhope.org/wp-content/uploads/2016/02/Policy_Paper_Eliminating_Third_Party_Control_Final.pdf [Accessed 5 June 2022].

Shared Hope (2017) 'Seeking justice: Legal approaches to eliminate criminal liability for child sex trafficking victims'. Available at: https://sharedhope.org/wp-content/uploads/2018/08/ANALYSIS-OF-STATUTORY-APPROACHES_ver7.pdf [Accessed 5 June 2022].

Shared Hope (2019a) 'National state survey: Child sex trafficking definitions'. Available at: https://sharedhope.org/PICframe9/statesurveycharts/NSL_Survey_ChildSexTraffickingDefinitions.pdf [Accessed 5 June 2022].

Shared Hope (2019b) 'National state law survey: Protective responses for juvenile sex trafficking victims'. Available at: https://sharedhope.org/PICframe9/statesurveycharts/NSL_Survey_ProtectiveResponsesforJuvenileSexTraffickingJuSTVictims.pdf [Accessed 6 June 2023].

Shared Hope (2020) 'Report cards on child & youth sex trafficking'. Available at: https://sharedhope.org/wp-content/uploads/2020/11/SHI_2020_Advanced-Legislative-Framework-Report_FINAL.pdf [Accessed 5 June 2022].

Smith, B.L. and Kercher, G.A. (2011) *Adolescent Sexual Behavior and the Law*, Houston: Crime Victims' Institute, Criminal Justice Center, Sam Houston State University.

STELLA (2013) 'Language matters: Talking about sex work'. Available at: https://www.nswp.org/sites/nswp.org/files/StellaInfoSheetLanguage Matters.pdf [Accessed 5 June 2022].

Strasburger, V.C., Zimmerman, H., Temple, J.R., and Madigan, S. (2019) 'Teenagers, sexting, and the law', *Pediatrics* 143(5): 1–9.

Swaner, R., Kabriola, M., Walker, A., and Spadafore, J. (2016) 'Youth involvement in the sex trade: A national study', Center for Court Innovation. Available at: http://www.courtinnovation.org/research/youth-involvement-sex-trade-national-study [Accessed 5 June 2022].

Williams, R. (2017) 'Safe Harbor: State efforts to combat child trafficking', National Conference of State Legislatures. Available at: https://www.ojp.gov/ncjrs/virtual-library/abstracts/safe-harbor-state-efforts-combat-child-trafficking [Accessed 6 June 2023].

PART III

Lived Childhoods

11

Childhood, Playing War, and Militarism: Beyond Discourses of Domination/Resistance and Towards an Ethics of Encounter

Sean Carter and Tara Woodyer

The military-industrial-entertainment complex is immensely powerful. War and peace are no longer highly differentiated zones in British and American societies. War has entered, uninvited, into our homes and taken up residence.

Bourke, 2014: 12

Introduction

Until relatively recently, the notion that children could be considered meaningful political actors was rarely considered within either academic studies or more generally in public discourse (see Beier, 2015). This chapter seeks to argue that, in part, this has been because of the ways in which political acts, (in this case, specifically resistance), have come to be defined and understood. Hughes (2020) has recently argued for a re-thinking of what counts as resistance, not least in relation to the 'logic of intention' that has, to date, formed a central part in its definition. When conceived only as an intentional act, with pre-determined outcomes and goals, it is difficult to recognize the potential capacity of children enacting such political agency. Here we use the example of children playing with war toys as one means of thinking differently about their political agency in general and their ability to enact resistance in particular.

The study of popular culture and global politics has also suffered at times from an unwillingness to ascribe political agency to the consumers of various forms of popular culture, and studies have frequently taken as their starting point that the power-laden ideological meanings of any given cultural text or artefact are capable of overwhelming audiences and consumers (for critiques of these positions, see Sharp, 2000; Dittmer and Gray, 2010). With regard to both the political lives of children and the politics of popular culture, there is a sense that the task of the critical academic is to uncover or decode the ways in which the lives of children, on the one hand, or the political lives of audiences and consumers, on the other, are overwhelmed or dominated by powerful external others. Resistance is sometimes offered as a possibility for critical or knowing audiences with regard to forms of popular culture, but it rarely features in accounts of the ways in which childhood and the political intersect. We briefly return to this theme in the conclusion.

In this chapter, we look at a specific toy range in the UK – Her Majesty's Armed Forces (HMAF), licensed by the UK's Ministry of Defence – as a departure point for thinking through the dynamic intersections of militarism and childhood, and the interplay between discourses of domination and resistance. The toy range was launched in 2009, in the midst of British military engagements in both Iraq and Afghanistan, and thus, in some ways could be considered as an ideologically charged homage to militarism, evident across a range of cultural processes and phenomena in the UK during the 'war on terror' (see Jenkings et al, 2012; Kelly 2013). However, our argument considers the specific role of children's play in the co-constitution of such cultures of everyday militarism: we address the toy not merely as a power-laden text to be 'read' for its ideological meaning, but rather as a thing-in-itself engaged with on an embodied level in children's everyday practices of play. This approach can present a powerful challenge to the idea that an inherent power embedded in the militarized toy is determinant of political outcomes, producing militarized childhood subjects, as is gestured towards in the opening quote from Bourke (2014). Our research, through a series of play ethnographies, attends to the demonstration of children's political subjectivity within play (for more on this, see Woodyer and Carter, 2020). This chapter thus begins with a brief discussion of some of the connections between play and global politics, and an overview of the research project that our empirical work draws upon. We then provide a couple of short vignettes from this research to explore how the experiential aspect of play with military action figures shapes the ethical demands it makes of the young player. We conceptualize such play as an embodied encounter, paying particular attention to issues of ambiguity, infidelity, and the contingency that materiality injects into children's everyday mediation of the power and ideas circulated through cultures of everyday militarism. The chapter concludes by linking back to recent ideas on both the political agency of childhood (especially Kallio, 2007, 2008) and the re-conceptualization of resistance (especially Hughes, 2020).

Playful subjects

Debates on the cultural geopolitics of childhood, or on the ways in which the geopolitical world 'out there', impinges upon daily life 'in here' have perhaps been most explored through the lens of war play. War play has a long and complex history, and one which is not always closely tied to forms of popular culture; a recent exhibition at the V&A Museum of Childhood, London, entitled 'War Play' opened, for example, with a glass cabinet featuring a wooden stick resembling the shape of the gun – a found object turned into a war toy through an act of the imagination. Alongside the cabinet, which also featured mass-produced cultural products targeted at a child audience, the following text was displayed:

> **Trigger happy?**
> The vast majority of children play with toy weapons. These might be convincing copies of the real thing, abstract versions constructed from building bricks, or simply sticks. The use of toy guns by children is often discouraged and is seen as glamorising and encouraging violence. However, the links between playing with toy guns and increased aggression are not clear.
>
> And are all toy guns equally bad? Realistic, mass-produced toy guns have an obviously violent purpose and it is hard for a child to move beyond this when playing with them. But a weapon constructed by a child encourages the use of abstract thought, important for a child's development. And these constructed 'weapons' often have more complex and imaginative uses than killing. They can teleport, transform or make people better.

This exhibition text gestures towards some of the issues that we wish to foreground and explore in this chapter. Firstly, it identifies the real and valid concerns that exist, in both public and academic discourses, around the potential negative effects of war play on children and childhood. This is a long-running debate, characterized by dichotomized perspectives (war play seen as either a good thing, preparing children for adult life, or a bad thing, teaching children that violence is the solution to problems) and a lack of compelling evidence on the direct links between playing war and wider impacts upon aggressive childhood behaviour (for example, Malloy and McMurray-Schwarz, 2004). Within academic debates, these concerns most often coalesce around the idea of the militarization of childhood and a concern that this helps to inculcate a sense of naturalness to militarized and violent solutions. If we understand militarism to be 'broadly understood as the preparation for war, its normalisation and legitimisation' (Stavrianakis and Stern, 2018: 3), then it becomes clear why war toys and war play are of such concern for critical scholars – they can easily be read and interpreted as yet one more domestic iteration of the military permeating the civilian sphere under the rubric of the military-industrial-media-entertainment complex, as Der Derian (2001) termed it (see also Turse, 2009). However, also contained in the exhibition text is a sense that other things might also be going on when children play war; that the act of playing itself is open-ended, experimental, and imaginative. We might go so far as to suggest that the act of playing affords opportunities for resistance and can be the location of childhood political agency, and it is to these possibilities that this chapter is oriented. In doing so, we do not seek to downplay or ignore concerns around militarization, but rather to offer a fuller account of childhood encounters with militarized forms of popular culture.

Playing war

Play has not featured heavily as a topic worthy of attention within the study of global politics, although there are recent signs that this is starting to change (see Hirst, 2019: Grzelczyk, 2022). More generally, play is often conceived as frivolous, and as intimately connected with children, childhood, and childish behaviour. As such, play is often understood as something that takes place at a particular stage of life, prior to the much more serious endeavours of adulthood. Where play has been analysed in relation to global politics, this has tended to relate to video games, for which there is a burgeoning literature (for example, Salter, 2011; Robinson, 2015; Berents and Keogh, 2018), exploring issues such as the relationship between gaming and weapons technologies, textual/discursive readings of the ideological intent of specific games, and to a lesser extent, the playing itself of these games. We would argue that foregrounding play itself is essential to fully understanding the links between play and global politics.

Our own research focuses not on video war games, but on the playing with war toys: more specifically the HMAF action figure range. Introduced in 2009 (to coincide with Victory in Europe Day), HMAF toys were directly licensed by the British Ministry of Defence and featured a range of model soldiers, vehicles, and other military paraphernalia. The initial flagship toys of the range were modern iterations of Action Man: 12-inch dolls outfitted in miniature uniforms accurately representing those of serving British troops. Produced by Character Group, the toys were commercially successful, with several new ranges added in subsequent years, such as dressing-up outfits and a Lego-style range, including a Reaper drone and operator set. One notable feature of the licensing agreement with the Ministry of Defence is that the advertising and packaging for the toy range featured the official insignia of the various branches of the UK military. The toy range harked back to earlier action figure ranges, such as Action Man (in the UK) and GI Joe (in the US), but with some notable differences. Firstly, the licensing agreement with the Ministry of Defence lent the range official state sanctioning, in contrast to those earlier ranges. Secondly, in its design and aesthetic, this range drew directly on contemporary conflict, unlike Action Man, for example, which tended to look back to World War II for design influences. Thus, the toy range featured military outfits, vehicles, and weapons that made direct reference to British military engagements in Iraq and Afghanistan The timing of the launch of this toy range can also be positioned within broader 'support the troops' initiatives taking place in the UK at the time, such as , Armed Forces Day (instigated in 2006), the charity Help for Heroes (launched in 2007), and the Invictus Games (established in 2014), and the prominence given in the UK media to repatriation ceremonies of UK military personnel killed in Afghanistan. Writing with regard to the latter, Jenkings et al (2012: 361), argued that these should 'be seen as part of a trend of the rehabilitation of the military in the aftermath of the Iraq war, and the legitimisation of the Afghanistan war'. While there is some literature on the links between action figures and wider political issues (for example, Machin and Van Leeuwen, 2009), there is even less focus on what actually happens during play with such toys than there is in the video game literature. A key part of the research project upon which this chapter draws (Ludic Geopolitics, funded by the Economic and Social Research Council, UK) was designed to begin to gain better insights into what actually takes place when children play with such war toys. To do this, we undertook a series of play ethnographies that captured children playing with the HMAF toy range in their own homes. Children were lent video cameras in order to film themselves playing, sometimes in the presence of a researcher, but most often on their own or with a friend or sibling. The research involved 20 in-depth studies with children aged four to eleven years old living in Hampshire and Surrey, UK. Each study typically involved spending one to two hours with each child per week for a period of six weeks, in addition to the children filming their own play between sessions. Across the many hours of recorded footage of children playing with the HMAF action figures (as well as other toys), here we would like to pick out just two brief examples or vignettes, which begin to call into question simplistic or overly deterministic interpretations of what is happening during war play. Of the two short vignettes briefly outlined here, the first is certainly 'more typical' of the data set as a whole, while the second represents one of the more unusual and obviously subversive play scenarios enacted by a child participant. That said, together these vignettes are broadly representative in two main ways. First, they both exhibit general features common with the majority of the play ethnographies – namely, they consist of a simultaneous combination of *fidelity* to the 'source material' of the militarized nature of the toys, and an *infidelity* to such 'in-built' meanings and uses of these toys. And second, they both exemplify a creative and playful scenario that defies easy categorization and description. At the same time, these chosen examples are unique, as indeed are all of the play ethnographies – while various patterns, themes, and motifs occur across the play scenarios, no two scenarios are quite the same.

Playful acts of resistance

The play ethnographies defy easy description or categorization. Each recorded session contains multiple scenarios being played out, conflicting narratives, and ambiguous dialogue. Often the play brings together incongruous elements. This incongruity can be thought of in a number of ways. For example, in a material sense, there are play scenarios that involve both designed war toys that seek some fidelity to the 'real world' (such as the HMAF toy range) as well as objects that do not 'fit' with this – dinosaurs, construction vehicles, bedroom furniture, to name but a few. This infidelity to the 'pre-existing context' that the design and promotion of the HMAF toy range refers is also expressed through, for example, narrative infidelity (the stories within these play events, even where discernible, do not always adhere to clear war or combat narratives), and geographic infidelity (such as the locations invoked and the nationality of the 'actors').

We do not have the space here to describe or examine the content of these play ethnographies in any detail. Rather, what we try to do is to give a brief flavour of some of the play scenarios as a means of illustrating the messiness and incoherence of playing with war toys. This undercuts, we would argue, any attempts to fix pre-determined meanings upon these encounters, not least the idea that war toys only ever act upon children in militarizing ways. Within the ambiguity of nonsense play also lie the possibilities of what McDonnell (2019) refers to as 'rupture', and which we seek here to consider as small acts of playful resistance.

Vignette #1: 2015-05-17 child 9 video clips 5 and 10

In this example, a child plays on their own with a mix of military-themed toys (tanks, soldiers), as well as non-military vehicles from their wider toy collection. The play is fractured, lacking any real coherence or over-arching narrative. There are elements that clearly fall into what might be commonly referred to as war play – the toy soldiers attack each other, the child makes the noise of gunfire and explosions while playing, and at various points military terminology is used. Alongside this, the play exhibits other characteristics: the child plays as both perpetrator and victim; there is no sense of one side being valorized at the expense of the other; categories of good and bad are blurred in the play; there is a recognition that war, and violence more generally, causes pain and suffering to participants; attention is paid to providing medical assistance to wounded bodies; and strategic decisions are taken to limit the loss of life. Similar themes are present in a second recording made by this child, in which the entire play scenario is based around the evacuation of the vulnerable and those in need. In this play encounter, rather than just using weapons, the child enacts the use of smoke bombs to provide cover for the evacuation.

While none of the collected play ethnographies could be described as 'typical', the kinds of ambiguities, complexities, and messiness of this example are common across many of them. Cases of clear, overt, deliberative 'resistance' to the narratives and materialities of warfare or combat are perhaps fairly rare, but moments of undercutting supposedly pre-determined narratives and sensibilities are commonplace. That said, on occasion, there were very clear subversions regarding the 'intended' use and meaning of military action figures.

Vignette #2: 2015-05-05 child 10 video clip 1

In this encounter, the child dresses the HMAF action figures with the help of TW [the researcher]. The child then lines the soldiers up in a row against the wall in the manner of a 'museum'. We see a line of at least five figures. The child then works out what hats/helmets fit each figure's head. Soon after, the child moves to a different room and prepares a number of (female) Barbie-type dolls to visit the museum. This is a domestic scene where the dolls are woken up, where they make their beds, tidy the house, arrange their hair, and apply make-up before the visit. The dogs, it is decided, cannot visit the museum, and neither will the horses. The doll family (one male figure, two female figures, and two babies) arrive at the museum entrance, upon which they are told by an HMAF figure 'guard' to park 'over there'. The child unpacks the dolls from the car and makes the larger dolls carry the smaller 'kids' dolls into the museum. The doll family visit the museum and are made to inspect the line of HMAF figures. After a repeat pass, the HMAF figures unexpectedly jump up, scare, and possibly attack the doll family. All of the dolls jump across the room and end up in a pile under the chair. The doll family are scared for their kids. The 'attack' by the HMAF figures is over, and the doll family work to put the figures 'back in their places' against the wall. The figures are also given back their respective guns. Having returned 'home', the doll family recount their visit to the museum to a doll that stayed behind.

Making sense of nonsense: playing as ethical encounter

When read as 'texts' for their ideological messages, war toys tell us some important things, but to fully understand their entanglement in war-related ethical considerations, we need to understand the interactivities that they encourage – what they *do* rather than what they say. While play scripts may mimic familiar socio-political narratives, as seen on TV or read about in books and comics, each enactment of these practices is original and open-ended, based on the specific interactivities of the unfolding play. They therefore contain the possible 'spark of recognition that things, relations, and selves could be otherwise' (Katz, 2004: 102). The reciprocal relations emerging within and through embodiment allow people and things to be set free of cultural coordinates, allowing 'fanciful recontextualisation' (Lutfiyya, 1987) or 'playful reconstruction' (Gilloch, 1996).

When playing, children are not merely rehearsing social roles and practices but 'playing with such things as power, control, symbol, gesture, and routine' (Katz, 2004: 97). Playing works through aspects of the mimicked activities that are somewhat mysterious; identities, social relationships, and socio-material practices are played with as details are tweaked or wildly (re)imagined (for rich examples, see Katz, 2004). 'Play is both a form of coming to consciousness and a way to become other' (Katz, 2004: 98). This is the motivation of play – the possibility of configuring alternate ways of being-in-the-world. Here we might usefully draw on the work of Walter Benjamin, who explains how this playful process is dependent upon the child's insightful way of knowing; a heightened perception of the surrounding environment based on a privileged proximity to things. This proximity is founded in a particular interaction with the material world that eschews the division between subject and object, creating reciprocal, non-hierarchical relations. Children 'do not so much imitate the works of adults as bring together, in the artefacts produced in play, materials of widely differing kinds in a new intuitive relationship' (Benjamin, 1979: 53). Benjamin accounts for this intuitive activity through reference to the immediate connection between thought and action within the child's consciousness. This amounts to a refusal to separate body and mind within cognitive experience. In this sense, children's cognition is not primarily contemplative, but rather tactile and hence tied to action. Rather than accepting the given meaning of things, children get to know objects by manipulating them and using them creatively, 'releasing', in Buck-Morss's (1989: 264) words, 'new possibilities of meaning'.

As a result, socio-political discourses shaping society are not simply absorbed into play through a practice of mimicking. Rather, children's play enters into these socio-political contours in different ways, offering the possibility of disrupting discourses and reconfiguring relations and social practices. Play, then, is as much about invention as mimicking, experimenting with how relations and selves might be otherwise. As Katz (2004: 102) remarks, '[m]aking that so is not child's play, of course', yet 'play is not immaterial to the task'. Toys and their themes can be understood partly through discursive reading, but it is their immersive quality – how they involve the player within their narratives – that acts as a mechanism for instilling, or otherwise, their geopolitical and military logics. This is not to disavow discursive or ideological approaches but to show other ways that play can and should be explored and developed in relation to conceptions of ethical agency. Examining what children actually *do* with military action figures requires us to appreciate how play, as an embodied practice, exceeds representation and rationality. It presents a powerful critique to conceptions of ethical agency as the impartial, rational enactment of instrumental reason.

We would argue, then, that play's possibility of configuring alternate ways of being-in-the-world may be seen as a form of resistance, even if the politics of playing are primarily bound up in experiencing vitality rather than strategic oppositional endeavour. Players are often primarily engaged in expressing themselves through enjoyable activities, not serious oppositional endeavours. By emphasizing vitality as the internal purpose of playing, this phenomenon is positioned as 'inwardly oriented', engaged with 'an expression of a different facet of power altogether. This power comes not from above – it is not ascribed – but from within – it is achieved' (Malbon, 1999: 148). Rather than evading power imposed by another, playing cultivates 'a form of micro-power or "vitality" that can be inhabited' (Malbon, 1999: 14). From this perspective, Barbie's day out to the museum to see the HMAF figures on static display discussed earlier was not motivated by a strategic opposition to ways we might expect toys to behave in particular ways. Rather, it was an embodied practice contingent on the interaction with the material objects and environment to hand and their place in a wider assemblage, including local museums and family films. Nevertheless, such practices have clear connections with recent debates concerning both the political agency of children and the re-conceptualization of resistance, as we look to explore in the final section.

Conclusion

The discussion above is an attempt to articulate the ethics of playing with war toys beyond various rigid dichotomies, such as good/bad or domination/resistance. Instead, we are arguing that the *playfulness* of play requires us to be more attentive to complexity, ambiguity, and emergence: that the outcome of play (even with apparently militarized or militarizing toys) cannot be determined in advance. More generally, this points towards two other conclusions: first, that it is worth reflecting upon what resistance might mean in the context of play and childhood; and second, that these brief examples point towards one way of acknowledging children as political actors in their own right, able to exercise elements of political agency. On this latter point we might usefully draw upon the work of Kallio (2007, 2008) and her arguments concerning the politics of childhood. Kallio (2007: 126) contends that 'children's politics is based on the autonomy they hold over their bodies. Although young people do not have autonomous positions at other political scales, the right and ability to control and command one's own body belongs to them as well'. We would argue that this autonomy and agency extends to their play, which is itself an embodied practice: the brief examples provided earlier in the chapter attest to the autonomous and imaginative ways in which children use their bodies in play, manipulating other objects in ways of their own choosing.

Elsewhere, Kallio develops these ideas, drawing particular inspiration from de Certeau and his distinction between strategic agency and tactical agency, arguing that 'children can participate and resist only through *tactical* agency' (Kallio, 2008: 286; original emphasis). While such tactical agency is necessarily prescribed and limited, working within the parameters of the structural agency operated by adults and institutions, nevertheless the recognition of this as a form of political agency opens the door for viewing children as political actors and, moreover, as capable of some forms of resistance. In Kallio's (2008: 288) words, de Certeau suggests that 'consumers can "ruse" the "proper" order by making use of opportunities and occasions (little gaps and caverns in the produced order)'. The range of ways in which children find to play with and subvert intended purposes and meanings of war toys, such as the HMAF range, seems a telling example of such a 'ruse'.

In viewing such actions as forms of resistance, we might also usefully draw on the recent argument of Hughes (2020), that resistance has often been defined and understood in unnecessarily narrow terms. In particular, she argues that across the social sciences, ideas on resistance 'have led to a *pre-determination of form* that particular actions or actors must assume to constitute resistance' (Hughes, 2020: 1142: original emphasis), and as such are 'wedded to particular co-ordinates – of intention, linearity and opposition – that serve to determine in advance what comes to be termed as resistance' (Hughes, 2020: 1142–1143). A key point here is that this pre-determination not only rules out certain *actions* in advance from definitions of resistance, but crucially, for our purposes, certain kinds of *actors*, namely children. When intentionality, linearity (understood as having a direct effect on that which is being resisted), and opposition (rather than accommodation or negotiation) are foregrounded as essential coordinates of resistance, it is hard to see how even the tactical agency we might afford to children can constitute resistance. Instead, what Hughes (2020: 1145) argues is that we need 'to open up our attention to more ambiguous, unremarkable and less coherent practices as resistance'.

In attending to the potential inherent within play and playing, we would thus want to highlight two specific issues that are pertinent for the study of childhood and global politics (both in relation to each other and independently of each other). First, in considering play as a creative act without pre-determined outcomes, it becomes possible to conceive of ways in which children can enact various kinds of political agency that, crucially, can include acts of subversion and resistance, however modest and circumscribed those might be. This in turn enables us to approach the study of the relationship between children and popular cultures (of militarism in this specific case), to go beyond the task of simply decoding the imposition of powerful discourses upon children, and to focus on the *encounter* that takes place in such moments. Second, play is of course not just an activity undertaken by children, but is an aspect of contemporary life that exists broadly across societies and cultures, with all kinds of attendant political and geopolitical ramifications (see Hirst, 2019). Thus, while recognizing the potential resistance present in the playfulness of children, we also ought to extend this possibility and seek to more fully explore the creative and resistant potentialities of play more generally. In so doing, we might better see both the political agency already possessed by children and the potential for playful resistance.

Acknowledgements
The fieldwork upon which this chapter draws was supported by the United Kingdom's Economic and Social Research Council under grant number ES/L001926/1.

References
Beier, J.M. (2015) 'Children, childhoods, and security studies: An introduction', *Critical Studies on Security* 3(1): 1–13.

Benjamin, W. (1979) *One-way Street and Other Writings*, London: Verso.

Berents, H. and Keogh, B. (2018) 'Virtuous, virtual, but not visceral: (Dis)Embodied viewing in military-themed videogames', *Critical Studies on Security* 6(3): 366–369.

Bourke, J. (2014) *Wounding the World: How Military Violence and War-play Invades our Lives*, London: Virago.

Buck-Morss, S. (1989) *The Dialectics of Seeing: Walter Benjamin and the Arcades Project*, Boston, MA: MIT Press.

Der Derian, J. (2001) *Virtuous War: Mapping the Military-industrial-media-entertainment Network*, Oxford: Westview Press.

Dittmer, J. and Gray, N. (2010) 'Popular geopolitics 2.0: Towards new methodologies of the everyday', *Geography Compass* 4(11): 1664–1677.

Gilloch, G. (1996) *Myth and Metropolis: Walter Benjamin and the City*, Cambridge: Polity Press.

Grzelczyk, V. (2022) 'The politics of toys: What potential for inter-Korean reconciliation?', *Asian Studies Review* 46(4): 668–684.

Hirst, A. (2019) 'Playin(g) international theory', *Review of International Studies* 45(5): 891–914.

Hughes, S. (2020) 'On resistance in human geography', *Progress in Human Geography* 44(6): 1141–1160.

Jenkings, K.N., Megoran, N., Woodward, R., and Bos, D. (2012) 'Wootton Bassett and the political spaces of remembrance and mourning', *Area* 44(3): 356–363.

Kallio, K. (2007) 'Performative bodies, tactical agents and political selves: Rethinking the political geographies of childhood', *Space and Polity* 11(2): 121–136.

Kallio K. (2008) 'The body as a battlefield: Approaching children's politics', *Geografiska Annaler: Series B, Human Geography* 90(3): 285–297.

Katz, C. (2004) *Growing Up Global: Economic Restructuring and Children's Everyday Lives*, Minneapolis, MN: University of Minnesota Press.

Kelly, J. (2013) 'Popular culture, sport and the 'hero'-fication of British militarism', *Sociology* 47(4): 722–738.

Lutfiyya, M.N. (1987) *The Social Construction of Context through Play*, Lanham, MD: University Press of America.

Malbon, B. (1999) *Clubbing: Dancing, Ecstasy and Vitality*, London: Routledge.

Malloy, H.L. and P. McMurray-Schwarz (2004) 'War play, aggression and peer culture: A review of the research examining the relationship between war play and aggression', in S. Reifel and M. Brown (eds) *Social Contexts of Early Education, and Reconceptualizing Play (II) Advances in Early Education and Day Care Volume 13*, Oxford: Elsevier, pp 235–265.

Machin, D. and Van Leeuwen, T. (2009) 'Toys as discourse: Children's war toys and the war on terror', *Critical Discourse Studies* 6(1): 51–63.

McDonnell, S. (2019) 'Nonsense and possibility: Ambiguity, rupture and reproduction in children's play/ful narratives', *Children's Geographies* 17(3): 251–265.

Robinson, N. (2015) 'Have you won the war on terror? Military videogames and the state of American exceptionalism', *Millennium: Journal of International Studies* 43(2): 450–470.

Salter, M.B. (2011) 'The geographical imaginations of video games: Diplomacy, Civilization, America's Army and Grand Theft Auto IV', *Geopolitics* 16(2): 359–388.

Sharp, J. (2000) 'Remasculinising geo(-)politics? Comments on Gearóid Ó Tuathail's Critical Geopolitics', *Political Geography* 19(3): 361–364.

Stavrianakis, A. and Stern, M. (2018) 'Militarism and security: Dialogue, possibilities and limits', *Security Dialogue* 49(1–2): 3–18.

Turse, N. (2009) *The Complex: How the Military Invades Our Everyday Lives*, London: Faber and Faber.

Woodyer, T. and Carter, S. (2020) 'Domesticating the geopolitical: Rethinking popular geopolitics through play', *Geopolitics* 25(5): 1050–1074.

12

Troubling Girl Power Environmentalism: Indigenous Girls, Climate Change Activism, and a Relational Ethic of Responsibility

Lindsay Robinson

Introduction

Under what is known as the girling of development (Hayhurst, 2011), girls have received unprecedented attention as global activists and empowered figures uniquely capable of addressing our world's most urgent crises. Early iterations of these programmes in the 1990s and early 2000s, such as Nike's *Girl Effect* and the World Bank's *Adolescent Girl Initiative*, focused on girls' unique capacity to end global poverty. Increasingly, however, girls are being called upon to save our planet from climate change. Girl Rising (GR), a US-based 'girl's education non-profit', has launched the Future Rising (FR) programme, described as 'a virtual fellowship for young activists working on environmental justice storytelling with a focus on women and girls' (Girl Rising, nd.c). FR fellows are to create a 'body of knowledge about how the drivers and impacts of climate change intersect with girls' education and gender equity' (Girl Rising, nd.b). Although many of the inaugural fellows' projects address the intersectional and global inequities of climate change, the FR programme itself – especially its promotional material and crafted lesson plans available to interested Global North teachers – remains committed to GR's broader liberal emphasis on individual educational investment to not only improve the life trajectories of Global South girls but also to address a broad array of grave social crises. As GR boldly claims, the 'future of our planet depends on investing in quality education for girls' (Girl Rising, nd.b).

FR is an example of girl power environmentalism: an individualistic, colonial, and capitalist version of (Southern) girls' personal responsibility for global planetary problems. Here, girls – because they are girls – possess a unique girl power waiting to be tapped into by Global North educational intervention and green employment initiatives. Under this thinking, girl power is all we need to address the climate crisis. Using what I refer to as decolonial feminism – a theoretical framework that encompasses Indigenous, decolonial, and anti-imperial feminist theorizing (Lugones, 2010; de Finney, 2014; Datta, 2015) – this chapter illuminates how FR constructs a limited, colonial, and capitalist version of girlhood informed by girl power environmentalism, one that works to conceal the variegated ways in which girls always already exist as political subjects in the world. Indeed, the choice-centred definition of agency and empowerment under girl power environmentalism – which often celebrates girls as hopeful futures, but only when they make the (right) choice to be empowered by not having babies and instead working in the global economy – should not be conflated with the recognition of girls' robust and embodied personhood. GR's depiction of girls' agency, in this way, is necessarily contained within her ability to stimulate economic progress along the stringent metrics of modern development. This reflects the development industry's long liberal objective to bring modernity to the lives of those considered distant, strange, and backward (Escobar, 2001), as well as its Enlightenment-based linear conceptualizations of time punctuated by a colonial ordering of space (McClintock, 1995). For GR, girls' empowerment and climate resilience become symbolic of their country's development progress. This chapter challenges such depictions of girlhood by highlighting other anti-capitalist and anti-colonial possibilities – specifically by showcasing the climate change activism of Indigenous girls.[1] This is not to collapse Indigenous girls into a homogenous or essentialized category, nor is it to suggest that they alone are exclusively responsible for protesting, addressing, and solving climate change – an argument that would eerily echo girl power environmentalism. Importantly, not all Indigenous girls are climate change activists. Yet, as Taft (2020: 12) argues, girl activists' involvement in politics is not unusual, but 'something that thousands of girls around the world are practicing and have been practicing for decades'. In this way, highlighting key figures in Indigenous climate change movements reveals Indigenous girls, like all girls, as agential, political subjects who have always existed in global politics – ones who do not need to develop their countries or engage with the global marketplace to be valued.

This decolonial feminist analysis sees modern logics – including those that suggest capitalism can be made green and pro-girl – as not only ill-equipped to address timely global crises but at the very root of them (Escobar, 2015). For decolonial feminism – and its attention to the racial, classed, and gendered nature of coloniality and modernity – gendered violence and environmental degradation are deeply entrenched in colonial and capitalist thinking, which prioritize the rational, scientific, male, and white over the spiritual, relational, female and queer, and racialized (Lugones, 2010). This chapter, thus, engages in the methodological praxis of what Mignolo (2009: 161) calls 'epistemic disobedience', described as a 'de-linking from the magic of the Western idea of modernity, ideals of humanity and promises of economic growth and financial prosperity'. First, this chapter analyses GR's official texts – including its promotional material, curated lesson plans, and video archive – by illuminating that girl power environmentalism harms girls through a superficial emphasis on their economic potential, which dismisses the complex and embodied nature of their political subjecthood. Second, this chapter turns to notable Indigenous girl activists who protest environmental destruction and climate change, epistemically delinking from GR's individualistic focus by appealing to an ethic of relationality that grounds our global responsibility to each other and to the planet on our embedded interconnections with all life (Datta, 2015; Escobar, 2015). In this way, decolonial feminism troubles whose voices and which knowledge counts as authoritative, effectively uncovering the 'epistemic silences of Western epistemology and affirming the epistemic rights of the racially devalued' (Mignolo, 2009: 162) and decolonizing the possibilities and expectations of girlhood, as well as the foundational responsibilities we have to our planet and to each other.

The girling of development and girl power environmentalism

While various development programmes operate under the rationale of 'invest in a girl and she will do the rest' (Moeller, 2013), GR has made a name for itself with its popular film by the same name that celebrates the power of girls' education. More recently, GR has leveraged this success to become an NGO that 'delivers research-proven educational programming' through content creation, outreach, and curricula (Girl Rising, nd.a). GR argues that educating girls 'is one of the world's best investments, changing lives and creating positive ripple effects throughout society', boasting that they have reached 5 million adolescent girls across 12 countries with the help of over 130 partners, some of which include Citi Bank, HP, the Obama Foundation, and USAID (Girl Rising, nd.a). As one of GR's newest programmes, FR is a virtual fellowship programme aimed at (mostly) girl activists involved in environmental justice, although it remains centred on the transformative power of education for girls' lives and for the planet. When referring to girl activists, GR means those of teenage age into young adulthood, reflecting the development sphere's definition of 'girl' as roughly between the ages of 16 and 24 (Saraswati and Beta, 2021).

The FR programme operates according to a particular formula common in the girling of development for realizing girls' empowerment: education, employment, and reproductive intervention (Girl Rising, 2021a). Echoing liberal feminism, education becomes the foundational input of girls' skills, opportunities, and success (Khoja-Moolji, 2018). GR claims there to be a strong causal relationship between years of education and environmental improvements, suggesting that 'for every additional year of schooling a girl receives, her country's resilience to climate disaster improves by 3.2 points' (Girl Rising, 2021a). The suggestion of such a relationship between girls' education rates and a country's disaster preparedness, of course, is overly sweeping, leaving out necessary details like whether a country has sufficient climate adapted infrastructure, effective disaster and emergency response policies, and climate action plans. More fundamentality, however, feminists have long argued that educational spaces are not necessarily inclusive or empowered spaces for girls (Bent, 2013). Rather, these spaces reinscribe gendered exclusions and harassment and perpetuate socio-economic dynamics and class hierarchies (Switzer, 2013). In addition, GR forgets that Greta Thunberg, and many young climate activists since, have walked out of the classroom as a global climate strike, protesting the apathy and inaction of political leaders on climate change.

Education, for GR, is not merely a girl's right but instrumentally important for girls' employment opportunities. As GR argues, both a 'gender equal future' and a 'green future' can be achieved through girls' employment in the new green global economy (Girl Rising, 2021a). Here, GR assumes that girls will advance ambitious climate goals and reduce carbon emissions through green employment, whether as politicians who pass ambitious climate policies or in STEM fields as climate innovators (Girl Rising, 2021a). Interestingly, GR recognizes that fossil fuel industries contribute to climate change, yet its programming falls short of proposing solutions that directly challenge our carbon-based capitalist economy – an important matter given that, as decolonial thinking highlights, capitalism relies on both environmental degradation (Escobar, 2015) and colonial, gendered exploitation (Lugones, 2010) for economic growth. GR, instead, has an individual focus on girls, as if their participation in green jobs will render capitalism both pro-girl and environmentally sustainable. Girl power environmentalism, in this sense, takes on the 'neoliberal girl power' of the broader girling of development, which conflates girls' 'economic capacities with their political empowerment' in a way that cultivates 'hard work, autonomous agency, and making the right decisions in a free market economy' (Bent, 2013: 10–11). Girls' economic empowerment, in this thinking, is not only about their financial success but is central to bringing progress, development, modernity – and now climate adaptation – to the Global South. That is, 'self-empowerment and girls' individual self-responsibility' become not only the answer to developing countries in the Global South (Hayhurst, 2011: 534) but can, rather conveniently, also address the dire issue of climate change.

Finally, GR makes a case for empowering girls through family planning, arguing that girls should be 'empowered to choose if and when to have children' (Girl Rising, 2021a.). The organization also claims that limiting pregnancies in the Global South 'would help avoid 85 gigatons of CO_2 emissions by 2050' (Girl Rising, 2021a). This is a bold claim to make, especially seeing as GR's projection lacks a citation and further data to support it, while they also do not explain how the (tenuous) link between future Global South babies and carbon emissions addresses the urgent nature of this crisis. Indeed, much reputable research on climate change links fossil fuel emissions with capitalist industries of the North (Hickel, 2020), not with poor girls of the Global South and their families. Most problematically, GR's claims contribute to persistent colonial discourses that have long characterized the Orientalist gaze towards the Global South (Escobar, 2001). Here, Global South girls are perennially at risk of falling victim to those 'ideologies and adult (men) who do not share the liberal Enlightened values of the Global North' (Berents, 2015: 517). This life of 'Third World Difference' (Mohanty, 1984) – where Southern girls' vulnerability and lack of reproductive choices is understood as oppositional to Northern girls' agency and ample opportunities (Bent, 2013) – is framed as having disastrous consequences for both girls and the planet. Given climate changes' immediacy and global reach, such claims support arguments in favour of 'the inherent "right" of the Global North to intervene' (Berents, 2015: 517). While 'conversations on sexual and reproductive rights and responsibilities', may be fruitful for girls' wellbeing and sexual health (Moeller, 2013: 619), GR's claims relating to population growth in the Global South only reinforce inaccurate and racist Malthusian arguments of resource scarcity. Such dynamics also raise 'feminist concerns regarding the racialized nature of seeking to control the reproductive and economic lives of particular girls and women' (Moeller, 2013: 615), which is made undeniably apparent when we consider that GR's panic about racialized babies is at odds with the ongoing distress in the Global North about declining (white) birth rates.

GR's definition of girl power, thus, sanctions only extremely narrow conceptualizations of girl agency and empowerment. It holds girls to unrealistic expectations to lift themselves out of poverty, develop their countries, and, while at it, resolve the climate crisis too. GR's framings of girlhood contribute to the common ways in which girls have been depicted in global politics as either heroes or victims (Berents, 2015); although in need of Global North educational interventions to save them from 'patriarchy, poverty, and victimization', girls still possess exceptional capacity and economic potential (Koffman et al, 2015: 160), what Switzer (2013: 350) has called 'adolescent female exceptionalism'. Yet it is only by adhering to the capitalist and colonial logics of GR, where girls embody 'individual autonomy, choice, and agency' (Khoja-Moolji, 2018: 99), that they are celebrated. This is a superficial version of girls' agency that is equated with individual choice, contributing to 'the quintessential girl power story where economic prosperity "naturally" occurs once girls "choose" to be successful' (Bent, 2013: 12). Of course, while GR frames girls' success as taking control of their economic and reproductive lives, these 'choices', rather than being inherently empowering for all girls, are more accurately how GR and its programming conceptualize empowerment. Girls, then, must constantly prove their empowerment and exceptionality by performing in alignment with girl power environmentalism – working and not having babies to solve the world's gravest crises on their own.

Despite the increasing visibility of girls in global politics, they are not intrinsically valued by GR as embodied subjects. Instead, Southern girls' agency remains embedded in their resilience and persistent survival of, and eventual triumph over, 'tribal, backward, and traditional' girlhood (Khoja-Moolji, 2018: 99). Even if we are to bracket aside the colonial underpinnings of this sentiment, such conceptualizations of Southern girl empowerment, economic agency, and, resilience cannot be equated with a full endorsement of girls' subjecthood; indeed, these are a 'necessary but not sufficient condition of genuine and robust political subjecthood' (Beier, 2015: 11). In this way, girls are prized by GR not because it thinks them to be exceptional subjects, but, quite the opposite, because their political subjecthood, agency, and activism are not taken seriously. Girls are, to use Taft's (2020: 8) language, considered 'harmless' because *'they are just girls'* (emphasis added). They are symbols of hopeful futures (Taft, 2020) who have overcome past tragedies with a girl power that can potentially be applied to the uncertain future of our climate. As hopeful symbols, though, they are not valued as fully embodied political subjects – certainly not as activists capable of levying serious political and economic challenges to the status quo. Thus, GR's confining definitions of empowerment and agency reinforce our colonial, market-based economic and political systems, those which undergird gendered, class, and racial inequalities (as well as environmental destruction) in the first place. As we will see, however, many girl activists are not convinced by such logics.

Indigenous girls, relationality, and decolonial knowledge

GR's constructions of girlhood can be troubled by looking to experiences of girlhood that are otherwise, specifically Indigenous activists protesting climate change.² Importantly, this chapter understands girlhood, and gender categories more generally, not as natural or self-evident, but rather as constructions that are always in the making (Khoja-Moolji, 2018), both by colonial knowledge-making processes and by girls themselves (de Finney, 2014; Saraswati and Beta, 2021). This chapter's focus on Indigenous girls challenges the persistent whiteness in much of girlhood studies, while it also confronts the colonial assumption that Indigenous girls are passive victims under colonial power (de Finney, 2014). Rather than romanticizing or essentializing Indigenous girls, this chapter embraces 'decolonising knowledge and decolonial knowledge-making' (Mignolo, 2009: 178) by centring 'knowledge and ways of being that flow outside the overwhelming Euro-Western perspectives that define girlhood, girl agency, and girl bodies' (de Finney, 2014: 21). There are five Indigenous girls and young women included in this analysis. They inhabit what is now known as the Americas, but which has been known by Indigenous peoples as Turtle Island, Anahuac, Abya Yala, and many other names. One young woman included in this analysis is a FR fellow, and another appears in various GR videos.

Tia Kennedy – an Afro-Indigenous young woman of the Oneida Nation of the Thames and Walpole Island First Nation – has an FR project aimed at clean water access in Indigenous communities (Girl Rising, nd.b). Her active social media presence signals a political stance that is critical of settler-colonial structures, challenging the Canadian government's apathy towards pressing issues facing Indigenous communities, such as lack of clean water, invasive and illegal pipeline projects, and the genocidal deaths of Indigenous children in residential schools. In another example, Xiye Bastida – who is an Otomi-Toltec activist – is featured multiple times in GR material, yet she regularly problematizes GR's superficial focus on education. In a GR video entitled 'Future Rising: A Girl Rising Earth Day Event', hosted by GR's CEO Christina Lowrey, Bastida questions what and whose knowledge is taught in standard Northern education, and specifically demands reform to the education system away from capitalism and individualism to relearn 'the whole narrative around what our purposes as humans on earth is' (Girl Rising, 2021b).

Indigenous girls also stress the effects of carbon-based economies and extractive industries. Although FR recognizes the relationship between fossil fuels and climate change, it is reluctant to place blame on corporations and industries that have been linked with heavy C02 emissions. For Indigenous girls, however, fossil fuels and extractive industries, and the capitalist logics of growth predicated on environmental exploitation, must be held responsible for environmental destruction. Indigenous girl activists, including Autumn Peltier (an Anishinaabe Indigenous activist from Wiikwemkoong First Nation on Manitoulin Island) and Ta'Kaiya Blaney (a Tla'amin First Nation activist) regularly critique the building of new pipelines and the state's reliance on and support of the fossil fuel industry (TEDx Talks, 2011; Parliament of World's

Religions, 2016; CBC News, 2018; Burton, 2019; McNulty, 2021). Nina Gualinga (of the Kichwa community of Sarayaku) also demands for 'the government to end its contracts with major oil and mining companies and to recognize the value of the Amazon Forest itself', calling for 'Ecuador to stop being economically reliant on fossil fuels' (WWF, 2018). Bastida similarly calls out capitalist extraction-based industries, especially the people who profit from 'hurting our communities', questioning the logics of 'infinite economic growth' while contrasting them with Indigenous beliefs 'of taking care of mother earth, of reciprocity' (Girl Rising, 2021b). In making critiques of oil and mining companies, girls suggest that we must renew our protective relationship with the earth and embrace our rightful role as custodians of our planet and all those who inhabit it: 'as humans, we have a responsibility to be caretakers' and to challenge the very ways in which we conceptualize and value non-human life (Parliament of the World's Religions, 2016). In so doing, Indigenous girls are creating a new story for our planet – one that reunites the human and non-human by using alternative thinking as a 'partial guide towards this goal of re-embedding ourselves within the earth' (Escobar, 2015: 27). Indigenous knowledges, here, challenge the logics of modernity, placing primacy on the ways in which their communities' teachings and understandings of the world, the environment, and Mother Earth must be revisited to combat environmental destruction. Indeed, girls appeal to intergenerational knowledge, citing their beliefs to the generations before them, including ancestors who they do and do not personally know.

For Indigenous girls, the environment is not understood as a set of resources to be exploited for economic productivity and growth, as is the case under modern ideologies. Instead, girls repeatedly afford an intrinsic value to the environment, describing it as sacred (UNIFY, 2014; CBC News, 2018a, 2018b; Burton, 2019; McNulty, 2021). The sacred nature of our planet, and all those beings and things inhabiting it, is understood through a relational onto-epistemology. As Escobar (2015: 18) describes relationality, '*nothing preexist the relations that constitute it.* Said otherwise, things and beings are their relations, they do not exist prior to them' (original emphasis). In alignment with relational thinking, Bastida continues by emphasizing our reciprocal relationship with the earth, something that demands we relearn how to rebalance a harmonious relationship with it, while Blaney has repeatedly shared her culture's understanding that 'everything is connected', where as much as water flows through river and streams, it flows through all of us to such an extent that we might even claim that 'we are water' (UNIFY, 2014). Peltier, too, shares a focus on the ways in which all life is connected, largely through water, in that water is the lifeblood for us, as humans as much as it is for Mother Earth. In one instance, she describes how we are conceived, made, and born in and through water: 'we come from our mother's water, and from her mother's water' (CBC News, 2018a). Here, humans are not above or outside of relations with the earth, its environmental processes, and other animals, but always already complexly embedded within them. This resembles what de Finney (2014: 19) calls 'presencing', the idea that: '"all relations" of ancestors, living things, trees, water, and other "powerful energies" draws on generations of communal knowledge'. It is 'a situated, collective, relational event', which is always 'intimately connected to place, to other forces, and to beyond-human relations' (de Finney, 2014: 19).

For Indigenous activists, environmental protection is not about empowering individual girls to do the work of saving our world, but about our shared responsibilities to act as the earth's caretakers. Indigenous girls problematize GR's individual solutions to climate change, not suggesting that they alone – through education, employment, and the right reproductive choices – are the key to addressing climate change. Indigenous girls, instead, advocate for alternative thinking, calling for collective care and activism when confronting environmental degradation, demanding structural changes to our carbon-based economies and enacting futures not imaginable under capitalism. Indeed, girls advocate for decolonizing our thinking away from capitalist modernity and unfettered economic growth based on extractive exploitation and destruction, where relationality and reciprocity become the foundations for imagining and enacting alternative realities and more egalitarian futures. Indigenous activists propose that since we are always already relationally intertwined with humans and non-humans, as well as land and the environment (Boulton and Brannelly, 2015), we share 'an ethic of mutual responsibility' (de Finney, 2014: 19). That is, these relations suggest we are 'spiritually interconnected, which makes one actor responsible to the other actors' (Datta, 2015: 2013). Rather than the individualistic thinking of girl power environmentalism, where we have 'lost our integral relation with the universe' (Escobar, 2015: 27), Indigenous girls see human life as deeply integrated with non-human life and other organic processes. As Bastida argues, 'the norm is not individualism; the norm should be cooperation', and we, as humans, must relearn values of reciprocity.

For matters of climate change, where its effects are both immediate and existing in a potential, future temporality that we do not yet know, relationality is an important intervention. This is because relationality and reciprocity extend beyond our present temporality and include those of previous and future generations, extending to all human and non-human life, even those who we might not personally know. That is, we all have a responsibility to act as guardians for the earth, for its processes, for the animals, and for any life that cannot speak for itself, not only because they possess an intrinsic value, but also because all our lives – even those we will never know – are in immeasurable relations that demand such responsibility. Arguably, then, these activists participate in what de la Ballacasa (2017: 110) refers to as 'speculative thinking', something that can be described as 'political imagination of the possible' or 'a mode of thought committed to foster visions of other worlds', resembling decolonial notions of pluriversality that suggest 'we are not metaphysically committed to a common world' (Rojas, 2016: 370). That is, Indigenous girls engage in what Rojas (2016: 370) calls 'emancipation-decolonisation' by challenging the limits of knowing and being that modernity imagines to be possible.

Conclusion

Thinking alternatively about girlhoods – not as individualized and empowered but as relational and community-based – reveals girl power environmentalism as limited in its reach, while illuminating the subversive power of Indigenous girl knowledge, especially when girls are supported by their communities and by many other relations. Simply, girls are not alone, nor are they individually and personally responsible for our planet. Caring for our world is a shared responsibility based in our embedded relationality with human and non-human life, and with the earth and its many complex processes. As Blaney aptly asserts, 'It isn't wrong to believe we can change the world, it's only wrong to believe we can change the world alone' (Parliament of World's Religions, 2016). This global climate emergency calls for the efforts of us all – Indigenous communities, non-Indigenous people, girls, boys, non-binary children, and adults – a truly intergenerational collective. In this way, this chapter not only encourages us to ask what we can and should do to support girls' activism, but it also prompts us to reflect on our shared responsibilities to girls and the planet.

Notes

[1] The term 'Indigenous' is an umbrella term used globally to refer to those who are the First Peoples of their lands – existing, living, and protecting these territories since time immemorial. Noting that there is much heterogeneity and complexity within the term Indigenous, when appropriate I refer to girls' specific Indigenous tribal and community identities.

[2] This chapter uses the terms 'girl' and 'young woman' interchangeably given that development programmes, including FR, target girls who are typically between the ages of 16–24, and because the activists reviewed are within this range. While this may potentially engage in the infantilization of adult women, this is also an important interjection into the false dichotomy often drawn between child and adult – especially since a strict demarcation between child as under 18 and adult as over that age misses the blurry, transitional life stage that characterizes late adolescence and early adulthood.

References

Beier, J.M. (2015) 'Children, childhoods, and security studies: An introduction', *Critical Studies on Security* 3(1): 1–13.

Bent, E. (2013) 'A different girl effect: Producing political girlhoods in the "Invest in Girls" climate', in S.K. Nenga and J.K. Taft (eds) *Youth Engagement: The Civic-political Lives of Children and Youth*, Bingley: Emerald Group, pp 3–20.

Berents, H. (2015) 'Hashtagging girlhood: #IAmMalala, #BringBackOurGirls and gendered representations of global politics', *International Feminist Journal of Politics* 18(4): 513–527.

Boulton, A. and Brannelly, T. (2015) 'Care ethics and indigenous values: Political, tribal, personal,' in M. Barnes, T. Brannelly, L. Ward, and N. Ward (eds) *Ethics of Care: Critical Advances in International Perspective*, Brighton: Policy Press, pp 69–82.

Burton, N. (2019) 'Meet the young activists of color who are leading the charge against climate disaster', *Vox*, 11 October. Available at: https://www.vox.com/identities/2019/10/11/20904791/young-climate-activists-of-color/ [Accessed 1 August 2021].

CBC News (2018a) 'Autumn Peltier, 13-year-old water advocate, addressed UN', [online video]. Available at: https://youtu.be/zg60sr38oic [Accessed 1 August 2021].

CBC News (2018b) 'The teen fighting to protect Canada's water – meet Autumn Peltier', [online video]. Available at: https://youtu.be/xqdE_7OZaqE [Accessed 1 August 2021].

Datta, R. (2015) 'A relational theoretical framework and meanings of land, nature, and sustainability for research with Indigenous communities', *Local Environment* 20(1): 102–113.

Escobar, A. (2001) *Encountering Development: The Making and Unmaking of the Third World*, Princeton: Princeton University Press.

Escobar, A. (2015) 'Thinking-feeling with the earth: Territorial struggles and the ontological dimension of the epistemologies of the South', *Revista de Antropología Iberoamericana* 11(1): 11–32.

de Finney, S. (2014) 'Under the shadow of empire: Indigenous girls' presencing as decolonizing force', *Girlhood Studies* 7(1): 8–26.

Girl Rising (nd.a) 'Girl rising'. Available at: https://girlrising.org/ [Accessed 1 August 2021].

Girl Rising (nd.b) 'Meet the future rising fellows', [online]. Available at: https://girlrising.org/future-rising-fellows [Accessed 1 August 2021].

Girl Rising (nd.c) 'Future rising'. Available at: https://www.girlrising.org/future-rising [Accessed 1 August 2021].

Girl Rising (2021a) 'Educate girls, protect our world', [online video]. Available at: https://www.youtube.com/watch?v=4YQRXD4qwrY [Accessed 1 August 2021].

Girl Rising (2021b) 'Future girling: A girl Earth Day event', [online video]. Available at: https://youtu.be/_xr7yeje7ts [Accessed 1 August 2021].

Hayhurst, L.M. (2011) 'Corporatising sport, gender and development: Postcolonial IR feminisms, transnational private governance and global corporate social engagement', *Third World Quarterly* 32(3): 531–549.

Hickel, J. (2020) 'Quantifying national responsibility for climate breakdown: An equality-based attribution approach for carbon dioxide emissions in excess of the planetary boundary', *The Lancet Planetary Health* 4(9): 399–404.

Khoja-Moolji, S. (2018) *Forging the Ideal Educated Girl: The Production of Desirable Subjects in Muslim South Asia*, Oakland: University of California Press.

Koffman, O., Orgad, S., and Gill, R. (2015) 'Girl power and "selfie humanitarianism"', *Continuum* 29(2): 157–168.

de La Bellacasa, M.P. (2017) *Matters of Care: Speculative Ethics in More Than Human Worlds*, Minneapolis: University of Minnesota Press.

Lugones, M. (2010) 'Toward a decolonial feminism', *Hypatia* 25(4): 742–759.

McClintock, A. (1995) *Imperial Leather: Race, Gender, and Sexuality in the Colonial Contest*, London: Routledge.

McNulty, L. (2021) '6 Indigenous climate activists we're celebrating this International Women's Day'. Available at: https://greenisthenewblack.com/indigenous-climate-activists/ [Accessed 1 August 2021].

Mignolo, W.D. (2009) 'Epistemic disobedience, independent thought and decolonial freedom', *Theory, Culture & Society* 26(7–8): 159–181.

Moeller, K. (2013) 'Proving "The Girl Effect": Corporate knowledge production and educational intervention', *International Journal of Educational Development* 33(6): 612–621.

Mohanty, C.T. (1984) 'Under western eyes: Feminist scholarship and colonial discourses', *Boundary* 12(3): 333–358.

Parliament of the World's Religions (2016) 'Ta'Kaiya delivers inspiring Parliament keynote', [online video]. Available at: https://youtu.be/Vj8xf8eBeoc [Accessed 1 August 2021].

Rojas, C. (2016) 'Contesting the colonial logics of the international: Toward a relational politics for the pluriverse', *International Political Sociology* 10(4): 369–382.

Saraswati, M. and Beta, A.R. (2021) 'Knowing responsibly: Decolonizing knowledge production of Indonesian girlhood', *Feminist Media Studies* 21(5): 758–774.

Switzer, H. (2013) '(Post)feminist development fables: The Girl Effect and the production of sexual subjects', *Feminist Theory* 14(3): 345–360.

Taft, J.K. (2020) 'Hopeful, harmless, and heroic: Figuring the girl activist as global savior', *Girlhood Studies* 13(2): 1–17.

TEDx Talks (2011) 'TEDxSTU Ta'Kaiya Blaney', [online video]. Available at: https://youtu.be/9ia5OIorFmc [Accessed 1 August 2021].

UNIFY (2014) 'UNIFY #LoveWater', [online video]. Available at: https://youtu.be/qORL2Ck1Kec [Accessed 1 August 2021].

WWF (2018) 'Activist Nina Gualinga on protecting the Amazon', [online]. Available at: https://www.worldwildlife.org/magazine/issues/winter-2018/articles/activist-nina-gualinga-on-protecting-the-amazon [Accessed 1 August 2021].

13

Children's Intifada: Children as Participants in a Violent Conflict

Timea Spitka

Introduction

On 23 November 2015, Wajih Awad, a 14-year-old from the Qalandiya refugee camp and her 16-year-old cousin Norhin Awad, entered West Jerusalem Mahane Yehuda market armed with scissors, with the intent to stab Israeli civilians. Wajih lightly wounded an elderly man and attempted to stab another civilian before the girls were both shot by an Israeli security officer. Wajih Awad was killed after being knocked on the ground by a passerby and then shot at point blank range by a security officer. Her cousin recovered from two bullet wounds in her stomach and is serving a 13-year prison sentence in Israel. Wajih, the 14-year-old 'terrorist', was apparently seeking revenge for the death of her brother, who was killed by Israeli soldiers after being shot at close range with a rubber bullet to the neck while protesting at a checkpoint. Her 16-year-old cousin claimed that she was accompanying her and did not intend to hurt anyone. Armed with scissors, these girls did not pose a serious threat; only the one man was slightly injured. However, within Israel, the shooting of the girls was considered fully justifiable. The attack by the teens was not an isolated case but was rather one of hundreds of incidents involving Palestinian youth seeking revenge against Israeli civilians subsequent to the 2014 Gaza war and ongoing realities of life under the military occupation. Because so many of the incidents were perpetuated by Palestinian youth lightly armed with scissors, screwdrivers, or knives, the wave of violence during 2015–2016 has often been referred to as the 'knife' or the 'children's intifada'.

Within an internal violent conflict where civilians are not far removed from combatants, children may engage as activists or perpetrators of violent acts, and they can volunteer or be coerced into conducting suicide missions. Although there is much literature on children's vulnerability regarding the effects of war and exploitation (Slone and Mann, 2016; Wessells, 2019), there is far less research into children as perpetrators of violence. Most of the research on children as violent perpetrators has focused on child soldiers abducted and trained by armed groups. Recent research has noted that modern armed conflict has increased the use of child soldiers (Nyamutata, 2020). Violent groups have practical reasons for targeting children for terrorist activities, which include attaining cheap soldiers and increasing the longevity of the groups. Empirical evidence suggests two broad methods of recruitment; the first is described as *predatory* and the latter as *structural* (Almohammad, 2018). Predatory recruitment includes the selection of a recruit based on his/her vulnerability, gaining access, developing emotional trust, ideological pre-schooling, and agency development. Structural recruitment takes place through schools, day camps, religious institutions, and the media (Almohammad, 2018).

Children, however, can also join armed resistance and become violently active due to personal trauma or for ideological reasons. Teens may take part in violent activities as an act of revenge, an escape from personal realities, or they may wish to contribute to national resistance or group aspirations. Within their own national group, children taking active part in violent conflict can be viewed as young heroes or martyrs, validating their engagement in armed resistance. In violent conflict, children from the opposing side are commonly considered to belong to the enemy, making the difference between adults and minors almost irrelevant (Van Reenen, 2006). Labelling children as lethal activists and terrorists, regardless of age or threat, can endanger them with immediate execution. What are the perceptions and justifications for children's engagement in violent conflict, and the rules of engagement towards children and youth suspected of involvement in violent activities?

This chapter will examine the perception and the realities of Palestinian children, or those under the age of 18, engaged in the Israeli/Palestinian conflict. To explore justification of violence against children, I utilize Maynard's typology of six recurring justification mechanisms: dehumanization, guilt attribution, threat construction, deagentification (militarily necessary), virtue talk, and future bias (Maynard, 2014). As noted by Maynard, the first three are about the victims, portraying them as subhuman, guilty, or threatening, which can justify their exclusion from protection. The last three are about the perpetrators, framing the violence as a military necessity, glorifying the perpetrators, or portraying the violence as essential for the future well-being of the group or the state. This can justify the acts by the perpetrators and shield them from repercussions.

Palestinian children living under Israeli military occupation have been on the front lines of the Palestinian–Israeli conflict, subject to shootings, bombings, detentions, and other severe security measures. Palestinian minors make up almost a quarter of all Palestinians injured, and many of the injuries create permanent disabilities. According to the United Nations Office for the Coordination of Humanitarian Affairs (OCHA), between 2008 and the end of 2019, 1,002 Palestinian boys and 244 girls were killed (OCHA, 2022). The majority were killed in Gaza by launched explosives or live bullets. During the same time period, 25,471 Palestinian boys and 2,213 girls were also injured (OCHA, 2022). Although some Palestinian children taking part in attacks have been targeted for recruitment by armed groups, increasing numbers have acted individually as 'lone wolves' in revenge attacks. The majority of the Palestinian children taking part in attacks have not been recruited or trained, using crude instruments to attack in vengeance after experiencing or witnessing a traumatic event. Attacks against Israeli security personnel and civilians have served as justification for severe security measures that infringe on the protection of Palestinians, including children. Palestinian children have also become the centrepiece of a propaganda war as the opposing sides utilize abuse of children to accuse the other of atrocities. Within Israel, most of the conflict-related deaths and injuries of children, including during demonstrations or escalations, involved Palestinian (Arab-Israeli) children. There is seldom an investigation into the shooting of demonstrators, even though many of the injuries result in death or permanent disabilities. Israel has justified its harsh responses against Palestinian children and youth by accusing Palestinians of not caring about their welfare and using their children as terrorists or as human shields.

'Children's intifada'

The wave of youth violence during 2015 and 2016, commonly labelled as the 'knife' or the 'children's intifada', refers to the attacks by mostly young Palestinians living in Israel, Occupied East Jerusalem, and the West Bank against Israeli civilians or security personnel. Between October 2015 and October 2016, there were at least 166 stabbing attacks and 89 attempted stabbings, conducted mostly by Palestinian youth (Shabak, 2022). Children's engagement in the intifada has been the centre of large propaganda campaigns. Pro-Israel propaganda group *Human Rights Voices* (HRV) stated that 'a society that encourages its own children to engage in violence, to become armed combatants, to kill and to maim in pursuit of their parents' ambitions ... is not ready, willing or able to accept the essentials of peaceful coexistence' (Human Rights Voices, 2018). Referring to the children as 'child terrorists', HRV noted that since October 2015 at least 174 Palestinian children carried out 142 separate terrorist attacks, killing 7 Israelis and wounding 58, placing full blame on Palestinians and the United Nations (Human Rights Voices, 2018). However, the HRV report failed to note the context or circumstances of these attacks, or that most of the minors did not pose a threat and were victims of extrajudicial killing. Many of the attacks took place subsequent to the 2014 Gaza war and ensuing clashes and escalations. The Gaza war and its unedited coverage in social media had a strong impact on the young population in the West Bank, East Jerusalem, and within the Arab-Israeli community in Israel. Tensions ran high across the Occupied Territories and included widespread demonstrations and daily clashes that also involved children and youth.

The children's intifada was not organized or directed, and although tensions were high, it came as a surprise to all authorities. Most of the stabbing incidents were linked to lone wolf attacks by individuals not influenced by or working for a particular terrorist organization or a national group. Israel Defense Forces (IDF) Chief of Staff Lieutenant-General Gadi Eisenkot noted that there was no early warning when it came to random knife attacks. 'We have had 101 such attacks over the past three months', he said, 'and have not been able to provide a warning in a single place' (Goodman, 2016: 4). Many of the youth went out of their way to distance themselves from their Palestinian leadership, whom they considered corrupt. At the funerals of the young martyrs, the bodies of the boys or girls were not draped in Hamas or Fatah flags but rather the Palestinian flag, linking the events to the Palestinian national movement rather than a specific group. In most cases, the youth appeared to be enraged by events of the Gaza war or other violent events which they witnessed personally or on social or public media, and they acted in revenge.

For example, two cousins – Hassan, aged 15, and Ahmed, aged 13 – took knives from their Jerusalem homes and attacked and injured civilians in a Jewish settlement. They stabbed and injured two Israelis, including a 13-year-old Jewish boy. Hassan was killed by police, while Ahmed survived being hit by a club and a car. Apparently, the boys decided to attack Israelis without knowledge from anyone, agreeing beforehand that they would only target army-aged men and not women or children. According to Ahmed, his cousin had said, 'Let's go scare them as they scare us' (Brooks, 2017). In an interview, their uncle, who still could not believe what the boys had done, said, 'Our children don't have normal childhoods ... from the minute they open their eyes they wake up into a reality of checkpoints, soldiers, settlers insulting their mom. They see the news from Gaza, children like them, bombed and homeless. They hear about a boy their age, burned alive by Israelis. They are sad and afraid. It's not a healthy environment' (Brooks, 2017).

Many youth involved in acts of violence typically had an awareness that death was a likely outcome of an attack, and in some cases this was also the goal. Although the cases above received much attention in Israeli media because Israelis were injured, in most cases, the lightly armed teens aiming to hurt Israelis were not successful in causing any injuries; however, the

Palestinian youth were often killed in the process. Some attacks by Palestinian youth have been attributed to suicide attempts by teens lacking opportunities or having personal or social problems, knowing they will likely be swiftly killed if they take out a knife or scissors in front of an Israeli soldiers or a security guard. For example, 13-year-old Bara'a Ramadan Owaisi from Qalqilya approached guards at a checkpoint in the northern West Bank without a weapon but did not adhere to orders to stop. She was shot in the leg and told the guards she 'came to die' (Times of Israel, 2016).

Israeli security has dealt with the rise of incidents by Palestinian youth in several different ways, including monitoring social media, arresting youth suspected or involved in violent attacks, and armed confrontation with the youth. Violent and non-violent activism of Palestinian kids and teenagers and fear of recruitment of Palestinian teens by radical groups has made them one of the primary targets for arrest and detention by Israel. According to UNICEF, approximately 7,000 Palestinian children have been detained, interrogated, prosecuted, or imprisoned within the Israeli military justice system in the past 10 years (UNICEF, 2013). Youth have also been shot or killed for looking or acting suspicious. Teens as young as 14 found to be holding knives or scissors have been killed on the spot by Israeli security personnel or vigilante civilians, even if they did not pose a treat. The general escalation in violence, political incitement, influence of social media, and vigilantism have all contributed to the killing of teens. Human rights organizations have noted that Israeli security officers and soldiers have been quick to shoot to kill instead of acting in a manner appropriate to the nature of each incident, and have criticized political and public support for extrajudicial killings (Adalah, 2015). The subsequent sections will examine Israeli and Palestinian rhetoric, justifications, and projection of blame regarding policies of prevention, security, safety, and well-being of Palestinian youth.

Israeli justifications, rhetoric, and projection of blame

Israeli leadership blames Palestinian leaders and parents for Palestinian children's injuries and deaths. Historically, most speeches by Israeli leadership about the welfare of Palestinian children blame the Palestinians for the deaths of their own children. Former Israeli Prime Minister Golda Meir famously thought to have said: 'We can forgive the Arabs for killing our children. We cannot forgive them for forcing us to kill their children. We will only have peace with the Arabs when they love their children more than they hate us' (Jewish Virtual Library, 2023). Current Israeli leadership justifies its harsh responses against Palestinian children and youth by accusing Hamas, and Palestinians in general, of not caring about the welfare of their own kids. In one of many Benjamin Netanyahu video clips on this topic, the Israeli

Prime Minister notes, 'A Palestinian father holds up his 4-year-old son. He pleads with Israeli border police to kill his own child. He shouts: shoot this little boy. His boy. ... Encouraging someone to murder a child let alone your child is probably the most inhumane thing a person can do. ... If parents don't respect their own children's lives how will they respect the lives of their neighbours?' (Netanyahu, 2016).

The children's intifada heightened justifications for more aggressive security against Palestinian minors and resulted in changes in legislation within Israel. In 2016, the Knesset approved a new bill that allowed a child 'terrorist' as young as 12 to be jailed within Israel (Dearden, 2016). The justification for the new legislation noted: 'The seriousness that we attach to terror and acts of terror that cause bodily injury and property damage, and the fact that these acts of terror are being carried out by minors, demands a more aggressive approach including towards minors who are convicted' (OCHA, 2016). Anat Berko, a member of Benjamin Netanyahu's Likud party, said that the law is born of necessity: 'A society is allowed to protect itself. To those who are murdered with a knife in the heart it does not matter if the child is 12 or 15' (Dearden, 2016).

The political rhetoric insinuated that Palestinians do not care about their children and have no problem sending their sons and daughters to the front lines to be killed (Gordon and Perugini, 2018). Danny Danon, Israel's ambassador to the United Nations, rebuffed international condemnation of shooting of live ammunition at unarmed Gaza demonstrators, including many children, and called on the Security Council to condemn Hamas for its use of children as human shields: 'During these protests, expected to escalate as part of the "Days of Rage" declared by the Palestinian leadership, Hamas, the internationally recognized terrorist organization, plans to exploit innocent Palestinian children as human shields and place them directly in harm's way' (Times of Israel, 2018).

Threat construction is prevalent within the Israeli ideological narrative as all Palestinians, especially those living in Gaza and Occupied West Bank, are commonly labelled as threatening. Children and teenagers are not exempt from this categorization. IDF shooting of unarmed demonstrators has been framed as a military necessity in order to show force and achieve victory. Former Southern Command IDF commander Brigadier-General Zvika Fogel noted 'They [Hamas] have patience and the only way to kill that patience is to bring it to their homes and not wait for a tunnel, kite, or rocket. We need to give them a bullet in the head and ensure quiet' (Cohen, 2018).

IDF General Fogel confirmed that when snipers shoot at protestors, including children, they are doing so deliberately under clear and specific orders, though not necessarily with orders to kill. 'I know how these orders are given. ... It is not the whim of one or the other sniper who identifies the small body of a child now and decides he'll shoot. Someone marks the target for him very well and tells him exactly why one has to shoot and what the threat is from that individual. And to my great sorrow, sometimes when you shoot at a small body and you intended to hit his arm or shoulder, it goes even higher' (Cohen, 2018). The children's intifada, similar to events of the Gaza war and the shooting of unarmed Palestinian demonstrators, was blamed on Palestinian leadership. PM Netanyahu noted, 'But I think President Abbas has to stop this incitement. You just saw examples of him lying, barefaced lies. "An innocent child executed by Israelis." No. He's not innocent and he wasn't executed. He tried to murder innocent people, almost succeeded' (Netanyahu, 2015).

Extrajudicial killings of Palestinian teens received widespread support both from the politicians and from much of the Israeli public. Once labelled as terrorists, young perpetrators of violence ceased to be viewed as children. Several members of the Israeli government praised the extrajudicial killings by the police, private security guards, and vigilante civilians. Interior Security Minister Gilad Arden stated that 'every terrorist should know that he will not survive the attack he is about to commit' (B'Tselem, 2015). MK Yair Lapid declared that 'you have to shoot to kill anyone who pulls out a knife or screwdriver' (B'Tselem, 2015). When it came to the children's intifada, some of the senior military officers took a more moderate tone than that of the politicians. They emphasized that killing youth who did not pose a threat was not appropriate behaviour for a soldier. IDF Chief of Staff Lieutenant-General Gadi Eisenkot emphasized that 'I don't want to see a soldier empty a magazine [to shoot] a young girl with scissors' (Amir and Hashavua, 2016). There has been little investigation, apology, punishment, or regret for the shooting of Palestinian children, which has most commonly been justified as a military necessity and blamed on Palestinian neglect. The key implication in Israeli rhetoric is that Palestinians do not love their children and send them out of neglect or sacrifice them to make Israel look bad.

Palestinian justifications, rhetoric, and projection of blame

Although the majority of speeches by Palestinian leaders focus on blaming Israelis for the deaths of Palestinian children, there is a significant difference in the justifications of attacks and the engagement of Palestinian children between Hamas and the Palestinian Authority (PA). Seeking international support, the PA leadership under Mahmoud Abbas has officially adopted an internationally sanctioned moderate position, taking a strong stand against terrorism while promoting and justifying Palestinian children's engagement only within the framework of non-violent resistance. Palestinian media, schools, and armed groups, however, have continued to encourage the engagement of children in the ongoing resistance and armed struggle. The death of Palestinian youth in violent confrontations with Israelis is commonly presented as a great victory. During matriculation in 2016, a front-page article in Al-Hayat Al-Jadida stated, 'The places of 16 students was not missing from yesterday's announcement of the general high school [exam] results … the occupation's bullets ended their lives and prevented them from taking their final exams, as they became martyrs in Paradise. Sixteen [students] passed the difficult [test] of dying as martyrs for the homeland, since dying as a martyr is the path of excellence and supremacy' (Memri, 2016: 119).

Glorification of martyrs or virtue talk has been utilized in the justification of violence by Palestinian perpetrators, including teens, who are generally portrayed and praised as martyrs. The June 2014 kidnapping and murder of the three Israeli teenagers living in a West Bank settlement was one of the sparks that escalated into the 2014 Gaza war. PA President Mahmoud Abbas denounced the kidnapping and called on Hamas and Israel to refrain from violence (Ravid, 2014). Although Hamas did not take responsibility for the attack, the leadership justified and praised the murder. The head of political wing of Hamas, Khaled Mashal, said that the teens, aged 16, 16, and 19, were 'settlers and soldiers in the Israeli army' (Miller, 2014). 'Blessed be the hands that captured them. … This is a Palestinian duty, the responsibility of the Palestinian people. Our prisoners must be freed; not Hamas's prisoners – the prisoners of the Palestinian people. … The three were not "youths", as Israel calls them, but first and foremost settlers … and not even regular settlers, but armed ones' (Ciralsky, 2014). Mashal referred to the Palestinian men who murdered the Israeli teens as 'martyrs' and employed guilt attribution when he said 'But Israel is killing our sons all the time' (Ciralsky, 2014). A senior Hamas official, Salah Arouri, boasted that the group's military wing was behind the attack on the Israeli youths. 'The al-Qassam's mujahedeen were the ones to carry out [the abduction] in show of support for the prisoners' hunger strike' (Khoury, 2014).

Hamas, under the political leadership of Khaled Mashal, has attempted to distinguish itself from terrorist organizations such as ISIS by justification of its methods as being militarily necessary, or deagentification: 'We do not target civilians, and we try most of the time to aim at military targets and Israeli bases. But we admit that we have a problem. We do not have sophisticated weapons. We do not have the weapons available to our enemy so aiming is difficult. We do promise you, though, that we will try in the future and we will warn people. We have given warnings to Israeli civilians. We promise that if we get more precise weapons, we will only target military targets' (Ciralsky, 2014). Mashal blamed military necessity and the lack of serious and precise weapons for the indiscriminate aiming of rockets which injure and kill Israeli civilians, including children. The head of Hamas in Gaza, Yahya Sinwar, has held a toddler dressed as a Hamas fighter, describing the sacrifice of Palestinian children 'as an offering for Jerusalem and the Right of Return' (Memri, 2018).

The support for the use of violence remains high among the Palestinian population, and in 2016 during the height of the attacks, public opinion polls showed 67% support and 31% opposition to the use of knives in confrontations with Israel (PSR Survey, 2016). About three quarters (73 per cent) of Palestinians, however, opposed the participation of young schoolgirls in the stabbing attacks, though a quarter of the population supported it (PSR Survey, 2016). Publicly, Abbas has argued for peaceful resistance by Palestinians, whether in Gaza, the West Bank, or Jerusalem. According to Abbas, Palestinian children should not take part in the confrontation with Israel because he doesn't want the Palestinian nation to become a deformed nation. He has, however, encouraged youth to be active in non-violent resistance. He has publicly called Ahed Tamimi, a 17-year-old Palestinian activist, a model for the Palestinian struggle: 'The Palestinian girl Ahed Tamimi is a model for the Palestinian struggle for freedom, independence and the establishment of our independent Palestinian state' (Rasgon, 2018). Ahed Tamimi became a symbol of Palestinian resistance when, at the age of 16, she slapped an Israeli soldier. The slap, which was caught on camera, cost the teenager a year in prison and made her a national teen hero. Tamimi, like many other Palestinian minors, wants to create better life for Palestinians, noting that she fights against the occupation: 'I always say I am a freedom fighter. So, I will not be the victim' (Holmes and Taha, 2018).

Conclusion

Cycles of violence and ongoing harsh policies of military occupation have made Palestinian children and youth not only vulnerable to being accidently injured and killed or recruited by extreme groups but also at times to becoming frustrated enough to take violent action. In light of the trauma endured by Palestinians under continuous policies of occupation and discrimination, including witnessing violent acts and the humiliation of siblings and parents, the actions of the youth are unsurprising. Acting alone without training or lethal equipment, youth commonly do not pose a serious risk to security or soldiers but have been frequently killed. While children and teens can be injured or killed attempting to do harm, youths can also be killed due to being profiled as terrorists. The shooting and killing of Palestinian children engaged in violent as well as non-violent activism has been publicly justified, adding fuel to the fire.

Several types of justification of violence against children have been utilized by Israeli and Palestinian policy makers. The militarily necessary argument and virtue talk have been most commonly used by Palestinian militants and governing institutions both to justify violent acts against Israeli youth and the engagement of Palestinian youth in violent activities. Dehumanization, guilt attribution, and threat construction have been commonly used by Israeli authorities to paint Palestinian minors as dangerous and justify their demise. Guilt attribution is also common, portraying all Palestinians, or those living within certain regions, guilty of collective terrorism. Children and youth who are not trained or armed with lethal weapons do not generally pose a serious threat, especially when attempting to approach armed soldiers or security guards. However, once labelled as terrorists, even when they do not pose danger, they may be killed. Justifications of the violence, a rhetoric of blaming the other, and lack of investigation or remorse into the deaths of Palestinian children and youth have been among the most crucial issues in the Israeli/Palestinian conflict. Fundamental changes have to be made to alter the current reality, end violence with impunity, and provide security to Palestinian children, even those engaged in violent activities.

References

Adalah (2015) 'Human rights organizations in Israel: Politicians' calls to police and soldiers to shoot rather than arrest endorse the killing of Palestinians', 14 October. Available at: https://www.adalah.org/en/content/view/8659 [Accessed 4 April 2020].

Almohammad, A. (2018) 'ISIS child soldiers in Syria: The structural and predatory recruitment, enlistment, pre-training indoctrination, training, and deployment', *The International Centre for Counter-Terrorism – The Hague* 8(14). Available at: https://www.icct.nl/publication/isis-child-soldiers-syria-structural-and-predatory-recruitment-enlistment-pre-training [Accessed 7 June 2023].

Amir, N. and Hashavua, M. (2016) 'IDF chief: No need to pump bullets into Palestinian girl with scissors', *Jerusalem Post*, 17 February. Available at: https://www.jpost.com/arab-israeli-conflict/idf-chief-no-need-to-pump-bullets-into-palestinian-girl-with-scissors-445237 [Accessed 26 October 2022].

Brooks, G. (2017) 'The dovekeeper and the children's intifada', *The New Yorker*, 27 May. Available at: https://www.newyorker.com/books/page-turner/the-dovekeeper-and-the-childrens-intifada [Accessed 26 October 2022].

B'Tselem (2015) 'Politicians' calls to police and soldiers to shoot rather than arrest endorse the killing of Palestinians', 14 October. Available at: https://www.btselem.org/press_releases/20151014_summary_execution_joint_statement [Accessed 10 October 2022].

Ciralsky, A. (2014) 'Interview with Hamas's Khalid Marshal on the Gaza war, tunnels, and ISIS,' *Vanity Fair*, 21 October. Available at: https://www.vanityfair.com/news/politics/2014/10/khalid-mishal-hamas-interview?fbclid=IwAR0fTI1kGdy0bxZy0CN9TckMk34Ob8KFYNsE56CUR9vDsx4aQPJswbzszDw [Accessed 15 October 2022].

Cohen, S. (2018) 'The solution to Gaza: "A bullet to the head"', *Arutz Sheva*, 6 June. Available at: http://www.israelnationalnews.com/News/News.aspx/247034 [Accessed 26 October 2022].

Dearden, L. (2016) 'Israel approves new law to jail child "terrorists" as young as 12', *Independent*, 3 August. Available at: http://www.independent.co.uk/news/world/middle-east/israel-approves-new-law-to-jail-palestinian-child-terrorists-as-young-as-12-human-rights-stabbings-a7170641.html [Accessed 25 November 2017].

Goodman, H. (2016) 'The knife and the message: The first 100 days of the new Palestinian uprising', in H. Goodman and Y. Kuperwasser (eds) *The Knife and the Message: The Roots of the New Palestinian Uprising*, Jerusalem Centre for Public Affairs. Available at: https://dokumen.tips/documents/the-knife-and-the-messagethe-roots-of-the-new-palestinian-din-the-first-100.html?page=1 [Accessed 7 November 2022].

Gordon, N. and N. Perugini (2018) 'The fallacy of Israel's human shields claims in Gaza', *Al Jazeera*, 18 June. Available at: https://www.aljazeera.com/indepth/opinion/fallacy-israel-human-shields-claims-gaza-180618085404724.html [Accessed 26 October 2022].

Human Rights Voices (2018) 'A Society not ready for statehood: Palestinian children who kill and their adult enablers', 6 September. Available at: http://www.humanrightsvoices.org/assets/attachments/documents/Report_on_Palestinian_Child_Terrorists._September_2018.2.pdf [Accessed 26 October 2022].

Holmes, O. and Taha, S. (2018) 'Ahed Tamimi: "I am a freedom fighter. I will not be the victim"', 30 July. Available at: https://www.theguardian.com/world/2018/jul/30/ahed-tamimi-i-am-a-freedom-fighter-i-will-not-be-the-victim-palestinian-israel. [Accessed 3 April 2023].

Jewish Virtual Library (2023) 'Golda Meir Quotes on Israel and Judaism'. Available at: https://www.jewishvirtuallibrary.org/golda-meir-quotes-on-israel-and-judaism [Accessed 26 June 2023].

Kelman, H.C. (2001) 'Reflections on social and psychological processes of legitimization and delegitimization', in J.T. Jost and B. Major (eds) *The Psychology of Legitimacy: Emerging Perspectives on Ideology, Justice, and Intergroup Relations*, Cambridge: Cambridge University Press, pp 54–73.

Khoury, J. (2014) 'Hamas claims responsibility for three Israeli teens' kidnapping and murder', *Haaretz*, 21 August. Available at: https://www.haaretz.com/hamas-admits-kidnap-murder-of-3-teens-1.5260283 [Accessed 26 October 2022].

Maynard, J.L. (2014) 'Rethinking the role of ideology in mass atrocities', *Terrorism and Political Violence* 26(5): 821–841.

Memri (2016) 'With publication of high school finals results, Palestinian Authority press notes deaths of students who carried out stabbing attacks, stresses: "Dying as a martyr is the path of excellence and superiority"'. Available at: https://www.memri.org/reports/publication-high-school-finals-results-palestinian-authority-press-notes-deaths-students-who#_edn1 [Accessed 1 September 2022].

Memri (2018) 'Hamas leader in Gaza Yahya Sinwar: Our people took off their military uniforms and joined the marches; we decided to turn the bodies of our women and children into a dam blocking Arab collapse'. Available at: https://www.memri.org/tv/hamas-leader-yahya-sinwar-our-people-took-off-their-uniforms-and-joined-the-marces [Accessed 11 October 2022].

Miller, E. (2014) 'Hamas chief claims three kidnapped youths were soldiers', *The Times of Israel*, 24 June. Available from: https://www.timesofisrael.com/hamas-chief-claims-no-responsibility-for-kidnapping-but-praises-it/ [Accessed 26 October 2022].

Netanyahu, B. (2016) 'This video shook me to the core of my being'. Available at: https://www.youtube.com/watch?v=j-kOwFA8xZ4 [Accessed 11 October 2022].

Nyamutata, C. (2020) 'Young terrorists or child soldiers? ISIS children, international law and victimhood', *Journal of Conflict & Security Law* 25(2): 237–261.

OCHA (2022) 'Data on casualties'. Available at: https://www.ochaopt.org/data/casualties [Accessed 1 November 2022].

PSR Survey (2016) 'Palestinian public opinion poll no-58'. Available at: http://www.pcpsr.org/en/node/625 [Accessed 17 September 2022].

Rasgon, A. (2018) 'Abbas hosts, praises soldier-slapper Ahed Tamimi amid celebration of her release', *The Times of Israel*, 29 July. Available at: https://www.timesofisrael.com/abbas-praises-soldier-slapper-ahed-tamimi-amid-celebrations-after-release/ [Accessed 11 October 2022].

Ravid, B. (2014) 'Abbas condemns kidnapping of Israeli teens, death of Palestinian youth', *Haaretz*, 16 June. Available at: https://www.haaretz.com/.premium-abbas-condemns-kidnapping-1.5252048 [Accessed 11 October 2022].

Shabak (2022) 'Terrorism statistics'. Available at: https://www.shabak.gov.il/english/pages/terror.html#=1 [Accessed 15 August 2022].

Slone, M. and Mann, S. (2016) 'Effects of war, terrorism and armed conflict on young children: A systematic review', *Child Psychiatry & Human Development* 47(6): 950–965.

Times of Israel (2016) 'Palestinian teen accused of attempting "suicide by soldier" denies wanting to die', TOI Staff, 23 September. Available at: https://www.timesofisrael.com/palestinian-teen-accused-of-attempting-suicide-by-soldier-denies-wanting-to-die/ [11 September 2022].

Times of Israel (2018) 'Israel demands UN condemn Hamas's use of children, civilians as human shields', *The Times of Israel*, 14 May. Available AT: https://www.timesofisrael.com/israel-demands-un-condemn-hamass-use-of-children-civilians-as-human-shields/ [Accessed 26 October 2022].

UNICEF (2013) 'Children in Israeli military detention: Observations and Recommendations', Bulletin No. 1, October. Available at: https://www.unicef.org/sop/reports/children-israeli-military-detention [Accessed 7 June 2023].

Van Reenen, P. (2006) 'Children as victims in the Israeli/Palestinian conflict: Policing realities and police training', in C.W. Greenbaum, P.E. Veerman, and N. Bacon-Shnoor (eds) *Protection of Children During Armed Political Conflict: A Multidisciplinary Perspective*, Oxford: Intersentia, pp 371–393.

Wessells, M. (2019) *Child Soldier: From Violence to Protection*, Cambridge, MA: Harvard University Press.

14

Children's Agency and Co-construction of Everyday Militarism(s): Representations and Realities of War in Ukrainian Children's Art, 2014–2022

Kristina Hook and Iuliia Hoban

Introduction

The Russian Federation's full-scale invasion of Ukraine in 2022 stunned the world with its brutal, targeted violence against civilians. Systematic war crimes by the Russian military have not spared children, who featured prominently as objects of violence in global media coverage (Falk, 2022). As children have been killed, trafficked, wounded, and maimed, this vulnerable group also comprises significant portions of the worst refugee and internally displaced person (IDP) crisis in Europe since World War II (Vierlinger, 2022). While many analysts trace how Russia's war against Ukraine is fundamentally changing the global geopolitical order, we note that this war is likewise profoundly shaping the youngest generation of Europe's largest country in ways that are still unfolding.

However, as we explore in this chapter, children's intersections and interactions with this war and its resultant militarism began nearly a decade ago. Although the current escalation has intensified the themes we explore in this chapter, we have elected to restrict our focus to 2014–2022 to explore how these latent realities shaped Ukrainian children and young adults today – including Ukraine's youngest soldiers who were in elementary school when this war began. The current war began when the Russian Federation annexed Ukraine's Crimean Peninsula and sparked armed conflict in the Donbas region of eastern Ukraine. Under the pretext of a separatist conflict, the Russian government funnelled military, financial, and political support to proxy forces, leading to protracted conflict that received muted global attention (Dunn and Bobick, 2014; Galeotti, 2016; Government of the Netherlands, 2018; Marten, 2019; Hook, 2020; Troianovski, 2021).

Even before February 2022, the United Nations estimated that at least 14,000 lives had been lost, 1.6 million IDPs driven from their homes, and approximately 30,000 people wounded (International Crisis Group [ICG], 2022). In 2020, the United Nations Children's Agency, UNICEF, estimated that the war had 'deeply affected' 580,000 children near the eastern frontlines and in areas controlled by Russia's proxy forces, with 200,000 children requiring urgent psychosocial support, another 200,000 driven from their homes, and a fifth of conflict zone schools damaged by kinetic violence like shelling, causing widespread disruption of education (UNICEF, 2020). Although these dynamics have significantly worsened, children in eastern Ukraine had experienced life-threatening conditions including fuel shortages; freezing temperatures; associated medical conditions like respiratory illnesses; nutritional deficiencies; and water, sanitation, and health access issues long prior to 2022. UNICEF noted that a polio outbreak was possible due to destroyed infrastructure and healthcare (UNICEF, 2020). As reported to the first author during ethnographic fieldwork in Ukraine in 2019, a frontline humanitarian worker in the Donbas conflict region recalled an interaction with a five-year-old child, whose entire lifespan had been impacted by wartime shelling and who incredulously asked if 'it was true that people used to walk outside whenever they wanted'.

More than statistics, these numbers indicate that compounding forms of disorientation were experienced by children growing up in the Donbas conflict areas as well as the Ukrainian regions that were once safer from military violence. Adding to direct violence, wartime mobilization since 2014 has transformed children's lived experiences in the national shadow of war, shifting childhood into a 'site for displacement and maneuvering for militarization', particularly surrounding narratives of the conflict itself (Agathangelou and Killian, 2011: 40). As violence limits important childhood development activities like play, spontaneity, exploration, social interaction, and routine-based intuition (Johnson et al, 1987), other forms of children's expression have grown in their formative influence, including art, literature, and media.

Even prior to Russia's escalation of the conflict, adult actions shaped children's developing awareness of what constituted 'normal' while consciously and unconsciously incentivizing children to reproduce the underlying militarization that had come to characterize prevailing social frameworks. As we explore how this conflict militarized everyday practices at the community level from 2014 to 2022, we focus on children's art programmes to demonstrate the complex nature of children's agency. Utilizing primary data gathered during ethnographic fieldwork by the first author during 2015–2019, this chapter explores sponsored art programmes created for the purpose of enabling Ukrainian children to process their wartime experiences. The investigation of this medium reveals the subtle, pervasive nature of militarization in hidden places of Ukrainian society – dynamics once possible when direct warfare was primarily limited to eastern Ukraine. Paradoxically, these art projects simultaneously impeded children's agency by reducing the boundaries of socially acceptable conflict interpretations and encouraging children to reproduce adult-generated conflict narratives while also providing spaces for children's agency and even resistance to these narratives to emerge in their artistic reflections and representations. As such, children not only reproduced but also co-constructed militarisms and conflict narratives through performative, meaning-making practices like artistic representations. Thus, by examining these art programmes and the works that children produced, this analysis elicits the tensions of children's agency 'as [children are] both potentially autonomous and a valued object of capture by other actors' (Beier, 2020: 13). Furthermore, we stress the power of children's performative involvement in war-related creative processes like art in this context and beyond. Significantly, performativity theory suggests that artistic depictions – like language – not only describe the world but operate as a form of social action that can bring new realities into being (Geertz, 1981; Hall, 1999).

Defying binary conceptions of children as either objects or subjects in the militarization process, we address the complexities of children's agency in the Ukrainian context and in other wartime contexts. As they participate in the co-construction of conflict narratives and interpretations, we highlight how the diffusion of militarization from the everyday sphere to national discourse to global geopolitics is also not a straightforward, unidirectional process (Henry and Natanel, 2016). Instead, children's art projects in Ukraine add further credence to the view of these dynamics as layered and multi-scalar, where the intimacies of everyday life are not merely impacted by the national or global but where instead military activities are themselves inherently born from these intimacies in the first place. Thus, this chapter continues an ongoing conversation regarding how children are 'engaged in encounters with militarism, wherein they are active in interpreting, negotiating, and resisting' (Beier, 2020: 13; see also McEvoy-Levy, 2018; Woodyer and Carter, 2020; and Chapters 2 and 11, this volume), with their actions reverberating beyond the local level. As we explore one example of children's activities in the midst of war and mobilization, we theorize more broadly about the complexities of children's agency in global political settings, enhancing our overall understanding of this unique population group's intersections and interactions with militarism, structural and direct violence, and socially supported security paradigms.

Theoretical considerations and existing literature

Building on compelling literature concerned with the intersection of popular culture and International Relations (Weldes, 2003; Grayson et al, 2009; Dittmer and Gray, 2010; Grayson, 2013; ; McEvoy-Levy, 2018; Woodyer and Carter, 2020), we analyse children's art as one of the sites 'in which identities, practices, institutions and objectives are discursively constituted' (Weldes and Rowley, 2015: 19). In their analysis, conducted in collaboration with young scholars, an observation is suggested that 'popular culture can be violent, racist, gender stereotyping' (McEvoy-Levy et al, 2020: 183). At the same time, it offers spaces for these ideas to be adapted, experimented with, and subverted, thus providing different 'modes of expression across political spectrums' (McEvoy-Levy et al, 2020: 183). Resonating with Kyle Grayson, this chapter explores children's art as an artifact that provides additional capacity to engage in 'political argument in terms and language' (Grayson, 2013: 378) that are more familiar to a given audience. Examining art as a medium of children's pop culture allows us to analyse narratives of power politics, practices of inclusion and exclusion that underpin 'us versus them' thinking, and memorialization strategies that inform politicization and even the militarization of childhood.

In this analysis, we therefore aim to contribute to the debate as to whether processes of militarization infiltrate the intimate spaces of children's everyday life under the shadow of an armed conflict once restricted to only one region of Ukraine (Enloe, 2002, 2007; Woodward, 2004; Bernazzoli and Flint, 2009; Dowler, 2012; Pain, 2015; Henry and Natanel, 2016; Wibben, 2018; Hoban, 2022). Influenced by Linda Ahall's (2016) observation that militarization practices dance their way into everyday life, this chapter examines performative meaning-making practices in children's art to explore the banality of militarization (Bernazzoli and Flint, 2009) in Ukrainian society prior to the 2022 escalation. We question whether art as a medium allows children to turn violence into play, thus broadening military influences into everyday civilian life (Enloe, 2002; Pain, 2015). At the same time, this chapter recognizes and draws on the contribution from literature on how children encounter and engage with militarism through interpretation, play, adaptation, disengagement, and resistance (McEvoy-Levy, 2018; Woodyer and Carter, 2020). Analysing narratives of militarisms – which intensified in Ukraine with Russia's first invasion and the onset of direct kinetic conflict in 2014 – across children's art, we investigate how children act as 'both agentic subjects and objects' (Basham, 2020: 138; see also Dowler, 2012; Basham, 2015; Ahall, 2019). This case study therefore contributes to the conversation on 'the complex entanglements of childhood, peace, and conflict and the ways in which children affect and are affected by them' as well as spaces to engage in resistance (Beier, 2020: 8). In the context of militarization in Ukraine during 2014–2022, this more complex picture of lived childhoods allows for a critical analysis, revealing spaces of everyday violence and the roles children perform in shaping them. Agathangelou and Killian (2011: 22), in their analysis of militarization of Cypriot childhood, for example, show how a 'child's emergence as militarized' represents a solution to geopolitical and social problems. Woodyer and Carter (2020), in their study of militarization of childhood through toys, reveal how the entanglement of childhood with geopolitics finds children engaged with militarisms as political subjects. In this chapter, we explore how art becomes the space in which children's agency is continuously negotiated and produced in relation to others.

Children's agency and art in wartime Ukraine, 2014–2022

This analysis is based on primary data in the form of ethnographic participant-observation and artwork photographs gathered by the first author during 2.5 years of fieldwork conducted across 32 cities, towns, and villages in Ukraine from 2015 to 2019, specifically her presence at both formal and informal exhibitions of children's artwork related to the armed conflict. We relied upon our own translations of these materials, aided by the second author's native language skills in Ukrainian. Given the complexity and sensitivity of the ongoing conflict during this period, this work was aided by additional contextual information gathered by the first author's interviewing and ethnographic fieldwork, including in war-affected regions, as well as feminist methodologies which guided us to question the gaps, silences, and erasures present in prevailing narratives and visual depictions of the armed conflict (Nast, 1994; Ackerly et al, 2006; Doucet and Mauthner, 2007; Woodward et al, 2017). After gathering these materials and associated metadata, visual data were organized and analysed systematically using observational data analysis techniques proposed by Russell Bernard, Amber Wutich, and Gery Ryan (2016).

Analysing underlying dynamics of sponsored art programmes for conflict-affected children

During the 2014–2022 phase of the Russia-Ukraine war, children's art that reflected on themes of war or war-linked art was regularly exhibited by Ukrainian and international actors, ranging from Ukrainian historical museums to displays sponsored by foreign embassies in Kyiv. One example of sponsored art projects for Ukrainian youth include the YouCreate project implemented by UNICEF in partnership with Terre des hommes-Ukraine, financially sponsored by the European Union Humanitarian Aid fund.[1] The Embassy of Lithuania similarly sponsored an art cooperation project for children in the war zone, based on an existing Lithuanian project.[2] Art by Ukrainian children travelled even further West, including an exhibition hosted at the Royal Museum of Natural Sciences in Brussels, entitled, 'Peace and War through the Eyes of Donbas Children'.[3] Ukrainian authorities also sponsored, hosted, and collaborated with such initiatives, with one representative example an exhibition connected to the 'Restoration of Donbas' project at the Center for Children and Youth Creativity in Zhytomyr in north-western Ukraine.[4]

As will be discussed further, art therapy is often linked with efforts to help traumatized children process complex emotions, with these international and Ukrainian art initiatives likely grounded in such motivations. Without calling such intentions into question, we note several ways in which such state or community-sponsored initiatives further commodified children's trauma and wove militarism into children's everyday lived experiences. Of note, art therapy projects, especially those funded by foreign embassies and multilateral organizations, can involve large financial investments, such as the Lithuanian embassy's declaration of €16,500 spent on the project described above through the Development Cooperation and Democracy Promotion Programme.[5] Particularly due to war-related Ukrainian currency plunges, this sum represents significant ground impact and likely fostered conditions in which children were strongly encouraged by authority figures in their environments to participate in these programmes. Also motivated by desires to receive positive attention and even celebrity as the art programmes were featured in local, national, and even international press and exhibitions, the specific depictions drawn by the children were filtered through internal calculations of how to 'succeed'. This scenario underscores many aspects in which children's participation in war-related art was not organic, nor an agency-based representation of them regaining control.

Furthermore, with the majority of human communication conveyed in non-verbal cues, descriptions of children's art exhibits in the media as well as similarities across the children's representations hint at other underlying power dynamics that allowed for the mediation of children's agency. Translated from Ukrainian, the media coverage of the Zhytomyr event noted that the art project organizers had first rejected the idea to hold an art competition, fearing that childhood trauma would result in pictures dominated by black and bleak imagery (for further discussions of war memorialization narratives in this context, see Danilova, 2015; Khrebtan-Hörhager, 2016).[6] Instead, children submitted more than 300 images, and the event is described as 'exceed[ing] all expectations – the children not only compared peace and war but also drew a happy future in which they live in a peaceful Ukraine'.[7] In the hindsight of Russia's brutal escalation in 2022, these subtle pressures on children to visualize only optimistic versions of the future are striking. Also of significance for this analysis, the media coverage notes, in 'the process of discussing the works and determining the winner, the jury members took into account not only the artistic value of the drawing but also their content and emotional load'.[8] Compounding these subtle, perhaps unintentional pressures, the transformation of war-related art into a competition further curated the content of children's pictures. The example of these dynamics, when the children likely received non-verbal signalling that 'dark' depictions of the war were not welcome or that the art exhibition would 'fail', illustrates another tensions between recognized aspects of children's agency, in this case images that visualize an optimistic future of the country and those that complicate adult assumptions (Basham, 2020).

Instead of depicting their war-related experiences in whatever way they chose, children's agency was constrained by adult delineations over the acceptable boundaries for filtering and portraying the war. The competitive framing also incentivized simplistic, non-subjective art that external evaluators could both understand and rank as valuable and impactful. Children were thus encouraged to depict their brutal wartime experiences and ideas about the future according to the norms, cues, rules, desires, and even aesthetic standards of the adult viewers of their work rather than having an unburdened space to visually communicate whatever they liked in whatever visual form they chose. Displacing children's agency over their own artistic depictions through subtle pressures and competitive rankings added to their overall loss of control in their environment and conflict narratives. Without being able to depict their traumas in such subjective, personal depictions as dashes, dots, and lines, the militarization of children was further deepened as depictions instead of non-symbolic war imagery – tanks, bullets, soldiers, and so on – flowed from their fingertips in response to the adult authorities' social, emotional, and financial cues. Wartime emotional processing (that is, 'black' depictions were not welcome) intuitively signalled to their young developing brains that there was a 'correct' way to process, communicate, and remember their own lived experiences, while one-dimensional future promises ('everything will be wonderful in the future') were instead unconsciously incentivized. Instead of allowing children agency, creativity, and space, such underlying structures furthered the militarized norms internalized by the young artists.

Children's agency in co-constructing and/or resisting wartime narratives through art

Still, children's war-related art in Ukraine simultaneously depicts how children maintain, regain, and resist efforts to co-opt their agency in other ways. In scholarly literature, particularly in childhood development studies, art has been suggested as an opportunity for children to control their space (Tanay, 1994). Although trauma can induce a disjointed relationship between a child's memory of a traumatic event and the child's ability to render it visually, images and symbols have been described as a vehicle for a child to emotionally defend against painful memories (for example, depicting a war memory non-literally as a monster, snake, or worm) and communicate trauma fixations (through visually representing 'stuckness' through symbol repetition, rows of lines, lines of dots, and so on). When promoting children's representation of wartime experiences through art, underlying goals and functions for encouraging children to communicate painful memories visually include environmental engagement, coping, new methods of communicating complex feelings and perceptions without words, remembering life before the war, and 'confront[ing] their problems [by developing] a personal strategy for solving them through art' (Tanay, 1994: 240). At a deeper level, art can also be a tool used to reproduce the idioms of their rights as a response to chaotic environments (Reynolds et al, 2006).

Despite the adult actions described above that consciously and unconsciously signal the boundaries and content of 'acceptable' conflict processing by children, their behaviours also established a standard against which a younger generation can communicate resistance through rebellion (Linke, 2002). The first author's presence at an exhibition of children's war-related artwork in Uzhgorod, western Ukraine, in April 2019 demonstrates this complex interplay of co-construction, agency, and resistance in children's artwork. Figure 14.1 provides an overview photograph of featured children's art, with many of the themes discussed in the preceding section apparent: bright colours, an overall sense of optimism for a nearly arrived military victory, aesthetically pleasing elements like Ukrainian folk elements and flowers, and recognizable symbols like doves.

Still, despite these incentivized elements, children's agency is immediately apparent in these artifacts in several ways. First, even within the incentivized parameters of bright colours and easily recognizable symbols, one young artist has depicted complex themes of desires for peace as contrasted to remembrances of shelling (Figure 14.2).

In addition, the children's personalization of the larger context is a recurrent theme, seen through frequent depictions of their family members and even pets like a cat in the artwork (see Figure 14.1). In so doing, the children's art hints that although they may not be willing initiators of the conflict, their mental compass of the world does now include placeholders of themselves and their families as actors in a militarized context (see Figure 14.3). Their artwork also reminds that military actors themselves emerge from the intimate contexts of local communities, thus pointing to complex, multi-directional relationships

Figure 14.1: Overview of children's art exhibit in Uzhgorod, Ukraine

Source: Photo by Kristina Hook

between the local, national, and international in armed conflict contexts. Further, even with overall themes of optimism pervading the art exhibit, as seen in the bright colours and depictions that portray Ukrainian military strength, the art in Figure 14.3 demonstrates how children's awareness of the terrible uncertainties and sacrifices of war coexist within the optimistic confines of wartime processing incentivized by adult actions as a family is depicted as saying a tearful goodbye. With Ukrainian trains now familiar to global publics through heartbreaking

Figure 14.2: Child's artwork in Uzhgorod exhibit

Source: Photo by Kristina Hook

photos of family separations and civilian evacuations, this drawing also reminds us that these realities of war have loomed large in children's experiences and imaginations long prior to the increased international attention from 2022. This artwork also illustrates a clear example of the child artist co-constructing militarized narratives through the artwork, as an angel is depicted upholding the Ukrainian national symbol of a trident. While no adult likely communicated this exact image verbally to the child, the young artist has both absorbed a militarized theme of divine support on the side of Ukraine and filtered this message in new symbolic terms through the depiction of the angel. The young artist therefore not only depicts this militaristic theme but actively participates in co-constructing and reproducing it in new ways.

Finally, although the adult-generated parameters of conflict filtering and their signalling as to what constitutes 'best art' appear to have influenced the overall artistic expressions of children's depictions of wartime, these tenets also underscore the reality that some young artists rebel against these standards. One such example is shown in Figure 14.4, where the young artist powerfully submits an artistic representation that deviates from nearly all of the adult-encouraged elements (for example, bright colours, easily recognizable symbols, literalism, optimistic victory). In this context, the young artist's deviation is made more apparent by being so

Figure 14.3: Child's artwork in Uzhgorod exhibit

Source: Photo by Kristina Hook

different from the other depictions (reference Figure 14.1) and results in drawing audience members' inward to take closer and longer looks at this work. With content ranging from the shocking (a hand dripping blood) to the politically charged (the European Union flag), both militarism and agency-driven rebellion against 'correct' conflict interpretations can readily be observed.

Conclusion

In this chapter, we examined how art programmes create settings where children's agency can be simultaneously controlled and directed, as well as how art can provide children with an opportunity for reflection, representation, and rebellion. We have also demonstrated how art projects create spaces for young participants to simultaneously internalize warfare dynamics while also generating new symbolic representations of them. War-focused art programmes also provide adults with opportunities to consciously and unconsciously delineate the acceptable parameters of war interpretations, yet in so doing, these boundaries emphasize the work of young artists who resist. Adding to these complexities, the young artists who rebel against the incentivized standards of 'good' war-related art are still reacting against the adult-generated cultural structures of power – allowing these standards to

Figure 14.4: Child's artwork in Uzhgorod exhibit

Source: Photo by Kristina Hook

still indirectly dictate their behaviour and choices. These nuances highlight the importance of thinking about childhood agency beyond the binaries of present/absent or activated/dormant. Agency, including for children in wartime, is inherently relational: produced in relation to others and existing in a continual flux as it is negotiated and shaped.

As we have examined children's agency, we have noted children's active, co-constructing roles in the everyday practices of militarization. Contributing to debates over whether military power permeates intimate spaces of local life, we find instead this process to be simultaneously multi-directional and multi-scalar. Instead of simplistic understandings of children turning violence into play or war into art, we suggest these childhood activities offer additional support to the idea that children, even with all their vulnerabilities and socio-political precarities, can exhibit methods of transforming violence into something else – even in situations where their overt agency remains limited (Beier, 2020; Woodyer and Carter, 2020). Such considerations are essential for any applied efforts to disrupt processes of militarization (Ahall, 2019). Future research in this direction may involve a closer investigation of children as active participants in construing, negotiating, co-constructing, or resisting against militarism through other childhood activities (Beier, 2020; Woodyer and Carter, 2020). Notably, the ability to envision the agentive role of children in conflict and perceive their centrality to processes of militarization creates new possibilities to transform these self-replicating processes (Watson, 2015; Lee-Koo, 2017; Beier, 2020; Hoban, 2022).

Acknowledgements
The authors would like to express gratitude to Sean Carter and Lindsay Robinson for their insightful comments on earlier versions of this manuscript.

Notes
[1] https://www.unicef.org/eu/stories/arts-project-gives-voice-teens-ukraines-conflict-zone
[2] https://en.unesco.org/creativity/policy-monitoring-platform/creative-partnerships-schools
[3] https://www.neweurope.eu/article/children-of-conflict-art-exhibition-shows-war-through-young-ukrainians-eyes/
[4] https://zt.20minut.ua/Kult-podii/yak-diti-malyuyut-viynu-i-mir-vistavka-malyunkiv-mir-i-viyna-ochima-di-10466810.html
[5] https://en.unesco.org/creativity/policy-monitoring-platform/creative-partnerships-schools
[6] https://zt.20minut.ua/Kult-podii/yak-diti-malyuyut-viynu-i-mir-vistavka-malyunkiv-mir-i-viyna-ochima-di-10466810.html
[7] https://zt.20minut.ua/Kult-podii/yak-diti-malyuyut-viynu-i-mir-vistavka-malyunkiv-mir-i-viyna-ochima-di-10466810.html
[8] https://zt.20minut.ua/Kult-podii/yak-diti-malyuyut-viynu-i-mir-vistavka-malyunkiv-mir-i-viyna-ochima-di-10466810.html

References

Ackerly, B., Stern, M., and True, J. (2006) *Feminist Methodologies for International Relations*, Cambridge: Cambridge University Press.

Agathangelou, A. and Killian, K. (2011) '(Neo) Zones of violence: Reconstructing empire on the bodies of militarized youth', in M. Beier (ed) *The Militarization of Childhood*, New York: Palgrave Macmillan, pp 17–42.

Ahall, L. (2016) 'The dance of militarisation: A feminist security studies take on "the political"', *Critical Studies on Security* 4(2): 1–15.

Ahall, L. (2019) 'Feeling everyday IR: Embodied, affective, militarising movement as choreography of war', *Cooperation and Conflict* 54(2): 149–166.

Basham, V. (2015) 'Gender, race, militarism and remembrance: The everyday geopolitics of the poppy', *Gender, Place & Culture* 23(6): 883–896.

Basham, V. (2020) 'From Hitler's Youth to the British child soldier: How the martial regulation of children normalizes and legitimizes war', in M. Beier (ed) *Discovering Childhood in International Relations,* London: Palgrave Macmillan, pp 135–155.

Beier, M. (2020) 'Introduction: Making sense of childhood in International Relations', in M. Beier (ed) *Discovering Childhood in International Relations*, London: Palgrave Macmillan, pp 1–21.

Bernard, H.R., Wutich, A., and Ryan, G. (2016) *Analyzing Qualitative Data*, Thousand Oaks, CA: SAGE.

Bernazzoli, R.M. and Flint, C. (2009) 'Power, place, and militarism: Toward a comparative geographic analysis of militarization', *Geography Compass* 3(1): 393–411.

Danilova, N. (2015) *The Politics of War Commemoration in the UK and Russia*, London: Palgrave Macmillan.

Doucet, A. and Mauthner, N. (2007) 'Feminist methodologies and epistemologies', in C.D. Bryant and D. L. Peck (eds) *The Handbook of 21st Century Sociology*, Thousand Oaks, CA: SAGE, pp 32–46.

Dowler, L. (2012) 'Gender, militarization and sovereignty', *Geography Compass* 6(8): 490–499.

Dunn, E.C. and Bobick, M. (2014) 'The empire strikes back: War without war and occupation without occupation in the Russian sphere of influence', *American Ethnologist* 41(3): 405–413.

Dittmer, J. and Gray, N. (2010) 'Popular geopolitics 2.0: Towards new methodologies of the everyday', *Geography Compass* 4(11): 1664–1677.

Enloe, C. (2002) *Maneuvers: The International Politics of Militarizing Women's Lives*, Berkeley and Los Angeles, CA: University of California Press.

Enloe, C. (2007) *Globalization and Militarism: Feminists Make the Link*, Lanham, MD: Rowman & Littlefield.

Falk, P. (2022) 'U.N. told of "credible" claims of sexual violence against children as Russia's war drives a third of Ukrainians from their homes', *CBS*, 13 May. Available at: https://www.cbsnews.com/news/ukraine-news-russia-war-children-sexual-violence-un-displaced-refugees/ [Accessed 24 May 2022].

Galeotti, M. (2016) 'Hybrid, ambiguous, and non-linear? How new is Russia's "new way of war"?', *Small Wars and Insurgencies* 27(2): 282–301.

Geertz, C. (1981) *Negara: The Theater State in the 19th Century Bali*, Princeton: Princeton University Press.

Grayson, K. (2013) 'How to read Paddington Bear: Liberalism and the foreign subject in "A Bear Called Paddington"', *The British Journal of Politics and International Relations* 15(3): 378–393.

Grayson, K., Davies, M., and Philpott, S. (2009) 'Pop goes IR? Researching the popular culture–world politics continuum', *Politics* 29(3): 155–163.

Government of the Netherlands (2018) 'MH17: The Netherlands and Australia hold Russia responsible', press statement, 25 May. Available at: https://www.government.nl/latest/news/2018/05/25/mh17-the-netherlands-and-australia-hold-russia-responsible [Accessed 28 March 2020].

Hall, K. (1999) 'Performativity', *Journal of Linguistic Anthropology* 9 (1–2): 184–87.

Henry, M. and Natanel, K. (2016) 'Militarisation as diffusion: The politics of gender, space and the everyday', *Gender, Place & Culture* 23(6): 850–856.

Hoban, I. (2022) 'Militarization of childhood(s) in Donbas: "Growing together with the Republic"', *Cooperation and Conflict* 57(1): 108–129.

Hook, K. (2020) '"When the Ukrainian world was destroyed": Genocidal narrative convergence and stakeholder interactions during national crises', PhD dissertation, Notre Dame, IN: University of Notre Dame.

International Crisis Group (ICG) (2022) 'Conflict in Ukraine's Donbas: A visual explainer', *ICG,* February. Available at: https://www.crisisgroup.org/content/conflict-ukraines-donbas-visual-explainer [Accessed 24 May 2022].

Johnson, J., Christie, J., and Yawkey, T. (1987) *Play and Early Childhood Development*, Glenview, IL: Scott, Foresman & Co.

Khrebtan-Hörhager, J. (2016) 'Collages of memory: Remembering the Second World War differently as the epistemology of crafting cultural conflicts between Russia and Ukraine', *Journal of Intercultural Communication Research* 45(4): 282–303.

Lee-Koo, K. (2017) 'Children, conflict, and global governance', in A. Burke and R. Parker (eds) *Global Insecurity*, London: Palgrave Macmillan, pp 159–174.

Linke, U. (2002) 'Archives of violence: The Holocaust and the German politics of memory', A.L. Hinton (ed) *Annihilating Difference: The Anthropology of Genocide*, Berkeley, CA: University of California Press, pp 229–271.

McEvoy-Levy, S. (2018) *Peace and Resistance in Youth Cultures*, London: Palgrave Macmillan.

McEvoy-Levy, S. with Byram, C., Lewis, J., Perry, K., Perry, T., Trujillo, J., and Whittemore, M. (2020) 'Between borders: Pop Cultural heroes and plural childhoods in IR', in M. Beier (ed) *Discovering Childhood in International Relations,* London: Palgrave Macmillan, pp 179–199.

Marten, K. (2019) 'Russia's use of semi-state security forces: The case of the Wagner Group', *Post-Soviet Affairs* 35(3): 181–204.

Nast, H. (1994) 'Women in the field: Critical feminist methodologies and theoretical perspectives', *The Professional Geographer* 46(1): 54–66.

Pain, R. (2015) 'Intimate war', *Political Geography* 44: 64–73.

Reynolds, P., Nieuwenhuys, O., and Hanson, K. (2006) 'Refractions of children's rights in development practice: A view from anthropology – Introduction', *Childhood* 13(3): 291–302.

Tanay, E.R. (1994) 'Croatian and Bosnian children's art in times of war', *Journal of Art & Design Education* 13(3): 235–240.

Troianovski, A. (2021) '"Threat from the Russian State": Ukrainians Alarmed as Troops Mass on Their Doorstep', *The New York Times*, 20 April. Available at: https://www.nytimes.com/2021/04/20/world/europe/-ukraine-russia-putin-invasion.html [Accessed 20 April 2021].

Ukrainian Independent Information Agency of News (UNIAN) (2019) '"Donbas war toll rises up to nearly 13,000" – UN.', UNIAN, 22 January 22. Available from: https://www.unian.info/war/10416549-donbas-war-death-toll-rises-up-to-nearly-13-000-un.html [Accessed 8 June 2023].

United Nations Children's Fund (UNICEF) (2020) 'Ukraine appeal: Humanitarian action for children'. Available at: https://www.unicef.org/appeals/ukraine#download [Accessed 20 April 2021].

Veirlinger, J. (2022) 'UN: Ukraine refugee crisis is Europe's biggest since WWII', *The Atlantic Council*, 20 April. Available at: https://www.atlanticcouncil.org/blogs/ukrainealert/un-ukraine-refugee-crisis-is-europes-biggest-since-wwii/ [Accessed 20 June 2023].

Watson, A. (2015) 'Resilience is its own resistance: The place of children in post-conflict settlement', *Critical Studies on Security* 3(1): 47–61.

Weldes, J. (2003) 'Popular culture, science fiction, and world politics', in J. Weldes (ed) *To Seek Out New Worlds*, New York: Palgrave Macmillan, pp 1–27.

Weldes, J. and Rowley, C. (2015) 'So, how does popular culture relate to world politics?', in F. Caso and C. Hamilton (eds) *Popular Culture and World Politics: Theories, Methods, Pedagogies*, E-International Relations.

Wibben, A.T. (2018) 'Why we need to study (US) militarism: A critical feminist lens', *Security Dialogue* 49(1–2): 136–148.

Woodward, R. (2004) *Military Geographies*, Oxford: Blackwell Publishing.

Woodward, R., Duncanson, C., and Jenkings, K.N. (2017) 'Gender and military memoirs', in R. Woodward and C. Duncanson (eds) *The Palgrave International Handbook of Gender and the Military*, London: Palgrave Macmillan, pp 525–542.

Woodyer, T. and Carter, S. (2020) 'Toying with militarization: Children and war on the homefront', in M. Beier (ed) *Discovering Childhood in International Relations,* London: Palgrave Macmillan, pp 155–179.

15

Centring the Demand for Critical Climate Justice Education

Bennett Collins and Ali Watson

Introduction

The lived experiences of children and young people and the actualization of their political agency – whether individually or collectively – remain largely under-recognized within wider policy frameworks, especially those that attempt to systemically address the ongoing climate crisis. In terms of current global priorities, the climate crisis is placing children and young people at the centre of both policy and advocacy, and there are now multiple examples of political spaces within a context in which they can be seen to be an important part of 'doing the work' (see, for example, Byrne et al, 2019). This chapter examines this centrality within the context of education, specifically arguing that children and young people are increasingly advocating for a 'critical climate justice praxis', as coined by Sultana (2022: 119), that 'demands systemic changes to address structural inequities and destabilize power systems that produce various climate injustices'. This is becoming more visible as a result of the political space that liberal institutions are allocating children and young people as moral authorities in addressing the climate crisis (Leggett, 2019) because they, and future generations, will be the ones witnessing its long-term impacts.

However, the demand for a climate justice praxis, and this moral positioning, clash with current educational frameworks for climate action in that, despite the widespread recognition by key stakeholders that critical climate justice education should involve radical critique, examination, and solutions, what currently exists is a framing that is neoliberal and colonial in nature. This chapter argues that alongside the very clear central role that children and young people play in climate action, what is required is a recognition that current frameworks of climate education are not, in fact, fit for the radical change that the climate crisis requires. Many of the education policies currently being promoted strip questions of justice, politics, and power from discussions of climate change and, in the end, deny children and young people the political space required to fully explore the causes and spectrum of responses to climate change. This is to say that the current policy environment sends a dual message that while children and young people are authorities in climate politics, they should not be given education that is critical of historical and enduring colonial and neoliberal structures, which remain the cause of the climate crisis.

The demand for a radical shift in climate education

Children and young people already engage in actions to address climate change that are radical and that recognize the need to centre justice-oriented approaches within climate narratives. Moreover, the direct political advocacy undertaken by children and young people in this regard is important because in this instance children and young people's voices are more likely to be listened to as a result of their 'moral authority'. Cocco-Klein and Mauger (2018: 95) argue that this is because, as representatives of the 'generation most affected', they have a unique role within climate mitigation policy.

In 1992, 12-year-old Canadian environmental activist Severn Cullis-Suzuki gave a speech at the United Nations Earth Summit in Rio de Janeiro that 'silenced the world for five minutes'.[1] In it she noted the hypocrisies of generational leadership wherein the liberal global status quo has traditionally allocated the agency in solving global crises to "adults":[2]

> 'Parents should be able to comfort their children by saying, "Everything's going to be all right; it's not the end of the world, and we're – and we're doing the best we can". But I don't think you can say that to us anymore. Are we even on your list of priorities? ... You grown-ups say you love us. But I challenge you, please, make your actions reflect your words.'

Almost 30 years later, in the lead-up to the 26th Congress of Parties (COP26) in 2021, Swedish teenage climate activist Greta Thunberg's famous 'Blah, blah, blah' speech in Milan hit a similar tone: 'Build back better. Blah, blah, blah. Green economy. Blah blah blah. Net zero by 2050. Blah, blah, blah. This is all we hear from our so-called leaders. Words that sound great but so far have not led to action. Our hopes and ambitions drown in their empty promises' (Carrington, 2021).

While coverage of youth climate activists has amplified these pushbacks and highlighted the intergenerational tensions at play, the focus of liberal institutions has nevertheless whitewashed and, to a point, de-radicalized much more meaningful conversations that are taking place, often with their origins in those places most impacted by climate crises. This was exemplified when, in January 2020, the Associated Press cut Vanessa Nakate, a then 23-year-old Black climate activist from Uganda, out of a picture taken alongside four white European climate activists, including Thunberg, at the World Economic Forum at Davos. She responded accordingly (Evelyn, 2020):

> 'Climate activists of color are erased ... I [had] activists who messaged me to tell me that the same thing happened to them before but they didn't have the courage to say anything ...
>
> Racism, classism and the erasure of marginalized voices isn't new. ... A photo crop-out is an easy way to describe it but it's really a metaphorical crop-out from the narrative of climate science in general.'

Nakate's words speak to a more radical truth so often ignored in liberal policy making: those most impacted by climate change are conveniently spoken for by those with the privilege of access. Not only have young climate activists like Nakate, Cullis-Suzuki, and Thunberg been the loudest in calling out the inadequacies of global liberal responses to industrial-induced climate change, they have often grounded their critique in the wider social injustices that remain unaddressed by current solutions. This is reflective of what Sultana articulates in her critical climate justice praxis framework. Echoing Freire's concept of praxis, or the 'reflection and action upon the world in order to transform it' (Freire, 1970: 51), Sultana (2022: 119) states that 'to have justice, it becomes imperative first to identify injustices that exist and then address underlying causes. Climate justice is in many ways inherently about praxis. ... In broad terms, critical climate justice praxis demands systemic changes to address structural inequities and destabilize power systems that produce various climate injustices'.

A focus on radical justice-oriented action, rather than solely ecological remedies, is something that researchers say is especially notable within the current young generation of climate activists. As Thew notes (Marris, 2019), 'More and more, they are talking about the problems for people and really recognizing that human–environment connection. ... They are not just concerned about the polar bear'.[3] Yet this is not new. Cullis-Suzuki's speech reflected a critical climate justice praxis centred largely on global wealth and power redistribution rather than solely on ecological loss:[4]

> 'In my anger, I'm not blind; and in my fear, I'm not afraid of telling the world how I feel. In my country we make so much waste, we buy and throw away, buy and throw away, buy and throw away and yet Northern countries will not share with the needy. Even when we

have more than enough we are afraid to share; we are afraid to let go of some of our wealth.'

Again, this is effectively a call for systemic change that is not a question of asking if 'the kids are all right' but rather if liberal institutions are ready to listen to, address, or even showcase the priorities of younger generations and their desire to dismantle generative structures of oppression and replace those structures with ones that they have an actual role in designing.

Luckily, with the advent of social media we are now able to hear directly from young climate activists basing themselves within a critical climate justice praxis. These young climate activists have shown that their priority is not solely scientific ecological loss and damage, but also their claims for agency in solving the wider social issues that caused this loss to impact particular populations over others. Nadia Nazar, a youth climate justice organizer and artist from Baltimore, US, notes:[5]

> We must make sure that we include everyone in our solutions because everyone needs to be uplifted. This movement led by Indigenous, frontline, and youth of color will win and achieve a livable planet for all. ... Together, the youth are shaking the systems that have supported the climate crisis, including racism, patriarchy, colonialism, and capitalism.

It should be noted that this increased advocacy for critical climate justice approaches is being informed by individuals coming from post-colonial countries in the Global South as well as racialized and minoritized communities in the Global North. Many climate solutions from the wealthier and predominantly white Global North reproduce colonial dynamics in the form of green capitalism, involving 'land grabbing, sacrifice zones, biofuels and mining dispossessions, [and] water contamination'. Raeesah Noor Mahomed, a youth climate activist attending Parktown High School for Girls in Johannesburg, perhaps summed this up best when she noted: 'I always say that my activism will never just be climate activism because everything is so intertwined and all the problems – climate problems will never just be climate problems, it will relate to racism, colonization, even gender-based violence and xenophobia'. When talking specifically about education she notes:[6]

> The school system also doesn't talk about other things that relate to climate change. It doesn't talk about the effects of colonization enough, it doesn't talk about the effects of apartheid enough. ... In general it's not decolonized enough. We don't do enough non-Western literature. We don't learn enough about non-Western people and activists and

historical events that are so important and have impacted us – like Black consciousness.

In a similar vein, SCOREscotland, an organization working 'with partners to address the causes of racism' and providing support to families and young people who struggle with its effects' and that has a number of sustainability-driven initiatives, has chosen to focus on climate justice as an opportunity for learning, especially in terms of supporting youth workers working with young people who are 'passionate about the climate emergency'.[7] Their work recognizes that it is children and young climate activists who appear to more clearly recognize that the climate crisis requires recognition of the underlying root causes of oppression and marginalization, and that addressing the climate crisis means connecting knowledge frameworks that have traditionally been siloed into addressing environmental injustice or gender injustice or racial injustice as separate issues. One young activist who was introduced to climate justice discussions by the work of SCOREscotland recognizes this when he notes:[8]

> I think climate justice ... when it comes to the harmful effects of climate change it's usually the countries who aren't the major emitters of greenhouse gases, those who aren't majorly responsible for what's happening, they're usually the ones who get affected the worst and aren't financially capable of bouncing back from whatever disaster happens.

In practice, there are numerous examples of children and young people working on these issues: Zero Hour, an organization whose website notes its mission as being 'to center the voices of diverse youth in the conversation around climate and environmental justice';[9] the Australian Youth Climate Coalition,[10] which promotes 'a climate justice narrative where children and young people are legitimate political actors responding to the climate crisis' (Hilder and Collin, 2022: 1); and the Rise Up Movement, founded by Vanessa Nakate, which aims to give 'African climate activists a platform for their voice to be heard in the world'.[11] In the face of the failure of liberal institutions to respond to the climate crisis, it is clear that children and young people are organizing around a more radical approach that moves beyond ecological solutions and into transformative and inclusive justice-oriented ones.

The problem: confining climate education in liberal praxis

In November 2021, the same month it hosted COP26, the UK released its 'Sustainability and Climate Change' draft strategy for the education and children's services system in England and Wales, noting that '[e]ducation is critical to fighting climate change. We have both the responsibility and privilege of educating and preparing young people for a changing world – ensuring they are equipped with the right knowledge, understanding and skills to meet their biggest challenge head on'.[12]

It argues for future green careers for children and young people and others; for a greater connection to nature; for the 'education estate' (school buildings) to be more sustainable; and for teaching on climate change to take place. There is, however, a key paragraph in this strategy that highlights a significant issue in the UK government's conception of climate change education:[13]

> Teaching about climate change and the scientific facts and evidence behind this, does not constitute teaching about a political issue and schools do not need to present misinformation or unsubstantiated claims to provide balance. ... [I]n climate education there may be relevant political issues and partisan political views, for example on social and economic reform, that should be handled in line with schools legal duties on political impartiality. Importantly, whilst schools should support pupil's interest in climate change and tackling both its causes and effects, it would not be appropriate to encourage pupils to join specific campaigning groups or engage in specific political activity, such as protests.

In other words, teaching climate change is about teaching 'objective' facts, not about the politics behind those facts or about supporting children and young people to step into the political space that youth climate crisis advocacy has opened up.

Of course, education, especially in the context of the West, has never been neutral and has always been developed with ulterior motives, many of them rooted within wider colonial and industrialization narratives. As Carl (2009: 503) notes, the needs of the market – in terms of both economic and political expediency – have always coincided with educational development. In addition, education has been used as an instrument of cultural erasure, providing children and young people with a dominant narrative that served to erase alternative narratives that might articulate the ways in which the state has served as an instrument of structural violence. Yuchi and Muscogee geographer Dan Wildcat (2009: 2) highlights how education was 'the most potent' instrument in carrying out the mission of colonialism on Indigenous children in the United States, noting that education has been 'the classic liberal solution to all social problems'. For non-reflexive and dominant societies that refuse engagement with notions of justice and that reject material critical of power hierarchies (for example, critical race theory in the United States or the absence of critical education around former empires across Western Europe), education continues to proliferate hegemonic epistemologies and ontologies such that colonial binaries are reproduced: the developed versus the undeveloped, the modern versus unmodern, the Global North versus the Global South. Within binary frameworks, non-Western societies can be developing, modernizing, and 'civilizing' themselves to achieve a Western status quo and, at worst, are incapable of achieving this and require Western saviourism. At the same time, there remains an unchallenged hierarchy of white racial supremacy whereby modernity and development are produced out of Eurocentric ontologies, with the status of white European and European-descendent peoples becoming the preeminent focus. As Sriprakash et al powerfully note (2022: 14), '[w]hiteness is thus a structural formation, shaped by the material interests of racial domination under colonialism and capitalism, and constantly reworked and reinscribed through the governance of social and political life'.

Education is part of that governance and has long been used as a tool of colonial oppression, with the main focus being on assimilation. Colonial education is thus a form of political action designed to control a colonized population; millions of children and young people are educated in such a way that they remain unaware of their exploitation, which in turn makes societal control easier (Althusser, 1971). The irony is that in such a model, a curriculum challenging such ideas is seen as peddling political demagoguery. For example, at the end of 2020 the UK government's Department for Education sent out guidance noting that anti-capitalism was an extremist stance and should not be included in the educational materials provided by English schools. At around the same time the UK's Equalities Minister, Kemi Badenoch, declared that the 'Government stands unequivocally against critical race theory'[14] limiting the discussions of race in schools and colleges in England and Wales.[15] Similarly, in Florida, the Department of Education has pulled a number of maths textbooks from the curriculum for reasons that 'included references to Critical Race Theory ... and the unsolicited addition of social emotional learning [SEL] in Mathematics' (Strauss, 2022). An SEL conducive space is about creating a learning community, including the ability to work with a diverse group of individuals. In a colonial model, however, education through a neoliberal approach is not directed towards the responsibilities of belonging to a community or even to the self-awareness of identifying as a member of a community. Rather, the neoliberalization of education centres largely on the success of the individual.

The neoliberal education model is an approach that results in a 'specific set of educational objectives and practices' (Patrick, 2013) that impact how children and young people are taught, what they are taught, and who teaches them (or whose voices are listened to within a classroom context). Brancaleone and O'Brien (2011) argue that this results in a technical rationalist approach to knowledge and its value where the emphasis is on a particular kind of education rooted in neoliberal values or, as Marcia McKenzie (2012: 165) describes it, 'individual over social, human over environment, and industrialized or 'developed' over non-industrialized'. Neoliberalism, as Tomlinson and Lipsitz (2013: 3) outline,

> is not just an economic system. Unimpeded capital accumulation requires extensive ideological legitimation. Neoliberal practices seek to produce neoliberal subjects through a social pedagogy that aims to naturalise hierarchy and exploitation by promoting internalized preferences for profits over the needs of people, a relentless individuation of collective social processes, a cultivation of hostile privatism and defensive localism based on exaggerated fears of difference, and a mobilization of anger and resentment against vulnerable populations that renders them disposable, displaceable, deportable, and docile.

This would seem to coincide with Hursh et al's (2015: 299) work, which notes in a discussion of environmental education, '[n]eoliberalism has become the dominant social imaginary, making particular ways of thinking and acting possible while simultaneously discouraging the possibility and pursuit of others'.

In terms of climate change education, the result of neoliberal dominance in education models is an inherent focus on the individual and upon individual consumption choice. The results of this in terms of climate action are twofold. First, children and young people are encouraged to reduce, re-use, and recycle, but without any wider learning on the ways in which big industry has driven consumption patterns in the first place, a type of learning that also reinforces the key mechanism by which children and young people have appeared to derive agency within the neoliberal system as consumers. As Dan Cook (2004) noted:

> [w]hat is most troubling is that *children's* culture has become virtually indistinguishable from *consumer* culture over the course of the last century. ... The children's market works because it lives off of deeply held-beliefs about self-expression and freedom of choice – originally applied to the political sphere, and now almost inseparable from the culture of consumption. Children's commercial culture has quite successfully usurped kids' boundless creativity and personal agency, selling these back to them – and us – as 'empowerment', a term that appeases parents while shielding marketers.

Second, that focus on the individual and on individual responsibility obscures not only the role of big industry but also the injustices that are so central to the outcomes of the prevailing neoliberal model. We thus find ourselves in a feedback loop with children and young people appearing to derive agency from their role as consumers, which in turn is fed back to them as a need to change their consumption patterns to address climate change – with either no reference to the role of the market or of producers, or indeed deliberate disinformation regarding their role in the climate change equation, and no sense that climate change is in fact linked to forms of oppression that it is vital that we address, and in a radical way. For example, as Zou (2017) notes in *The Guardian*:

> Decades of documents reviewed by the Center for Public Integrity reveal a tightly woven network of organizations that works in concert with the oil and gas industry to paint a rosy picture of fossil fuels in America's classrooms. Led by advertising and public-relations strategists, the groups have long plied the tools of their trade on impressionable children and teachers desperate for resources.

Additionally, the solutions to climate change given in the classroom are often framed in terms of the market. Schools and higher education institutions are encouraged to have sustainability goals, but again these are largely framed as market-based, often focusing on supply chain issues and procurement.[16] Neoliberalism appears to divorce economics from politics, creating an economic approach that is purported to be apolitical when the reality is that it is anything but. We can see this within existing climate education frameworks, where climate change education can most often be found rooted within a science curriculum, with a focus on individual action. We would argue that a different approach is required.

Critical educational approaches towards climate justice

We would argue that it is in developing alternative ontologies and epistemologies that centre sustainability and the value of place beyond the market that the opportunity for real climate education, and in turn the opportunity for increased climate action, can be seen. Although there are undoubtedly a number of ways of doing this, this chapter will focus on three: land education, intergenerational collaboration, and community creation. Land education remains in the margins as a pedagogical approach to climate education, but it is reasonable critique that place-based education is able to de-centre colonial lived realities of place. Tuck et al (2014: 13) note the importance of such an approach:

> Land education puts Indigenous epistemological and ontological accounts of land at the center, including Indigenous understandings of land, Indigenous language in relation to land, and Indigenous critiques

of settler colonialism. It attends to constructions and storying of land and repatriation by Indigenous peoples, documenting and advancing Indigenous agency and land rights.

They also note that in the context of the climate crisis, place-based education and its main occupation of 'facilitating relationships to place' is 'necessary to cultivate the humility needed to ensure the future of places' (Tuck et al, 2014: 14). Similarly Datta et al (2022) see land-based environmental education as an 'intercultural and intergenerational space to overcome climate change challenges'.

While neoliberal policies reduce the responsibilities of the state to its citizens (and even more so to its non-citizens), replacing those responsibilities with policies that reinforce the idea that individuals are responsible for their own well-being, place-based education instead rests responsibility on the shoulders of community. Developing humility, responsibility, and meaningful connections to land remains an educational approach that challenges the neoliberal model and its focus on the primacy of the market. One practical example of land education is provided by *BYTE – Empowering Youth Society* a 'by youth, for youth' organization focusing on youth empowerment and engagement in the Yukon and northern Canada. Its workshop *This is Our Land*, highlights a different approach:[17]

> We hear about climate change all the time, but what's really happening to the land around us? In this workshop, we encourage youth to look closely at the land they live on and to connect with community members and knowledge holders to answer this question. We ask youth what the land means to them and how they can watch over it. Youth consider how their own lives and culture are intrinsically linked to the land and how they, in turn, can change their environment for the better or for the worse.

Studies have found that this kind of education, which strengthens connection to land and highlights the impact of climate change on that land, is important for both Indigenous and non-Indigenous learners.[18]

This kind of learning is also related to a route to critical climate justice education that is both intergenerational and collaborative (echoing Datta et al, 2022). Land education often includes collaboration between youth and elders, with the older generation teaching on heritage and place. Lawson et al have noted the unique perspectives that children have on climate change, being potentially better equipped to 'navigate the ideologically fraught topic of climate change with older generations in ways that inspire action' (Lawson et al, 2018: 204).[19] This is something that we ourselves found in a series of workshops with schoolchildren in Fife using digital storytelling as a common ground to talk about various social injustices being brought forth from the climate crisis. When faced with the question of who they would like to produce digital stories on topics around climate justice for, one key audience group was their own parents, as they sought to pass on their own knowledge to older generations (Hepburn, 2021).[20]

Finally, finding an alternative ontology and epistemology is also about creating a community of learners such that not only is there space for critical climate justice education but also for sustainable climate action. There are numerous examples of this – from the Community Climate Collaborative, which aims to build a community engaged in individual and community responses to climate change, to Classrooms for Climate Action, where 'teachers support their students in learning about climate change in order to build their hope and agency by taking local climate action'. In Rethinking our Classrooms, Au et al (2007, x) talk of classrooms as places of hope where students and teachers get a glimpse of the society that could be. Yet while there are educators doing great work in terms of anti-oppressive practice both within and outwith orthodox educational spaces, the dominant educational frameworks remain those that sterilize climate change to be a phenomenon or crisis born out of an inevitable trajectory of human progress instead of a product of ongoing systems of oppression.

Conclusion

The problem we have outlined is that children and young people demand a more radical response from education systems to better understand both the scientific and social origins and effects of the climate crisis. Liberal institutions have responded by placating and tokenizing 'youth voice' – as a necessary one at the proverbial table, but one that should wait for a system response. While children and youth are highlighted as central to the management of the climate crisis when education is being touted as necessary for climate action, the current educational status quo around climate education fails to meet the mark. The continuing domination of neoliberal and colonial educational models of climate education downplay the question of how we got here and silence the message that systemic change is both possible and necessary. Our suggested response is for climate education to remain reactive rather than static in its position in relation to youth. A dynamic approach is not only in keeping with the ways in which critical classroom praxis should take place but would also be one way of challenging the intergenerational hierarchies that can suppress communication across generations; that is, indeed, if such challenge is an appropriate course of action and not itself a reinforcement of what can sometimes be seen as the white Western tendency to challenge cultural hierarchies on the liberal ethos of equality. Opting for a critical climate justice education praxis rejects neoliberal and colonial education approaches and can also centre the ongoing experiences and the physical, mental, and spiritual well-being of children and young people as those who must live with the reality of the climate crisis longer than any other generation to date.

Acknowledgements

The authors would like to thank Kemisso Alebachew, Marshall Beier, Helen Berents, and Jennifer Riggan for their detailed comments on drafts written at various stages of the editing process, as well as the other authors in this volume for their comments during the workshop process. The authors would also like to thank their colleagues and partners in the Third Generation Project for their part in the process of developing the methodology outlined here.

Notes

1. Lootens, F. (2018) 'New voices after 26 years of "The girl who silenced the world for 5 minutes"', Earth Charter, 25 May. Available at: https://earthcharter.org/new-voices-after-26-years-of-the-girl-who-silenced-the-world-for-5-minutes/ [Accessed 8 June 2023].
2. Suzuki, S. (1992) 'Speech at U.N. Conference on Environment and Development', American Rhetoric. Available at: https://www.americanrhetoric.com/speeches/severnsuzukiunearthsummit.htm [Accessed 8 June 2023].
3. Marris, E. (2019) 'Why young climate activists have captured the world's attention', 18 September. Available at: https://www.nature.com/articles/d41586-019-02696-0 [Accessed 8 June 2023].
4. Suzuki, S. (1992) 'Speech at U.N. Conference on Environment and Development', American Rhetoric. Available at: https://www.americanrhetoric.com/speeches/severnsuzukiunearthsummit.htm [Accessed 8 June 2023].
5. Burton, N. (2019) 'Meet the young activists of color who are leading the charge against the charge against climate disaster', October 11. Available at: https://www.vox.com/identities/2019/10/11/20904791/young-climate-activists-of-color.
6. Climate Justice Coalition (2020) 'Just Us and the Climate', Episode 5: 'They don't really care about us', September. Available at: https://pod.link/cjc/episode/e034c9017150c2aa253d2dd755be5062
7. Ba, Jennifer (2021) 'Addressing Climate Justice: National Youth Conference 2021'. Available at: https://www.scorescotland.org.uk/update-addressing-climate-justice/ [Accessed 8 June 2023].
8. Von Moltke, A. (2021) 'Realities of climate justice education in Scotland: Speaking with Mahmoud Makkawi'. Available at: https://www.thirdgenerationproject.org/mahmoud-makkawi-interview/ [Accessed 8 June 2023].
9. See the Zero Hour website at: https://www.thisiszerohour.org
10. See: https://www.aycc.org.au
11. Rise Up Movement. Available at: https://www.instagram.com/riseupmovement1/?hl=en
12. Department for Education (2021) 'Sustainability and Climate Change: A draft strategy for the education and children's services systems', November. Available at: https://www.eyalliance.org.uk/sites/default/files/scc_draft_strategy.pdf [Accessed 8 June 2023].
13. Department for Education (2021) 'Sustainability and Climate Change: A draft strategy for the education and children's services systems', November. Available at: https://www.eyalliance.org.uk/sites/default/files/scc_draft_strategy.pdf [Accessed 8 June 2023].

14 OldQueenTV (2021) 'Kemi Badenoch on critical race theory'. Available at: https://www.youtube.com/watch?v=3vf7yX9ESRc [Accessed 8 June 2023].

15 In Scotland, education is a 'devolved matter', with education seen as a flagship policy differentiating Scotland from the rest of the UK. Indeed, in the Scottish Government's White Paper on Independence, published in 2013, the claim was made that education in Scotland reflected a focus upon social justice principles rather than the principles of the market that is the focus in English schools.

16 In our own institution, the University of St Andrews, the sustainability focus is currently on achieving net zero, with a particular emphasis on procurement policies, travel, and increased energy efficiency, as opposed to, for example, seeing sustainability as being linked to wider questions of inclusion and ongoing colonization. Justice is rarely mentioned, and when it is, it is couched in terms of Rawlsian equality rather than upon system change.

17 Yukon Youth. Available at: https://www.yukonyouth.com/workshops/ [Accessed 8 June 2023].

18 See for example: Global Environmental Education Partnership, 'This is Indigenous land: An Indigenous land-based approach to climate change education'. Available at: https://thegeep.org/learn/case-studies/indigenous-land-indigenous-land-based-approach-climate-change-education [Accessed 8 June 2023].

19 See: Lawson, D.F., Stevenson, K.T., Peterson, M.N., Carrier, S.J., Strnad, R., and Seekamp, E. (2018) Intergenerational learning: Are children key in spurring climate action? *Global Environmental Change* 53: 204–208.

20 See: https://www.tes.com/magazine/analysis/general/why-teaching-hope-key-tackling-climate-change. See also Thomas and Silva (2022) for a real-world example of the impact that children and young people can have on an older generation, in this case a parent.

References

Althusser, L. (1971) *Lenin and Philosophy and Other Essays*, New York: Monthly Review Press.

Au, W., Bigelow, B., and Karp, S. (2007) *Rethinking Our Classrooms: Teaching for Equity and Justice, Volume 1*, Milwaukee: Rethinking Schools.

Byrne, E., Bowman, B., and Buckley, C.G. (2019) 'Climate change: Children are carving out a place in politics, now adults must listen and act', *The Conversation*, 20 September. Available at: https://theconversation.com/climate-change-children-are-carving-out-a-place-in-politics-now-adults-must-listen-and-act-123704 [Accessed 14 November 2022].

Carl, J. (2009) 'Industrialization and public education: Social cohesion and social stratification', in R. Cowen and A.M. Kazamias (eds) *International Handbook of Comparative Education*, Springer International Handbooks of Education, vol 22, Dordrecht: Springer, pp 503–518.

Carrington, D. (2021) '"Blah, blah, blah": Greta Thunberg lambasts leaders over climate crisis', *The Guardian*, 28 September. Available at: https://www.theguardian.com/environment/2021/sep/28/blah-greta-thunberg-leaders-climate-crisis-co2-emissions

Cocco-Klein, S. and Mauger, B. (2018) 'Climate change: What can we learn from child-led initiatives in the U.S. and the Pacific Islands?', *Children, Youth and Environments*, 28(1): 90–103.

Cook, D. (2004) 'Lunchbox hegemony', *Consumers, Commodities & Consumption*, 5(2). Available at: https://csrn.camden.rutgers.edu/newsletters/5-2/Cook.htm [Accessed 12 November 2022].

Datta, R., Kayira, J., and Datta, P. (2022) 'Land-based environmental education as a climate change resilience', in E.M. Walsh (ed) *Justice and Equity in Climate Change Education: Exploring Social and Ethical Dimensions of Environmental Education*, New York: Routledge, pp 214–233.

Evelyn, K. (2020) '"Like I wasn't there": Climate activist Vanessa Nakate on being erased from a movement', *The Guardian*, 29 January. Available at: https://www.theguardian.com/world/2020/jan/29/vanessa-nakate-interview-climate-activism-cropped-photo-davos?CMP=gu_com [Accessed 14 November 2022].

Freire, P. (1970) *Pedagogy of the Oppressed*. Reprinted 2005, New York: Continuum.

Hepburn, H. (2021) 'A climate of hope', *Times Educational Supplement*, October.

Hilder, C. and Collin, P. (2022) 'The role of youth-led activist organisations for contemporary climate activism: the case of the Australian Youth Climate Coalition', *Journal of Youth Studies* 25(6) 1–19.

Hursh, D., Henderson, J., and Greenwood, D. (2015) 'Environmental education in a neoliberal climate', *Environmental Education Research* 21(3): 299–318.

Lawson, D.F., Stevenson, K.T., Peterson, M.N., Carrier, S.J., Strnad, R., and Seekamp, E. (2018) 'Intergenerational learning: Are children key in spurring climate action?', *Global Environmental Change* 53: 204–208.

Leggett, K. (2019) 'Why children have such powerful moral authority', *Washington Post*, 1 March. Available at: https://www.washingtonpost.com/outlook/2019/03/01/why-children-have-such-powerful-moral-authority/ [Accessed 12 November 2022].

Mackenzie, M. (2012) 'Education for y'all: Global neoliberalism and the case for a politics of scale in sustainability education policy', *Policy Futures in Education* 10(2): 165–177.

Marris, E. (2019) 'Why young climate activists have captured the world's attention', *Nature*, 18 September. Available at: https://www.nature.com/articles/d41586-019-02696-0 [Accessed 12 November 2022].

O'Brien, S. and Brancaleone, D. (2011) 'Evaluating learning outcomes: In search of lost knowledge', *Irish Educational Studies* 30(1): 5–21.

Patrick, F. (2013) 'Neoliberalism, the knowledge economy, and the learner: Challenging the Inevitability of the commodified self as an outcome of education', Hindawi Publishing Corporation, ISRN Education, 108705. Available at: https://downloads.hindawi.com/archive/2013/108705.pdf [Accessed 12 November 2022].

Sriprakash, A., Rudolph, S., and Gerrard, J. (2022) *Learning Whiteness*, London: Pluto Press.

Strauss, V. (2022) 'Florida releases four prohibited math textbook examples. Here they are', *Washington Post*, 21 April. Available at: https://www.washingtonpost.com/education/2022/04/21/4-math-textbook-problems-florida-prohibited/ [Accessed 12 November 2022].

Sultana, F. (2022) 'Critical climate justice', *The Geographical Journal* 188(1):118–124. Available at: https://www.farhanasultana.com/wp-content/uploads/Sultana-Critical-climate-justice.pdf

Thomas, M. and Silva, M. (2022) 'Climate change: How to talk to a denier', *BBC News*, 24 June. Available at: https://www.bbc.co.uk/news/blogs-trending-61844299?at_medium=RSS&at_campaign=KARANGA [Accessed 14 November 2022].

Tomlinson, B. and Lipsitz, G. (2013) 'Insubordinate spaces for intemperate times: Countering the pedagogies of neoliberalism', *Review of Education, Pedagogy, and Cultural Studies* 35(1): 3–26.

Tuck, E., McKenzie, M., and McCoy, K. (2014) 'Land education: Indigenous, post-colonial, and decolonizing perspectives on place and environmental education research', *Environmental Education Research* 20(1): 1–23.

Wildcat, D. (2009) *Red Alert! Saving the Planet with Indigenous Knowledge*, Golden: Fulcrum Publishing.

Zou, J.J. (2017) 'Pipeline to the classroom: How big oil promotes fossil fuels to America's children', *The Guardian*, 15 June. Available at: https://www.theguardian.com/us-news/2017/jun/15/big-oil-classrooms-pipeline-oklahoma-education [Accessed 12 November 2022].

Index

A

'abandoned children' 50
Abbas, Mahmoud 186–187
action figures 158–159
Addis Ababa, Ethiopia 114–126
Agathangelou, A. 194, 197
age assessment procedures 135
age of military enlistment 60–61, 63–64, 102–103
age-determination procedures 24, 27
agency
  in armed conflict 101–113
  child soldiers 58–70, 107–108, 130–131
  children in the sex trade 141, 143–144, 148
  children's agency in global political studies 4–5
  children's sexual agency 147
  consumer agency 217
  consumption of popular culture 155–156
  ethical encounters 162–163
  girl power environmentalism 167–179
  girls' (generally) 170–171, 172
  global health governance 75–76, 77, 79, 81
  migration 18, 23, 24–26, 27, 114, 123, 130
  non-agentic children in armed conflicts 102–104, 107–110
  in participation 34, 35, 37, 40
  and play 158, 164–165
  reconciliation and reporting spaces 37–42
  refugees 114, 123
  strategic versus tactical 164
  Ukrainian children's art 193–209
  in years leading up to 18th birthday 109
Agenda 2021 89
Agenda 2030 78, 89
Åhäll, L. 196, 205
Ahmed, S. 96
Allsopp, J. 130
Almohammad, A. 181
Althusser, L. 216
ambivalence 23
'anchor babies' 18, 20–23
'anchor children' 18
Anderson, B. 26
Andrews, M. 47
apolitical child, myth of 35
Arce, M.C. 34
Arden, Gilad 186
Arouri, Salah 187
art 193–209
art therapy 198
asylum seekers 24, 25, 127–139
Au, W. 220
Australia 102–103, 109, 110
Australian Youth Climate Coalition 214
autonomy 2, 61, 102, 164
  see also agency
Awad, Wajih and Norhin 180

B

Badenoch, Kemi 216
Baines, E. 32
Bamberg, M. 47
Bastida, Xiye 173, 174, 175
Baylis, J. 104
'becomings' children as human 4
Beier, J.M. 5, 24, 37, 88, 90, 96, 155, 172, 195, 197, 205
Bellamy, A.J. 105, 111
Benjamin, W. 162
Bent, E. 170, 172
Berents, H. 19, 26, 102, 103, 111, 123, 171
Berko, Anat 185
Bernard, R. 197
best interests of child 17, 18, 19, 20–24, 130
Bhabha, H. 18, 23, 24, 92, 114, 130
birth certificates 49–50
Bloodsworth-Lugo, M.K. 22, 23
Bourke, J. 155, 156
boys in the sex trade 144
Brahm, E. 33
Brancaleone, S. 216
Brett, R. 61
Brexit 128, 132, 136
Brooks, G. 183
Brounéus, Karen 33
Buck-Morss, S. 162

Burnet, J. 48
BYTE – *Empowering Youth Society* 219

C

Cairns, E. 40
Canada 24, 33, 219
Carl, J. 215
Carpenter, R.C. 106, 111
Carrington, D. 211
Carter, S. 156, 196, 197, 205
Cederborg, A. 130–131
Chase, E. 130
CHEGA! comics 38–40, 41
child protection discourses
  child migrants 18–19, 133
  child soldiers 58, 63, 64, 66
  coverage of armed conflicts 103
  global governance of migration 91
  protectionist frameworks of children's participation 34, 35
  unaccompanied migrant children 133
  United Nations (UN) 18, 63, 66, 105, 107
  see also vulnerability discourses
child soldiers 58–70
  Children and Armed Conflict (CaAC) agenda 107–108
  definition of childhood 102
  as focus of existing IR studies 5–6, 103–104
  non-agentic children in armed conflicts 101–104, 107–110
child-friendly reports (from TRCs) 35–36
childhood, definitions of 2, 17, 59, 61, 102–103, 109
childhood development studies 199–200
Childhood Studies 123
Children and Armed Conflict (CaAC) agenda 36–37, 101–113
children's geographies 5
citizenship
  'anchor babies' 18, 22–23
  children's contribution to knowledge 37
  Eritrean refugees in Ethiopia 117
  global citizenship 81
  global health governance 81
  obligations to children 32
  Somali refugees in Ethiopia 118
Classrooms for Climate Action 220
Clayton, E.W. 146
climate change activism 168, 170, 171, 173, 174, 175
climate justice education 210–224
Cocco-Klein, S. 211
co-construction 193–209
Collin, P. 214
colonialism 60, 168, 170–173, 215–216, 220
Committee on the Rights of the Child 76, 89
Community Climate Collaborative 220

Comprehensive Refugee Response Framework 116
constructive turn in political theory 89–90, 106
Cook, D. 217
Cook, P. 35–36
Council of Europe 77, 80
  Council of Europe Action Plan on Human Rights and Technologies in Biomedicine 77
counter-narratives 45–57
COVID-19 73, 79, 82
Critical Childhood Studies 4–5
critical climate justice education 210–224
critical global health studies 76–77
critical security studies 3, 102
Cullis-Suzuki, Severn 211, 212

D

Danon, Danny 185
Datta, R. 168, 169, 175, 219
de Certeau, M. 164
de Finney, S. 168, 173, 175
decolonial feminism 168, 169, 173
definitions of childhood 2, 17, 59, 61, 102–103, 109
Denmark 25, 131
Denov, M. 58, 59, 60, 62, 64
deportations 21, 135
Der Derian, J. 158
developmentalism 4, 95, 106
digital storytelling 219–220
Disarmament, Demobilization and Integration (DDR) programmes 104
Disch, L. 89, 90
discourse analysis 131–132
Donbas conflict 194, 198
Drumbl, M. 58, 59, 60, 62, 63, 67
Dubs Scheme (Section 67) 135

E

education
  child soldiers 66
  colonialism 215
  critical climate justice education 210–224
  decolonizing 213–214
  girls' 169, 170
  neoliberalism 216–218
  refugee children in Addis Ababa 114–126
Eisenkot, Gadi 183, 186
Elgström, O. 110
empathy 41, 134
Enloe, C. 5, 196
environmental justice 167–179, 210–224
Eritrean refugees in Ethiopia 116, 117–124
Escobar, A. 168, 169, 174, 175
ethical encounters 161–165
Ethiopia 114–126
ethnography 47, 50, 115, 159–160, 194, 195, 197

INDEX

European Court of Human Rights 17, 24
European Return Platform for Unaccompanied Minors 21
European Union (EU) 21, 80, 127, 129
European Youth Federation 80
everyday sphere, importance of 115, 123, 156

F

family planning 171
family reunification 17, 18, 20–21, 22, 25, 135–136
fatherless children 50
feminism 115, 141–142, 168, 169, 170, 173
fiction, as data source 46–47
Finding Cholita (Isbell, 2009) 46–47, 50–53
Finland 20–21, 22
Finnemore, M. 106
Flynn, D. 147
Fogel, Zvika 185
forced marriage 66
Foucault, M. 47
Francis, D.J. 102
Freire, P. 212
Future Rising (FR) 167–168, 169–170, 173

G

G7 80
Gamboa, Rebeca 52–53
gender
  child migrants 23, 130
  child soldiers 60
  children in the sex trade 141, 144
  education 170
  gender-based violence 23
  prosecution of statutory rape in US 147
  symbolic technologies 106
Gilloch, G. 162
Girl Rising (GR) 167–168, 169, 173
girls
  child soldiers 60, 62
  girl power environmentalism 167–179
  girling of development 167, 169–172
global citizenship 81
Global Compact for Safe, Orderly and Regular Migration (GCM) 88, 90–95, 96
Global Forum on Migration and Development (GFMD) 88, 90–95, 96
global health 73–86
Global Health Youth Foundation 80
Global South
  binaries 216
  child soldiers 60, 102, 103
  environmentalism and climate change 167–168, 171, 213
  meaningful participation from 95
  migration 20, 95, 114–115, 116, 123
  post-colonialism 102, 111, 213
  post-conflict societies 103
  'world child' archetype 110

Godwin, M. 105
Goodman, H. 183
Goodwin, M. 129
Grayson, K. 196
Gualinga, Nina 174
Guinea-Bissau 61

H

Hayhurst, L.M. 167, 171
Hayner, Priscilla 41
health 73–86
Hedlund, D. 130–131
Heidbrink, L. 130
Hepburn, H. 220
Herz, M. 22, 130
Hettihewa, J.A. 73
Heykoop, C. 35–36
Hilder, C. 214
HMAF action figures 156, 158–161
Holzscheiter, A. 22, 34, 39, 73–74, 87, 88, 89, 90, 96
Hughes, S. 155, 156, 164
human rights 17, 33, 107, 142, 182–183
  see also rights
Human Rights Council 107
Human Rights Voices (HRV) 182–183
humanitarianism 21, 103, 114–115, 116
Hursh, D. 217
hypermasculinity 104

I

'ideal childhoods' 4, 103, 136
identity
  childhood as 3
  hypermasculinity 104
  national identity 117
  and representation 95
  universalizing discourses of 67
  in/visibility 118–123, 124
images of children in coverage of armed conflict 103
images of suffering children 101
images of young people in global health 80–81
'impostor children' 18, 24–26, 144
Indigenous knowledge 174, 218–219
Indigenous people 52, 172–176, 215–216
individualism 61, 168, 169, 173, 175, 217
'innocent children'
  in conflict discourses 58, 59, 103
  media 24, 25, 27
  in migration discourses 18, 24, 25
  pictures of 26
  UN peacekeeping 63
Inter-American Court of Human Rights 17
International Federation of Medical Students' Associations (IFMSA) 80
International Labour Organization 142

227

international law
  child migrants 17–18
  child soldiers 59
  children in the sex trade 142
  norm diffusion in conflicts 106
International Migration Review Forum (IMRF) 91
International Organization for Migration 87
International Relations (IR)
  childhood in 1, 3–4, 5, 6, 73–74
  feminist IR 115
  global health governance 78
  non-agentic children in armed conflicts 102, 103
  norm entrenchment 106
  and popular culture 196
International Youth Health Organization 80
intersectionality 6
intifada 180–192
in/visibility 118–123, 124
Isbell, Billie Jean 46–47, 50–53
Israeli/Palestinian conflict 180–192
Iusmen, I. 135

J

Jenkings, K.N. 159
Johnson, D. 63
Josefsson, J. 24–25, 26, 88, 89, 90

K

Kallio, K. 115, 123, 156, 163–164
Katz, C. 162
Kendall, E. 22
Kennedy, Tia 173
Khoja-Moolji, S. 172, 173
Killian, K. 194, 197
Kim, J.K. 22
Kurdi, Alan 26
Kwon, S.A. 34, 90, 93, 95

L

la Ballasca, M.P. de 175
Laffey, M. 101, 104, 105–106, 110
Lalander, P. 22
land education 218–219
Lapid, MK Yair 186
Lawson, D.F. 219–220
Lederer, J. 22
Lee-Koo, K. 17, 36, 38, 60, 102, 103, 104, 109, 111, 205
Lemberg-Pedersen, M. 21, 135
Lems, A. 131
LGBTQIA+ children 144–145
liberal feminism 170
Lidén, H. 131
Lind, J. 18, 22
Lipsitz, G. 217
'lost childhoods' 35
Ludic Geopolitics 159

Lugo-Lugo, C.R. 22, 23
Lutfiyya, M.N. 162

M

Mahomed, Raeesah Noor 213
Malbon, B. 163
Mali 65
Manta and Vilca case, Peru 49–50, 55n28
Margolin, C.S. 89
Marris, E. 212
martyrs 187
Mashal, Khaled 187
Mauger, B. 211
Maynard, J.L. 181
McDonnell, S. 160
McEvoy-Levy, S. 196
McKenzie, M. 217
McLaughlin, C. 131
media
  images of children in coverage of armed conflict 103
  images of suffering children 26, 101
  images of young people in global health 80–81
  'innocent children' 24, 25, 27
  social media 173, 184, 212–213
Meir, Golda 184
Mejía, Nicanor 49–50
memorialization processes 47–48, 53, 196
Mignolo, W.D. 169, 173
migration
  'anchor babies' and 'impostor children' 17–30
  child/youth representation in global governance 87–100
  family reunification 17, 18, 20–21, 22, 25, 135–136
  global governance of migration 115–117
  refugee children in Addis Ababa 114–126
  unaccompanied migrant children 18, 20–22, 91, 127–139
Migration Youth and Children Platform (MYCP) 93
militarism 155–166, 193–209
Millazzo, C. 129
Moeller, K. 169, 171
Monitoring and Reporting Mechanism (MRM) 105, 108
Moon, C. 48
moral authority 211

N

Nakate, Vanessa 212, 214
narratives
  conflict narratives 185, 195
  counter-narratives 45–57
  memorialization processes 47–48
  power of 47
  storytelling 31–34, 37–40, 167, 219–220

Ukrainian children's art 199–203
victimhood 141, 146
  see also storytelling
Nazar, Nadia 213
neoliberalism 95, 170, 212–213, 216–218, 219, 220
Netanyahu, Benjamin 184–185, 186
New York Declaration for Refugees and Migrants 116
NGOs 63, 67, 87, 90, 91, 101, 105, 143
non-performativity 96
norm transfer 101–113
Norway 131

O

Obama, Barack 21, 25
O'Brien, D. 216
One Third Facebook 92, 94
Ormonde, M.E. 20, 22
OSRSG-CaAC (Office of the Special Representative of the Secretary-General for Children and Armed Conflict) 101–113
'other' 20, 23, 91–92, 117–118
'out of sequence' childhoods 35

P

Palestine 180–192
partnership discourses 36–37
patriarchy 3, 62, 171
Patrick, F. 216
peace and peacebuilding 31–44, 58–70, 109, 110
Peltier, Autumn 173, 174
performativity theory 195
Peru 45–57
Philpott, D. 31, 41
play 35, 155–166, 197
Podestá, Cecilia 53
Polaris 145
political geography 5
political representation 89–90, 92–95
popular culture 196
post-colonial contexts 102, 106, 213
post-developmentalist Childhood Studies 6
power
  barriers to participation 96
  and childhood 4
  global health governance 77
  of narratives 47
  and play 156, 162–163
  popular culture 156
  redistribution 212, 215–216
  social navigation 62
praxis 212, 214–218
'presencing' 175
protection and care of children *see* child protection discourses
Pruitt, L. 129, 131, 133

Q

Quinn, J.R. 31, 37, 41
Qvortrup, J. 4

R

race
  children in the sex trade 144, 145
  climate change activism 212
  critical race theory 215, 216
  racism 60, 96, 212, 213–214
  white supremacy 216
radicalization 180–192
Rana, S.S. 38
rape
  children born of 23, 45–57
  prosecution of statutory rape in US 146–147
reconciliation and reporting spaces 31–44
refugees 24, 26, 114–126, 194
reproductive rights 171
Responsibility to Protect (R2P) mandate 105
right to family 17
rights
  agency in migration 18, 21–23, 24–26, 88–89
  to citizenship 22
  global governance of migration 88, 89
  human rights 17, 33, 107, 142, 182–183
  institutionalization of 88
  non-performativity 96
  right to non-discrimination 17
  right to participation 34, 39, 74
  UN peacekeeping 63
  UNCRC (United Nations Convention on the Rights of the Child) 17, 18
  violated by treating children as adults 24
Rise Up Movement 214
Rojas, C. 176
Romeo and Juliet laws 147
Rosen, D.M. 102, 104
Rowley, C. 196
'rupture' 160
Rwanda 48

S

Safe Harbor laws 140–152
Saward, M. 89, 90, 95
Schierup, C.U. 87, 90, 95
Schmidt, S. 22–23
Schwartz, S. 38
SCOREscotland 214
Scott, J.C. 75
Scott, K. 77
secondary migrations 116
Security Council Resolution 1460 37
Security Council Resolution 1612 108
Security Council Resolution 2250 109
sex trade 140–152

sexting 147
sexual violence 45–57, 60
  see also rape
Shalhoub-Kevorkian, N. 146
Shared Hope 142, 143
Shusterman, J. 105
Sierra Leone 33, 34–37, 63
Sikkink, K. 106
Silverman, S.J. 24
Sinwar, Yahya 187–188
social capital 41
social media 173, 184, 212–213
social navigation 60–62, 64–65, 66–67
social technology, childhood as 6
Somali refugees in Ethiopia 116, 117–124
Somers, M.R. 47
Specht, I. 61
Sriprakash, A. 216
Starmer, Keir 132, 133
Stavrianakis, A. 157
stereotypes 66, 109, 117, 122, 124, 131
Stern, M. 157
Stewart, B. 32
storytelling 31–32, 33–34, 37–40, 167, 219–220
'Straight 18' principle 102, 109
Strauss, V. 216
Stretmo, L. 20
substitute parent, state as 133, 134, 135
suicide 184
Sultana, F. 210, 212
Sustainability and Climate Change draft strategy (UK) 214–215
Sustainable Development Goals 74, 76, 77, 78, 90
Sweden 25, 130–131
Swedish National Youth Council 92
Switzer, H. 172
symbolic technologies 105–106, 107, 108, 110
Syria 108

T

Tabak, J. 5, 37, 58, 59, 60, 62, 63, 66, 67, 103, 108, 110
Taft, J.K. 168, 172
Tallberg, J. 87, 95
Tamimi, Ahed 188
Tanay, E.R. 200
Tapaninen, A.M. 21, 22
'terror babies' 23
terrorism 23, 156, 180–181, 182–184, 185, 186, 187
Theidon, K. 54n1
Thunberg, Greta 170, 211, 212
Timor-Leste 33, 37–42
Tomlinson, B. 217
toys 155–166, 197
trafficking 21, 133, 141–142, 146, 147–148

Trafficking and Victims Protection Act (TVPA) 142
transitional justice scholarship 31, 33, 45, 47–48
trauma 46, 132, 141, 181–182, 198–199, 200
Trojanowska, B.K. 110
Trump, Donald 22, 25
Truth and Reconciliation Commissions (TRCs) 31–44, 45–57
Tuck, E. 218–219

U

UK 127–139, 155–166, 214–215
Ukraine 193–209
unaccompanied migrant children 18, 20–22, 91, 127–139
unchilding 146
UNCRC (United Nations Convention on the Rights of the Child)
  child participation 74
  children's rights focus 89
  definition of childhood 17, 18, 102, 103
  laws on trafficking 142
  normative guidelines for children's participation in transitional justice 34, 39
United Nations (UN)
  Agenda 2021 89
  Agenda 2030 78, 89
  child protection discourses 18, 63, 66, 105, 107
  Children and Armed Conflict (CaAC) agenda 36–37, 101–113
  children/youth as 'major group' 87
  Committee on the Rights of the Child 76, 89
  Development Program 109
  Earth Summit 211
  Economic and Social Council (ECOSOC) 80
  High Commissioner for Refugees (UNHCR) 115, 116, 127, 129, 130
  Inter-agency Network on Youth Development 109
  Major Group for Children and Youth (UNMGCY) 79, 89, 92–93, 94
  Migration Network 93
  Monitoring and Reporting Mechanism (MRM) 105, 108
  Office for the Coordination of Humanitarian Affairs (OCHA) 182, 185
  peacekeeping 58–70
  Security Council 37, 105, 108, 109, 111
  Security Council Resolution 1460 37
  Security Council Resolution 1612 108
  Security Council Resolution 2250 109
  Sustainable Development Goals 74, 76, 77, 78, 90
UNICEF 36, 59, 63, 78, 87, 91, 92, 103, 184, 194, 198

INDEX

Youth, Peace and Security (YPS) agenda 103, 109
Youth Strategy 2030 89
Uprichard, E. 4
Urbinati, N. 89, 95
US
 'anchor babies' 22–23
 children in the sex trade 140–152
 critical race theory 215, 216
 'impostor children' 25
 migration 21, 25

V

victimhood
 child migrants 131
 child soldiers 60, 62, 63–64
 children in the sex trade 140–141, 142, 143–145, 146, 147–148
 girls' 172
 Indigenous girls 173
 memorialization processes 48–49
 unaccompanied migrant children 135
 victims of children's violence 181–182
video games 158, 159
Vigh, H. 61–62
violence
 child soldiers 63
 children as perpetrators of 180–192
 children born of rape 23, 45–57
 gender-based violence 23
 sexual violence 45–57, 60
 Ukrainian children's art 193–209
 war play 155–166
visibility/invisibility 118–123, 124
Vitus, K. 131
vulnerability discourses
 child as 'vulnerable other' in migration governance 91–92

child soldiers 61, 63–64
imagined childhoods 2, 59
UN 110
unaccompanied migrant children 133, 135
see also child protection discourses

W

Wall, J. 88
war
 child agency 60–62
 children born of 46
 children's agency and art in Ukraine 197–203
 discourses on childhood and 59–60
 OSRSG-CaAC 101–113
 playing war 155–166
'war on terror' 156
Weldes, J. 101, 104, 105–106, 110, 196
Wernesjö, U. 130
Wildcat, Dan 215
women, children conflated with 5, 106
Wong, B.L.H. 81
Woodyer, T. 156, 196, 197, 205
'world child' archetype 103, 108, 110
World Health Assembly 80

Y

YouCreate project 197–198
Youth, Peace and Security (YPS) agenda 103, 109
youth hubs 80
youth pre-summits in international organizations 79–80
'youth tokenism'/'youthwashing' 96

Z

Zero Hour 214
Zou, J.J. 218
Zvobgo, K. 38

www.ingramcontent.com/pod-product-compliance
Lightning Source LLC
Chambersburg PA
CBHW051537020426
42333CB00016B/1977